THE FINISHING SCHOOL

THE
FINISHING
SCHOOL

Earning the Navy SEAL Trident

DICK COUCH

Foreword by Bob Kerrey

THREE RIVERS PRESS

NEW YORK

Originally published in hardcover in the United States by
Crown Publishers, an imprint of the Crown Publishing Group,
a division of Random House, Inc., New York, in 2004.

Library of Congress Cataloging-in-Publication Data
Couch, Dick, 1943–
The finishing school : earning the Navy SEAL Trident /
Dick Couch; foreword by Bob Kerrey. — 1st ed.
1. United States. Navy. SEALs. 2. United States.
Navy—Commando troops—Training of. I. Title.
VG87.C67 2004
359.9'84—dc22   2003019803

ISBN 0-609-81046-4

Printed in the United States of America

Design by Leonard W. Henderson

10 9 8 7 6

First Paperback Edition

To

Aviation Boatswain's Mate First Class Neil C. Roberts
Killed 3 March 2002, Takur Ghar, Afghanistan
BUD/S Class 184

Chief Hospital Corpsman Matthew J. Bourgeois
Killed 22 March 2002, Kandahar, Afghanistan
BUD/S Class 162

Radioman First Class Thomas E. Retzer
Killed 26 June 2003, near Gardez, Afghanistan
BUD/S Class 198

Photographer's Mate First Class David M. Tapper
Killed 20 August 2003, near Orgun, Afghanistan
BUD/S Class 172

SEAL Warriors who died in the defense of
our nation in the war against terrorism

ACKNOWLEDGMENTS

This is a book about how SEALS train for war. It is a deadly business, and one that calls for the highest measure of dedication and professionalism. For the most part it is a dirty, difficult, dangerous, and unglamourous business—very unlike anything one might see in the movies. The men you will be reading about fought in Afghanistan and in Iraq, and are still engaged in the fight against terrorism worldwide. Many of them are at this moment in harm's way. Others are deployed in distant, seemingly nonhostile parts of the world, waiting for terrorists to show themselves. They all stand on guard for us and allow us to go about our post-9/11 lives in relative peace and security. Thanks, guys. To the extent that al-Qaeda and their ilk have to worry about your suddenly appearing in the middle of the night, they are less likely to bring terror to America.

But Navy SEALs do get a great deal of recognition as one of America's premier special operations forces. Many others within the Naval Special Warfare community do not. So I'd like to recognize our brother warriors, the Special Warfare Combatant Craft crewmen, as well as the communicators, the intelligence specialists, the technical specialists, and the support personnel who make the business of Naval Special Warfare possible.

I'd be remiss if I didn't thank the families of all those who go in harm's way. Ours is an all-volunteer, professional military force. As illustrated in Afghanistan and Iraq, our military has no peer in the world. But this preeminence comes at a price. These warriors are away from home a great deal; their kids often ask, "When is Dad [or Mom] coming home?" There is a growing gulf between the American people and the military that so capably serves them. This is to be expected; much about America is the pursuit of happiness, and much about the business of being a warrior is about sacrifice and hardship. This gulf applies to the family of a warrior, too. So as we occasionally thank our warriors, we must also thank their families for their sacrifice as well. And I'd like to thank my family—my wife, Julia, who waited while I was away, following our SEAL warriors as they train for war.

And finally to the platoon SEALs, the guns in the fight, thank you for allowing me to tell a part of your story.

CONTENTS

FOREWORD

Following their heavy use in the 2001 Afghanistan and the 2003 Iraq wars, American special operations forces have received considerable attention and praise. The words of praise, while richly deserved, often become rhetorical mythmaking. Dick Couch has written a book that gives readers an opportunity to separate fact from myth about one of these special operations groups: the United States Navy SEALs.

The facts of their current training and the details of their current missions take warfighting as mankind's most serious business. It is one worth avoiding, if possible; but if necessary, it must be fought with a professionalism that is constantly on guard against overconfidence and constantly alert to the mistakes that become a vital lesson taught with blood.

Dick Couch's story makes it clear that today's SEAL must have great physical strength and endurance. Further, today's SEAL must have the intellectual capacity to master technical details that seem comparable to those required of medical or engineering students. Imagining what it takes to become SEAL qualified inspires great respect and even a little awe.

However, what struck me in reading Dick Couch's story is the importance and value of human characteristics that have nothing to do with either physical strength or intellectual capacity. I was impressed with the emphasis on the character of these remarkable trainees. Today a man's character is more likely to disqualify him from earning a SEAL's Trident than any physical or mental failing.

Character includes such things as self-discipline, modesty, teamwork, consideration for others, and the ability to dial down as quickly as dialing up the aggression needed to be a successful warrior. SEALs are taught to do a job right the first time, to subtract complaints from their verbal arsenals, to accept real-time criticism of performance, and to never cease the active effort to learn how to do their jobs better.

A few years back, during my second term in the United States Senate and within a few days of each other, I heard two men with strikingly different careers address the importance of character with great eloquence and passion. The first was the commandant of the U.S. Marine Corps, General Charles Krulak. The second was investor and Omaha, Nebraska, native Warren Buffett.

Commandant Krulak was convinced that character could and should be taught to his Marines. He was urgently including character skills in the basic and advanced training for recruits and veterans. He believed that good character was nothing more or less than establishing and articulating rules that could not be broken no matter what the circumstances. Rather than making a man less flexible and unwilling to change when change was needed, good rules increased the chances that a Marine would be able to perform at the highest level possible by avoiding debilitating distractions and temptations.

General Krulak was most excited about a summer program designed to give inner-city youth a taste of what character building could do for them. Some of these young people would later become Marines, which would be beneficial for the Corps. Some would return to their neighborhoods with a life-altering understanding of the power of good character to build a happy and successful life.

Warren Buffett's attitude was identical to the commandant's. At a conference attended by Nebraska high school students who had gathered to study the relationship between savings and wealth (something about which Mr. Buffett knows a great deal), he was asked this question: "Mr. Buffett, sir, no disrespect to you, but aren't most wealthy people jerks?"

His answer, which I thought of as I read Dick Couch's book on SEAL training, was remarkable. "No," he said. "My experience is that wealth merely allows you to be a little more of what you already were. So that if you begin as a jerk and then become wealthy you can be a really big jerk. But if you begin as a person with good character, you can use your wealth to do good."

Mr. Buffett went on to say that three human characteristics were of dominant importance to a happy life: physical energy, intelligence, and character. He observed that the first two are most likely to be the genetic gifts of your parents and that all of the students in his audience appeared to have plenty of both. The third one, character, is completely within our power to create. We do so one choice at a time. Finally, he said, to improve the chances that you will make the right choice at the moment when the fork in the road appears before you, it is best to establish rules ahead of time. Live by those rules until and unless something or someone persuades you the rule needs changing.

That, it seems to me, is the secret to the training described by Dick Couch in his lively, informative, and intimidating book. Character counts, and today's U.S. Navy SEAL is taught to believe and act it every step of the way.

Bob Kerrey

THE FINISHING SCHOOL

A steady eye and an MP5 submachine gun. A Navy SEAL covers a suspect during urban-battle drills. *Photo by Cliff Hollenbeck*

INTRODUCTION

On 11 March 2002 more than a thousand people gathered at a memorial service in the chapel on the Navy base at Little Creek, Virginia. Many of them were Navy SEALs. They had gathered to honor the memory of Petty Officer Neil Roberts. There are a number of things worth noting about the passing of Neil Roberts, not the least of which is the heroic manner in which he died.

In support of Operation Anaconda in the mountains of Afghanistan, Neil was a member of a special operations element that was to be inserted on a reconnaissance and scouting mission. When the big CH-47 Chinook helicopter flared for a landing, it came under heavy machine-gun and rocket fire. Three RPG rockets ripped through the helicopter, but they did not explode. Had they done so, the helo would have become an instant fireball. In addition to the RPG strikes, the fuselage was raked by machine-gun fire. The pilot fought for control, knowing that his aircraft was mortally wounded. There was confusion in the troop compartment of the helo, and the deck was slick with fluid from ruptured hydraulic lines. A crewman slipped from the exit ramp and dangled from his nylon tether. Neil Roberts immediately went to his aid and hauled him back into the aircraft. In doing so, Neil fell from the helicopter just as the pilot regained control and veered away from the enemy fire. The helicopter pilot was able to crash-land his aircraft a few miles from the insertion site. All aboard were safe—all except Neil.

He activated his beacon to let his teammates know he was alive, and crawled away from the insertion site. There were more than sixty well-armed al-Qaeda fighters around him. Prudence, let alone self-preservation, would dictate that he go to ground and wait for help. But the machine-gun emplacement that had so devastated the Chinook was still active. When his teammates came back for him, as Neil knew they would, they would face another round of deadly fire. So Neil Roberts attacked. He maneuvered some two hundred yards to a position above and behind the al-Qaeda gunners. With his grenades, he destroyed the machine gun and killed the gun crew. Then the al-Qaeda came for him. Outnumbered, outgunned, and wounded several times, he fought until he exhausted his ammunition. He was cut down, and the al-Qaeda fighters dragged his body away. But SEALs never abandon their own. In less than two hours, Navy SEALs, assisted by other British and American special operations personnel, were on the ground. After eight hours of fierce, close-quarter combat, Neil's body was recovered by his teammates. More than three hundred al-Qaeda died at the hands of the American and British special operators. Six other Americans were to die in the battle; two Navy SEALs were seriously wounded. A stiff price, but thanks to the sacrifice of his special operations brothers, Neil could go home to his family.

Neil Roberts was one of twelve children, including a twin brother. He leaves a widow and an eighteen-month-old son. Before Neil deployed to Afghanistan, he left a letter with his wife and instructions that it be opened only if he were killed. Kathy Roberts made that letter public, wanting everyone to know of her husband's devotion to his nation and his brother warriors. In part, the letter read:

> *My family is the reason I am the person I am today. They supported and cared for me in the best way possible. Although I sacrificed personal freedom and many other things, I got just as much as I gave. My time in the teams was special. For all the times I was cold, wet, tired, sore, scared, hungry, and angry, I had a blast. I loved being a SEAL. I died doing what made me happy. Very few people have the luxury of that.*

Extraordinary, yes. Unique, not really. As you will see in this book, the Navy SEAL teams produce extraordinary warriors on a regular basis. They are courageous, disciplined, and very highly trained. They prize integrity, accountability, reliability, and a commitment to team. They do all these things with a passion. These men live in a world where personal honor is as important as professional military skill. It is with a great deal of pride and humility that I call Neil Roberts a teammate and a fellow warrior.

That others willingly risk mortal combat to recover the remains of a fallen comrade is difficult to understand for many Americans. I'm sure it is a burden for the families of those men who died to bring Neil home. Yet this is not new, nor is it an inconsequential aspect of the American warrior culture. A number of lives were lost during the *Black Hawk Down* battle in Mogadishu, Somalia, simply because we were unwilling to abandon our dead to the enemy. We will leave no one behind. But why is this? What is this covenant among our warriors that requires our remains be carried from the battlefield, even at great risk to the living? This point was the central theme of the bestselling book *We Were Soldiers Once . . . and Young,* by Hal Moore and Joe Galloway. The book resulted in the movie *We Were Soldiers,* starring Mel Gibson. Both recounted the battle in the Ia Drang Valley in 1965, the first main-force slugfest of the Vietnam War. Three hundred and five Americans were lost in that engagement, along with some eighteen hundred North Vietnamese soldiers. I personally asked Brigadier General Hal Moore (USA Ret.), the man who led the First Battalion of the Seventh Cavalry in and out of that deadly valley, about this.

"Dick," Hal Moore told me, "those of us who are left meet every year at The [Vietnam Memorial] Wall. And every year my men tell me the same thing; they followed me into that god-awful battle because I told them that I would leave no man behind. It was a sacred promise. They believed me, and I kept my promise."

This may mean little to a widow or even to the extended family of a warrior who perished while fighting to recover the body of a fallen comrade, but it means everything to the men who have to do the fighting. They want to come home—alive, if they can, but they want to come home. It's very important to men for whom facing death is an occupational reality. Teammate, buddy, shipmate, platoon mate: By whatever term used by these bands of brothers, it simply means that I love you; I will, if necessary, die in an effort to preserve your earthly remains for the sake of others who love you—your nonmilitary family. It is not a business ethic or even an American cultural ethic; it is a warrior ethic.

The death of Neil Roberts is significant for other reasons. His fighting and dying may well have been the first such action recorded live. An orbiting Predator drone saw it all and flashed this drama to commanders in Afghanistan and in the Pentagon. We may never see the actual footage of Neil's final moments, but I'm sure they would make a mockery of the reality-TV combat programs. No posturing or trash talk here, just courage and professionalism in the face of certain death. There is, however, one thing that bothers me, and other SEALs I talk with share my concern. Navy SEALs are all about teammates and commitment to team. We're pack animals. In his last battle, Neil Roberts fought and died alone. Somehow, more than anything else, this seems an injudicious end for a magnificent warrior.

Navy SEALs have died in nearly all conflicts since the first SEALs were commissioned in 1962. But among all those who have perished in combat, Neil Roberts will share a distinction with another fallen SEAL in the history of the teams: He was the first to die in his war. On 16 June 1964, Petty Officer Billy Machen was killed in a firefight in the Rung Sat Special Zone—the first SEAL to die in the Vietnam War. Before that conflict ended, forty-seven of Machen's brother warriors had fallen in combat. The number of SEALs who will be claimed in the war that began on 11 September 2001 is the stuff of future SEAL lore. Neil Roberts died over there, in Afghanistan, because a deadly and resourceful enemy has brought his fight over here, onto American soil. This war, unlike most American conflicts of the twentieth century, is not to help some other nation with its problems; this is our war—a war from which we can neither walk away nor negotiate a settlement. It has to be won, and it is imperative that this war be fought and won on the *enemy's* ground, not ours. The reason is obvious: We go to great lengths to avoid civilian casualties in war. The primary objective of al-Qaeda and those who support them *are* American civilian casualties.

Today there are twelve sixteen-man platoons of Navy SEALs deployed around the world, as well as various Naval Special Warfare combat and support elements. There are SEAL Delivery Team platoons and special SEAL strike elements. Many of them are in harm's way. The current war on terrorism is very different from the one that the first SEALs fought some thirty-five-odd years ago. The stakes are higher; our national interests are clearly threatened. We Vietnam veterans are fond of saying, "We deserved a better war." The current conflict may be just that for today's SEALs. But I am no less saddened by the prospect that Neil Roberts may be only the first of many to die before the threat to America from terrorism and those who support terrorism has been defeated. How we train and prepare our Navy SEALs to do this important work is related in the pages of this book.

In September 1999, I began work on *The Warrior Elite,* which detailed Basic Underwater Demolition/SEAL Training, or simply BUD/S. The reader followed BUD/S Class 228 as its members negotiated the basic thirty-week course that every man must complete to earn a Navy SEAL Trident pin. This basic course and the famous BUD/S Hell Week—along with the parade of cold, wet, sandy trainees staggering down the beach—is fairly well known. This course is more of a testing ground than a training course, as the high rates of attrition would suggest. The reality, if not the philosophy, of basic SEAL training is that if you want one good man, begin with five good men. When that one good man emerges from BUD/S training, the serious business of molding a Navy SEAL begins. It takes a little more than seven months to complete the BUD/S course. Without question, it is a rite of passage—a process that seeks to find men who would rather die than quit. Such a rendering of the human spirit identifies men like Neil Roberts on a regular basis. But it only scratches the surface of that unique, professional military skill set that a young warrior must master to become a Navy SEAL.

In the fall of 1999, ours was a rich nation at peace and enjoying an unprecedented economic expansion. We were then worried about Y2K and consolidating gains in our stock portfolios. The senior leadership in Naval Special Warfare was concerned about the number of veterans who were leaving the teams. The political climate then did not favor the military. There didn't seem to be any work for warriors, and corporate America was paying (and still does pay) top dollar for former Navy SEALs. So I was allowed to roam freely among the training and operational commands as I compiled my research for *The Warrior Elite*. As a retired SEAL, I enjoyed special access to the men and the unique culture that thrives in the Navy SEAL teams. I felt like an old grad on a visit to his fraternity house on a homecoming weekend.

The climate today is much different. Fewer SEALs are leaving the Navy. Many who had submitted their resignation papers have pulled them, and several SEALs recently released from active duty are returning to the teams—they want in this fight. In 1999, I watched fine young men struggle in BUD/S to become Navy SEALs. That was their goal—to become a Navy SEAL and to stand with the best. Now their goal is to *fight* with the best. The road to becoming a SEAL has changed little since 1999, but what lies at the end of that road has changed dramatically, perhaps forever. The climate for a writer, even a former member of this exclusive club, has changed. I still enjoy the trust and goodwill of those SEALs on activity duty, without which my work would be impossible. *The Warrior Elite,* I am proud to say, has strengthened this trust. "Dick," they tell me about my description of BUD/S training and Class 228, "you got it right." I believe Randy Wallace, the screenwriter and director of *We Were Soldiers,* got it right. I heard Hal Moore tell him so. It's a powerful thing when those you admire and respect feel that you tell their story well.

But 9/11 changed much, and it changed how writers like myself tell our stories. I no longer enjoy the unlimited freedom I had when I did the research for *The Warrior Elite*. My movement among the various SEAL commands is still allowed, but access to training venues and the operational components is closely monitored. This is no longer basic training. This is about the finishing school where the combat skills of Navy SEALs are taught. There are tactics, methods, and procedures that I observed, but will be restricted from putting in print. The Navy SEALs in this book are real, but their names, for the most part, have been altered. This is for their protection as they prepare to go in harm's way and for the well-being of their families, who must wait for their safe return. These are restrictions I welcome. These are my brothers, and we are at war.

In my research for this work, I observed SEALs in advanced and predeployment training during the year that led up to the Iraqi War. As I put the finishing touches on the manuscript, the SEALs who fought in Iraq were just being rotated home. All indications are that they completed a marvelous chapter in the battle history of the teams. The men in these pages fought in that war. By the time this volume on SEAL training reaches the bookshelves, these Navy SEALs will be moving on to other campaigns in the war on terrorism.

The Warrior Elite was a book about endurance, courage, and testing the human spirit—to find men who will never quit. *The Finishing School* is about all that, and more. It is how we train Navy SEALs for war—to fight and win at all costs. In addition to the seven months that it takes a man to get through BUD/S, it will take another two years to make him a combat-ready, deployable Navy SEAL. After thirty-some months of the most intense military training in the world, he is considered an apprentice in the SEAL teams—a new guy. After his first deployment, he is then a journeyman in the business. To replace a man like Neil Roberts, it takes someone with courage, training, *and* experience—combat experience. Men like Neil are never easy to find, but the system that found and trained Neil Roberts is in place. And we live in a world that provides ample opportunity for Navy SEALs to gain experience in combat. For the men that you will soon read about in SEAL Qualification Training, combat is at least two years away. For those you will meet in the West Coast operational SEAL teams, it is much closer. This is how they train. This is how the Navy takes the raw steel from BUD/S and tempers this material to make a modern SEAL warrior.

CHAPTER 1

The Prerequisites

THE BASIC COURSE

There are a number of things a young man must do before he begins the serious business of SEAL finishing school. Before the Navy or Naval Special Warfare will invest the time and money to train a man to be a Navy SEAL, they want to know two things: Is he smart enough and is he tough enough for this business? SEAL candidates are screened carefully for mental aptitude, and most have the required mental ability. Basic Underwater Demolition/SEAL training, or BUD/S, is designed to test whether these SEAL hopefuls have the toughness. What we are talking about here is what the SEALs call Hack It School, or Pain 101.

In the culture of the Navy SEAL teams, it all begins at BUD/S. Perhaps no other military training carries with it the mystique—and pain—associated with this training. *The Warrior Elite* focused on this basic course. It is the crucible that takes qualified young sailors and naval officers and makes them candidates for SEAL training. Note that I used the term *candidates* for SEAL training. But BUD/S

Post-BUD/S pain. SQT students wade into Alaskan waters to cool off after a trek in the snowfields. *Photo by Dick Couch*

is where the real making of a Navy SEAL begins. Granted, the price of admission to the qualification course is steep. The coin of this culture is counted in terms of sweat and pain. Men are vetted in BUD/S for their commitment and determination; it's a measure of heart. It is an accomplishment in itself to successfully complete BUD/S, but the basic course is no more than an admissions slip to advanced SEAL training—the finishing school.

The eternal debate about BUD/S is whether this is a training program or a testing ground. In reality, it is both. First of all, it is an elaborate, tradition-bound screening process that seeks to find men who would rather die than quit. This is accomplished with a punishing diet of physical conditioning, cold water, and lack of sleep—the same conditions in which Navy SEALs are expected to operate. BUD/S trainees learn early on that unless they can come to terms with being cold and miserable for extended periods of time, they don't belong here. The training is brutal by design.

BUD/S also lays the foundation for basic SEAL operational skills. Many of these skills are fundamental, military/special operations tradecraft, and others are maritime-centric skills. The Navy SEAL is a versatile animal, capable of many of the disciplines of other SOF (special operations forces) components. The other SOF components, such as the Special Forces, the Rangers, and the Air Force Special Tactics Teams, also conduct diving and small-boat training, but no special operator in the SOF community is as comfortable in the water as a SEAL. For the others, water is an obstacle; for SEALs, it is a refuge. While SEAL capabilities do not stop at the water's edge, SEALs are, and will remain, the primary special operations maritime force. Before a man can become a SEAL, he must first become a frogman. He must excel in a variety of military skills, but it is essential that he be comfortable in and under the sea. Again, it all begins at BUD/S.

This basic course, start to finish, is a thirty-week endurance test. The attrition is dramatic as many young men discover that they have neither the heart nor the physical stamina for this life. Only about one man in five who passes the screening test and is admitted to

BUD/S training will qualify to wear the Navy SEAL Trident. BUD/S is conducted at the Naval Special Warfare Center in Coronado, California. The Center, as it is called, is on the Naval Amphibious Base, a naval base that straddles a sand spit that connects the near-island of Coronado to the city of Imperial Beach, situated just north of the U.S.-Mexican border. This famous sand spit is know as the Silver Strand, or simply the Strand.

INDOC

BUD/S training is conducted in three phases: First Phase—physical conditioning; Second Phase—diver training; and Third Phase—land warfare. In order to prepare trainees for phase training, SEAL candidates must complete a pretraining course called the Indoctrination Course, or Indoc. Officially, the purpose of Indoc is "to physically, mentally, and environmentally prepare qualified SEAL candidates to begin BUD/S training." Prior to the beginning of Indoc, trainees arrive at the Naval Special Warfare Center. For the most part, this is physical conditioning without pressure—a time to tune up for the ordeal ahead.

BUD/S trainees come to the Special Warfare Center from a variety of backgrounds. Newly commissioned ensigns come from the Naval Academy, the Naval Reserve Officer Training Corps (NROTC), and a few from Officer Candidate School. Most classes include fleet officers—lieutenants or junior-grade lieutenants—who come to BUD/S after a tour aboard ship. The leadership of these seasoned officers is often critical to the success of a BUD/S class. Many of the enlisted men come from boot camp, usually by way of a Navy school that will help them qualify in their rate, or naval technical specialty. They joined the Navy with the goal of becoming a Navy SEAL. Some enlisted men come from the fleet with shipboard experience or a tour at a shore facility. The leadership of these petty officers is also critical to the success of a BUD/S class. And some SEAL candidates, both officers and enlisted men, come from other services. The challenge of BUD/S training draws men from other SOF components and from the Marine Corps.

The Indoctrination Course is currently a five-week curriculum. Here the trainees will learn the rules and conventions of BUD/S training, and about the culture and ethos of this warrior class. Indoc is also designed to physically and mentally bring the class together. Most of the students have prepared for this individually. Now they will live and train as a class—as a team. The days are long with liberal doses of timed beach runs, soft-sand conditioning runs, group physical training (known as PT sessions), and a great deal of time in the water. There are standards of performance—individual times that trainees must achieve or face being dropped from the course. BUD/S classes that work together and demonstrate teamwork will not necessarily have an easy time of it, but they can avoid a great deal of discretionary pain. Team play, and the lack of it, never escapes the watchful eyes of the BUD/S instructors.

A day in the life of an Indoc trainee begins at 0530 for pool training or for a four-mile beach run. After breakfast, his morning could be taken up by calisthenics, the obstacle course (called simply the O-course), or practical work with basic SEAL equipment. The afternoon could begin with a conditioning run in the soft sand, more pool work, or classroom sessions on subjects ranging from first aid to proper nutrition. There may or may not be a training evolution after the evening meal. Many times throughout the training day, the trainees are sent into the surf, usually in their fatigue uniforms and boots. Now they are cold and wet. On their return from the surf, they are made to roll in the sand. Now they are cold, wet, and sandy—a normal condition for a BUD/S trainee. There is a price to pay for meals as well. The round-trip from the Center to the chow hall is two miles. That's six miles of running, often after a trip to the surf, just to get three squares a day. This will continue, in one form or another, for the next six months.

At the conclusion of Indoc, the attrition has already begun. Five percent of the candidates quit before they even begin Indoc; they simply become intimidated by the whole process. Up to 20 percent will voluntarily drop from training during Indoc—a few from injuries, some from the pain of the moment, but most because they now understand that this pace and the cold water will not end for months and months. In truth, it will never end. Most of these men are physically capable, but they lack the mental toughness to continue. Most still want to be Navy SEALs. They simply didn't understand the price of admission to this club.

FIRST PHASE

First Phase training presents a different set of instructors and a new set of challenges for the BUD/S class. First Phase is quite similar to Indoc, but the intensity is turned up a notch—perhaps two notches. It begins on day one with a killer PT session. After a trip to the surf and a roll in the sand, each trainee will do more than five hundred push-ups and sixty pull-ups before First Phase is an hour old.

Each man is expected to lower his run, swim, and O-course times. There are new challenges like surf passage and log PT—a game in which the teams of trainees juggle sections of telephone poles. They undergo a drown-proofing test with their hands and feet bound, and an underwater fifty-five-yard swim without fins. In First Phase, the days are longer than in Indoc, with less time for sleep. The weekends, which provide much-needed time for battered bodies to rest and heal, seem shorter.

And for First Phase trainees, the prospect of an upcoming Hell Week hangs over them like a dark cloud. Pre–Hell Week training is devoted to toughening a class and preparing it for Hell Week. Post–Hell Week training must allow for healing and teaching skills the class will need before it moves on to the advanced phases of BUD/S training. This balance is not easy to achieve. Hell Week may be one of the most intense and demanding challenges, both physically and mentally, in the armed forces of any nation. A class may lose 20 to 40 percent of its number in the days before Hell Week. During Hell Week alone it can be as high as 60 percent. I closely followed Class

228 during the writing of *The Warrior Elite*. Ninety-eight men began Indoc with Class 228. Of those ninety-eight, nineteen finished Hell Week. Of those nineteen, ten graduated with Class 228.

A tradition that begins during Indoc and carries over into First Phase is intense competition within the class. The competition is driven in large part by the fact that in BUD/S it pays to be a winner. On most evolutions, the individuals or boat crews who finish first will be given a few minutes rest or spared a trip into the cold surf. Those who are not winners are losers, and losers pay the price: more push-ups, more cold water, more unwanted attention from the instructors. This is not a trivial concept or a game. Those who survive BUD/S and go on to the teams will always strive to win. On an actual SEAL operation, winning will take the form of completing the mission, planting the explosives, or surviving the gunfight. Losing is failing the mission and/or death.

Outside the First Phase training office there is a ship's bell lashed to a stanchion, just off the PT grinder. At any time, a trainee can quit, or DOR—drop on request. To do this he rings the bell three times and puts his helmet on the grinder. He's finished—no longer a BUD/S trainee. He will be assigned other duties in the Navy. There will be no more cold water, no more punishing PT sessions, and no soft-sand conditioning runs. And no chance of becoming a Navy SEAL. The line of green helmets grows throughout First Phase, but that growth takes a dramatic spurt during Hell Week.

"Ringing out," as it is called, is a curious custom. This public declaration of failure has been challenged by some as demeaning and unnecessarily humiliating. Others contend that it serves no purpose, and may even lead to the emotional scarring of an unsuccessful trainee. I agree—in principle. But it is a custom that serves this warrior culture. All trainees, at one time or another, consider quitting. I did when I went through BUD/S.

But the act of walking across that grinder and ringing that bell is a difficult one, even when you're cold, wet, sandy, and very, very tired. It is a hurdle that got many of us past that time when we felt we couldn't go on. BUD/S training is not about self-esteem or personal disgrace. It's about sorting out those who think they want to be warriors and those who are willing to pay the price to achieve that goal.

Hell Week begins sometime on Sunday evening and continues through early Friday afternoon. The trainees do the same things they have been doing the past several weeks—pool evolutions, log PT, the O-course, beach runs, surf passage, and ocean swims. They make the two-mile round-trip to the chow hall three times a day. They are cold, wet, and sandy all the time. But two things are different. The Hell Week trainees carry their 185-pound rubber boats with them everywhere. They run with them on their heads—to the pool, to the chow hall, even as they run the O-course. One more thing: They don't sleep, or their sleep is severely limited. The instructors are on them in three shifts, around the clock. Hell Week is designed to see if these apprentice warriors have the heart to perform when they are cold, wet, and sandy *and* haven't slept in a few days. These same conditions, the trainees are reminded, are often present on actual SEAL combat missions. The mechanics of this around-the-clock training is a production of sorts, very well formatted and choreographed. The instructors watch the trainees' every move. The medical supervision is continuous. Trainees are granted but two or three sleep periods totaling four to five hours for the entire week. They will be on the move for sixty hours before they are granted an hour or two of sleep. Throughout this ordeal, they have to work as a team. During Hell Week, each boat crew is a team. On the water, they paddle as a team. On the land, they carry the boats on their heads as a team. And it's not just survival; they must perform. The sun comes up, the sun goes down, one evolution to the next—cold, wet, and sandy. It's a screening process of the heart and the spirit.

The line of helmets by the bell continues to grow. Oddly enough, most of those who ring out do so during the first twenty-four hours of Hell Week. Why not the second day, or the third? After a single night and day of this punishment, a man gets very cold and extremely tired. And then he thinks, *I'm dying! Four more days of this? I don't know if I can do it!* Those with the heart for this kind of intense training keep going. The rest ring the bell and put their helmet on the grinder. Most who DOR are physically capable. They simply lack the will or the desire to go on. Sometime Friday afternoon, the much-reduced class hears the magic words: "Gentlemen, Hell Week is over; you are secured." A small, tattered, weary-beyond-words band of men will then muster the strength to hug each other and celebrate their victory. Many will go on to qualify as Navy SEALs, but not all. Hell Week is just one step in the process, but an important step, one worth close examination.

One First Phase instructor described Hell Week as a "speed bump" during BUD/S. One has to consider the scope of the training and the requirements of this warrior culture to fully appreciate the perspective of this statement. In one respect, Hell Week is but one week in thirty at BUD/S, one step along the way to earning the SEAL Trident. Yet no other military training in the world has this vigorous a check mark in its basic training curriculum. In reality, it is more than that—much more. Hell Week is the soul of the SEAL culture, and it binds us all together—young and old, seaman and admiral, active warriors and retired warriors. How important is it? Every SEAL *knows* that on a combat mission he can, if he has to, endure incredible hardship and go for days without sleep. More than that, he knows that his SEAL brother fighting alongside him can do the same thing.

Hell Week is a curious and unique event, and it changes a man forever. Future challenges and many of life's triumphs are now calibrated by this experience. For a few souls, Hell Week is their zenith, and they have a difficult time getting past it. For them, making it through Hell Week is the end goal. But for most BUD/S trainees, it is a learning experience and becomes a powerful engine for future physical and mental growth. Hell Week, like BUD/S itself, has its roots deeply imbedded in tradition.

When Lieutenant Commander Draper Kauffman, the father of the Navy frogmen, first began to train the Naval Combat Demolition Units (NCDUs) in the summer of 1943, he visited the Naval Scouts and Raiders training camp, then colocated at Fort Pierce, Florida, with the NCDUs. He took their eight-week physical conditioning program and compressed it into a single week of training. This first week was called Indoctrination Week, but it quickly became known as Hell Week. The theory behind this grueling initial week was to weed out the weak men early on and train those who remained. Since then, Hell Week has been moved from week one to several weeks into what is now First Phase training.

This train-the-best, discard-the-rest philosophy was not the only legacy of Draper Kauffman. Kauffman and his officers went through the first Hell Week with their NCDU enlisted volunteers. The idea that officers have to train and suffer with their men, especially endure suffering on this scale, is unique in American military service. Today, officer trainees, like SEAL platoon officers, have to lead while under pressure, and have to suffer the same hardships as their men. SEAL work is a harsh, physically demanding business. If an officer is to lead from the front, he needs to be, at a minimum, as physically capable as the men he expects to follow him.

The history of Hell Week is a microcosm of the history of the teams and of SEAL training. The Navy SEAL is quite young—barely forty years old. His evolutionary cousin, the Navy frogman, just turned sixty. Both the frogmen and the SEALs were born out of necessity, as was Hell Week. The slaughter of young marines on the beaches of Tarawa in 1943 underscored the need for beach reconnaissance prior to amphibious landings. Volunteers for this dangerous work had to be recruited and trained quickly. Hell Week soon became the crucible—a way to quickly find the right kind of men for this task. Once chosen, they were hastily organized and rushed overseas to clear the obstacles for the amphibious landings at Sicily. Those who went ashore to clear the beaches at Normandy for the D-day invasion suffered terrible casualties. On Omaha Beach alone, 52 percent were killed or wounded. The NCDUs were consolidated into Underwater Demolition Teams, or UDTs, shortly before the end of the war. As UDTs, these first American frogmen saw action across the Pacific as American forces fought their way to Japan. Later in Korea, they served with distinction, raiding coastal targets and performing critical hydrographic reconnaissance prior to the landings at

Inchon in September 1950. Throughout the war in the Pacific and the Korean War, the Navy frogmen were defined by Hell Week.

January 1962 marked the commissioning of SEAL Team One in the Pacific Fleet and SEAL Team Two in the Atlantic Fleet. Training SEALs, like training frogmen, demanded a rigorous Hell Week. The new SEALs focused on duties that included unconventional warfare, operational deception, counterinsurgency, and direct-action missions in maritime and riverine environments. During the Vietnam War, SEAL direct-action platoons and advisory teams compiled an impressive record of combat success. At the height of the Vietnam conflict, there were never more than 500 Navy SEALs on active duty. At any given time, there were seldom more than 120 SEALs deployed in the combat zone. Since Vietnam, changing missions and increased operational tempo have prompted the UDTs to be redesignated as SEAL Teams and SEAL Delivery Vehicle (SDV) Teams.

Hell Week, and all of BUD/S training, is a work in progress. If Hell Week has changed over the years, it's only been a refinement of the basic theme. In 1969, with Class 45 in Little Creek, Virginia, I remember being so cold that to this day I cringe when I read about the exploits of Shackleton and Scott. I think I truly understand what it is to be cold. I thought those terrible five days would never end. If I slept four hours, I was lucky. Our ordeal was similar to the modern version of Hell Week. We carried the same rubber boats everywhere on our heads. One night we ran all night and another night we paddled from sundown to sunrise. Clearly, there is better medical supervision and treatment today, but this also allows current BUD/S instructors to safely take the trainees a little closer to the edge. Today's Hell Week is bound in tradition, but that tradition is continually made better and more relevant to the needs of today's SEAL requirements. Each of the sixty-some evolutions in the current Hell Week are tightly scripted and continually adjusted in small ways to make them more challenging and effective.

I am often asked, "How does Hell Week today compare to yours?" It's not an easy question; mine was a long time ago. Time heals wounds and trauma. I'd like to say it was much harder in my day, but that is not the case. Hell Week has evolved over the past thirty years, and so have the young men who come to BUD/S. Today's BUD/S students are clearly stronger and more athletic than those in the past. It's obvious that many who arrive at BUD/S have logged more than a few hours in the weight room. Yet it can be argued that the current raw product is less ready for this kind of punishment and discipline than previous generations. Life in America is good and, often, soft. On balance, the feel-good generation may be less mentally prepared for the crucible of BUD/S than their predecessors. So where do they come from, these young men who volunteer for this duty? Adjusted for population density, most of them come from smaller, inland communities. It seems the calling of a maritime warrior is less attractive for those who live on the coasts or in a large city. Perhaps small towns in Middle America, because of lesser economic opportunity or a greater patriotic feeling, send more of their sons off to serve their country. It was much the same in my BUD/S class.

BUD/S training is lengthy, expensive, dangerous, and difficult. Far fewer trainees graduate than are reassigned back to the fleet. So just what makes a successful BUD/S trainee? I get asked this a great deal as well. And since Hell Week has the largest share of attrition in BUD/S, what does it take to get through Hell Week? Psychological profiling is now a part of the BUD/S process, but this screening is designed only to weed out those with pathological tendencies. Other tests have been developed that have a high degree of predictability for success at BUD/S. But since there are no absolutes in predicting who will or will not make it, they are used as guides to influence training rather than as screening tools. The current consensus, based on my interviews with BUD/S instructors and curriculum specialists, is that most classes break out something like this: Perhaps 10 or 15 percent of those who arrive simply do not have the physical tools to make it through the training or Hell Week. They cannot meet the performance standards, or they break down physically. There is another 5 or 10 percent who, unless they break a leg or are otherwise seriously injured, will make it no matter how difficult it becomes. But the other

70 to 85 percent are up for grabs. If this large percentage of trainees can find it within themselves, or are properly motivated by the BUD/S training cadre, they can make it; they have the physical tools. Why more of them don't has to do with that elusive quality that is the heart of a warrior. Is this elaborate, tradition-bound process the only way to find out who has grit and who does not? The only way to determine who will stand tall in a firefight and who will come up short? Until there is a multiple-choice test for heart or essay questions to determine courage, I believe it is.

I also believe one of the strongest motivators is the desire to belong. In the case of the young men fighting their way through BUD/S, it is the desire to belong to an elite group—to be a part of this exclusive warrior culture. Those who succeed have high expectations of themselves, and they want to associate with others who share those expectations. They want to be the best, and they want to serve with the best. I also believe that success at BUD/S is based on intelligence. I'm sure that many would disagree or even argue to the contrary: that no intelligent individual would put up with this kind of abuse. But intelligence, in part, is the ability to think ahead and to clearly visualize one's personal goals. Hell Week is a mental gauntlet as well as a physical one. Those who have a clear goal of where they are going, and know why they're going there, are less likely to surrender mentally to the physical pain.

After Hell Week, the final weeks of First Phase are devoted to hydrographic reconnaissance, mechanics of cartography, and small-boat navigation. The Hell Week survivors begin on the following Monday with classroom work, but by the end of the week they are back in the water—cold, wet, and occasionally sandy.

SECOND PHASE

Second Phase is the dive phase. Throughout this phase, the students will still do PT every day. They will be expected to lower their times on the O-course, the four-mile runs, and the ocean swims. The new wrinkle in this phase of BUD/S training is diving—or, more specifically, learning to become combat swimmers. The first few weeks of Second Phase will be spent in the classroom, learning diving physics and diving physiology. Trainees learn about the U.S. Navy diving and treatment tables. All must pass rigorous exams on these subjects before they begin diving instruction. They will also be tested in a recompression chamber for their ability to breathe pure oxygen under pressure. In the Center dive tower, they will dive to fifty feet for knot-tying drills and make free ascents.

The third week of Second Phase is called pool week. The trainees use scuba rigs similar to those used by sport divers, except the tanks are fitted with double-hose regulators. During pool week, the Second Phase trainees learn to scuba dive. After mastering the basics, the trainees then learn to perform specific underwater routines in a proscribed manner. These include ditching and donning their equipment and swapping their equipment with their swim buddy. When they become proficient at this, the trainees are ready for their pool competency testing, during which they must defend these underwater skills under stress. The BUD/S trainees call this pool harassment. This is a major hurdle and the defining moment in Second Phase, and the only time a trainee will be underwater without the constant presence of his swim buddy. Each trainee goes one-on-one with an instructor on the bottom of the pool. Instructors tumble their trainees, pull off their fins and masks, tangle their hoses, and turn off their air. Trainees must reestablish their airway and repair the damage—underwater. Only as a last resort do they abandon their rig and go to the surface.

Next, the BUD/S trainees begin work with a diving rig that will be their constant underwater companion during their SEAL careers: the Draeger LAR (lung-activated rebreather) V scuba. This is a closed-circuit, 100 percent oxygen scuba. The Navy designation for this rig is Mk-25; in the teams, the SEALs refer to it by its manufacturer's name—the Draeger. The advantages of this rig for SEAL operations is that there are no telltale bubbles, it has many times the underwater endurance of open-circuit scubas, and it is lightweight. During their final weeks in Second Phase, the BUD/S trainees will train with the Draeger, learning underwater navigation, pace count, and combat-swimmer skills. They also learn how to care for and maintain these tactical scubas. Each day they will conduct a dive in San Diego Bay to learn a new skill and build on those mastered during previous dives. Once they become proficient during a daytime dive, they do it at night.

As a BUD/S class works its way through Second Phase, the pace never lets up. Most are still healing from Hell Week and the punishment of First Phase, but BUD/S trainees have to train with pain, just as operational Navy SEALs must be prepared to fight when they are hurt. For some, it's stress fractures in their legs. For others, it's tendinitis or low-grade infections or cracked ribs. But the training grinds on. They often don't get to the barracks before midnight or one o'clock, and are up at five—day in and day out. They know the most difficult part of BUD/S is behind them, but they still have a long way to go. The harassment and the punishment of BUD/S may end, but they will always train. And they will often be wet and cold. The BUD/S instructors have been telling them this since Indoc. Now, as they face their final phase of training, they're starting to believe it.

On their last day in dive phase, they swim from the Naval Special Warfare Center south to the pier at Imperial Beach—five and a half miles of open ocean. It's a long swim in cold water, but it's the last evolution of Second Phase. They are still BUD/S trainees, but they are well on their way to becoming frogmen.

THIRD PHASE

Third Phase is the Demolitions and Tactics Phase—often called the Land-Warfare Phase. During the nine-week Third Phase training, the class will learn the basics of land warfare—the land-warfare skills of the naval commando. The first order of business for the class is to draw field equipment: H-gear (combat, weight-bearing harness), canteens, ammunition pouches, rucksacks, and sleeping bags. Next, as if they were a bunch of boot-camp trainees in the Army, they have to learn how to adjust and wear their basic load-bearing equipment. They are now sailors learning the basics of soldiers. As in Second Phase, the class will be timed on runs, ocean swims, and the O-course, but the cutoff times are again lowered; Second Phase times are no longer good enough. Many of the conditioning runs will be made with full rucksacks and field gear.

The first week of Third Phase is largely devoted to land navigation. The class learns how to read a map and how to use a compass, and to walk a line of bearing while measuring distance by pace count. Week one also introduces them to weapons. They begin with pistols—the SEAL team standard-issue Sig Sauer 9mm automatic. After classroom work on land navigation and weapons safety, the class leaves the Naval Special Warfare Center for the Naval Special Mountain Warfare Training Facility at La Posta, a rugged military reservation in the Laguna Mountains some eighty miles east of San Diego. Here the class will conduct day and night navigational practicals and qualify on the pistol range with the Sig Sauer.

Week two brings more weapons training, including weapons safety, and shooting qualifications. The BUD/S trainees are introduced to the primary SEAL weapon, the M4 rifle. The M4 is a variant of the standard military M16, but with a shorter barrel and a collapsible stock. Third Phase trainees spend close to a week at the SEAL shooting range at Camp Pendleton, California, and qualify with the M4. Trainees also get a chance to shoot various shotguns and submachine guns in the SEAL weapons arsenal. The end of the second week features the class top-gun shooting competition. Two at a time, the student shooters must engage and hit two targets. They begin by standing with their M4s at the ready. On the signal from the instructor, the two shooters drop to one knee and engage a metal silhouette at twenty-five meters. Once a shooter registers a *ping,* he goes to the prone position and sights in on the second target, a silhouette at fifty meters. The first shooter to get two *pings* is the winner. By single elimination, the best shooter in the class is determined. For this honor, he claims a plaque-mounted Ka-bar knife that will be engraved with his name as the class top gun.

Weeks three and four are back at the Center and the classroom for demolitions training. SEALs must know a variety of military and improvised demolitions, and how to safely handle explosives on land and in the water. They learn the basics of priming charges both electrically and nonelectrically. Basic firing assemblies with blasting caps can be prepared and detonated on the beach near the Naval Special Warfare Center, but the serious demolition training is conducted on San Clemente Island.

In many ways, San Clemente Island *is* Third Phase. San Clemente is one of the Channel Islands off the southern California coast. It's a rugged, boulder-strewn strip of land sparsely covered with scrub grass, ice plant, and cactus—lots of prickly pear and golden snake cactus. On a clear day, Santa Catalina can be seen to the northeast. On the northern tip of the island is Camp Al Huey, the BUD/S training facility. Here the BUD/S classes have everything they need to train: barracks, chow hall, armory, weapons cleaning stations, and classrooms. There are shooting ranges, demolition ranges, hand grenade ranges, and an O-course. Four weeks of training on San Clemente Island are all that stand between the trainees and their BUD/S graduation, but they are four very long weeks. On San Clemente, they will work seven days a week for the entire period without a break.

Weapons training continues on San Clemente. The trainees learn combat shooting techniques with the M4 rifle and the Sig Sauer pistol. Combat shooting requires shooting fast and accurately, changing magazines and continuing to get rounds on target. It requires expert marksmanship and magazine manipulation. Then the shooting training moves into immediate-action drills, or IADs. IADs are used to train SEALs how to break contact in a firefight or quickly assault an enemy position. The IADs require that a SEAL squad leapfrog in two elements, with one element maneuvering while the other element lays down a base of fire. This means that someone on your flank and slightly behind you is shooting at a target in front of you. This training involves a great deal of trust. IAD training is highly choreographed and closely supervised by the Third Phase staff. Trainees will walk through these drills before they run, and they will do them in the daylight before they do them at night.

On San Clemente, BUD/S trainees learn basic SEAL land-warfare skills such as ambushes, hasty ambushes, structure searches, prisoner handling, reconnaissance techniques, and raid planning. They learn these skills in the classroom, rehearse them in the field in the daylight, then go out and do them at night in simulated tactical situations.

The trainees take what they learned at the Center and apply it to heavy demolitions on the island. The class prepares nonelectric firing assemblies that are carefully timed to allow a margin of safety. Then they lay out the demolitions and rig them with a detonation cord or primacord. Finally, they cap them into a demolition field laid out on the shoreline, and it's "Fire in the hole!" They will prime and blow haversacks of C-4, Mk-75 hose, and bangalore torpedoes—up to five hundred pounds a shot. Each shot has an objective and several teaching points, not the least of which are safety in the handling, priming, and detonation of the explosives. With the same basic tools learned in Third Phase during demolitions week, Navy SEALs deployed in Afghanistan blew up tens of thousands of pounds of al-Qaeda weapons, ammunition, explosives, and equipment. Following their work with heavy demolitions, the trainees learn to set and prime claymore mines and set ambushes using claymores and improvised demolitions. From there it's an afternoon of grenades, both the 40mm, shoulder-fired type and the hand-thrown varieties.

The final week at San Clemente is taken with field training exercises (FTXs). Each morning, a squad is given a problem—a truck park, a rocket launcher, an enemy base camp—and the trainees begin to plan the mission. These could be reconnaissance missions, direct-action strikes, demolition ambushes, or raids. Throughout the day, they plan, brief, rehearse, and prepare.

At night, they conduct simulated combat missions, one squad per target. After the operation, they are back in the classroom. Each squad leader debriefs his squad, and the instructor staff critiques the evolution. If the trainees are lucky, they catch a few hours of sleep and begin another combat problem.

Each mission begins and ends with an OTB. Over-the-beach operations are a key SEAL tactic that the trainees were introduced to in First Phase. At BUD/S, they begin with OTBs in daylight, then do them over and over again at night. First, they paddle to the objective area and anchor their IBSs (inflatable boats, small) several hundred yards offshore. Next they send in scout swimmers to recon the beach. Only then is the entire squad brought ashore. The squad scurries across the sand and crawls into hiding just past the high-water line. SEALs are most vulnerable when coming ashore, so they practice these sea-to-land crossings over and over, in full combat gear with weapons. During the combat exercises on San Clemente, they wear fins that fit over their boots and partially inflate their life jackets to carry their combat load. Once ashore, they strap the fins to their H-gear for land travel. It's cold, wet, dirty work, and it must be learned well. These future SEALs will do this again and again in advanced training and in their SEAL platoons.

Friday of week nine in Third Phase is graduation day. It's a big day for the surviving trainees and a big step on their journey to becoming Navy SEALs. The Naval Special Warfare Center is turned out in flags and bunting. Proud parents watch their young men cross the podium and receive their graduation certificates. The current Indoc class stands to one side in formation, watching the proceedings with admiration and apprehension; their ordeal is just beginning. The featured speaker is an active or retired SEAL who is on hand to recognize the new BUD/S graduates and pass on a few words of inspiration as they move on to their advanced training. It's a moving time for graduates and speakers alike. I know; I have been honored to speak at two BUD/S graduations.

I remember the first time I took my wife, Julia, to a BUD/S graduation. Among all the pomp and ceremony that accompanies this event, there was a small group of men in white dress uniforms talking quietly among themselves, waiting for the proceedings to begin.

"Well, dear," I told her, "there they are, our future Navy SEALs."

"You mean that group of sailors! Those are the guys who are going to graduate?" I nodded. "No way!" she replied. "They look so average—and so young."

She was right; they did look like average young sailors. You wouldn't necessarily pick any one of them from a group of Navymen in a ship's complement or aviation squadron as being anything special. But they are special—very special. These young men are apprentice warriors, and already they are a breed apart. Now they begin the serious work of learning the tradecraft of the Navy SEAL operator. Ahead of them is Army airborne training and SEAL Qualification Training—the finishing school. With BUD/S graduation, they have completed a major step on the way to earning the Trident. One by one, the new BUD/S graduates leave the awards platform with their graduation certificate. Each receives a personal congratulation from a waiting line of BUD/S instructors—along with an admonishment to stay focused and keep working. It will not get easier, they tell them one last time; training is never over. But for today, their graduation day, these newest BUD/S graduates can celebrate their achievement. Their parents and the Navy SEAL community at large will celebrate along with them. The ceremony concludes with the class leader "ringing out" the class. He rings the BUD/S bell three times, and another BUD/S class leaves the Naval Special Warfare Center. It's a very special day. I remember my BUD/S graduation as if it were yesterday, but it wasn't. It was 2 May 1969.

INTO THE AIR

After BUD/S training, the entire class will enjoy a week or two of leave. Some will go home to visit their families; others will remain in the area and enjoy the simple freedom of not having to be up and on the run

before the sun rises and not being cold and wet for most of their waking hours. Many BUD/S graduates carry some lingering injury from the
basic course. While by now they are almost impervious to cold water
and lack of sleep, they're weary and a little beat up. The luxury of
unlimited sleep, nourished by the euphoria that comes with having
graduated from BUD/S training, is indescribably delicious. It's been
more than a few years since I graduated from this program, but I can
still easily recall the cold and fatigue followed by those marvelous few
days when I could sleep as much as I wanted and stay dry and warm.
Back then, we went straight to the teams for advanced and predeployment training. Today, BUD/S graduates remain assigned to the Naval
Special Warfare Center. They are still in "the schoolhouse"; training is
not over. They get time off but are told to stay fit and to prepare themselves mentally for some very important training ahead.

After this brief break, the BUD/S graduates go as a class to Army
Airborne School—or, as it's more commonly called, jump school.
This training is conducted at Fort Benning, Georgia. It's a three-week
course that trains and qualifies men in the basics of military static-
line parachuting. There are a few in each BUD/S class who are
already jump qualified and don't have to go to Fort Benning. But this
qualification has to be a military certification; civilian parachute or
free-fall training and experience does not count. During the course of
this instruction, the BUD/S graduates, along with their Army jump-
school classmates, will complete five qualifying parachute jumps,
including an equipment jump with rucksack and rifle. In doing so,
they will earn their Army silver jump wings and learn the basic
mechanics of mass troop parachute operations.

Jump school is a tradition-bound, methodical course of instruction
designed to take earthbound soldiers and turn them into paratroopers.
So there is a great deal more going on than simple instruction of military parachuting. The course is designed to build spirit and pride in the
Army, and a certain elitism goes along with wearing the silver wings.
Pride runs deep in Army airborne units, and it all begins at Fort Benning. We all saw this pride and professionalism in the 101st Airborne

in Iraq. Among numerous examples was the case of Captain Tony Jones. After being seriously wounded in the grenade "fragging" incident in Kuwait, Jones was confined to a hospital bed. On hearing that the 101st was about to move out into Iraq, the good captain slipped out of the hospital and hitchhiked to his unit—wearing only boots, a hospital gown, and a flak vest. The BUD/S graduates arrive at the huge Army base with their own idea of what is elite and special. Yet they must fall in ranks with their Army classmates and again become basic students. The physical demands and training regime of jump school seem trivial to the Navymen. Occasionally, the BUD/S graduates demonstrate excessive or improper spirit as they learn to parachute the Army way. They have been known to proffer cigars on a run or crank out fifty push-ups when they are dropped for ten. The sergeant instructors, or Black Hats, have seen this before. They tolerate it up to a point, and when appropriate, they know how to rein in the BUD/S graduates.

While the mechanics of Army parachuting are valuable, most SEALs will never use the mass parachute-drop techniques common to Army airborne operations. And three weeks may be too long for what the SEAL trainees get from this training. Plans are under way at the Center to develop an in-house parachute training course for BUD/S graduates designed around the requirements of the maritime special operator. It will provide training in free-fall, high-altitude-low-opening (HALO) parachuting, as well as static-line jumping. This training is still on the drawing board, but it is estimated that the course will last four weeks and provide the BUD/S graduates with five static-line and up to thirty day and night HALO jumps.

The BUD/S graduates arrive back in Coronado and the Naval Special Warfare Center wearing their new silver wings. Once they have another five parachute jumps for a total of ten, they will qualify for the gold Navy and Marine Corps jump wings. At this juncture on the road to the Trident, the enlisted men and officers of a BUD/S class will part company. As a group, the enlisted men will join the next convening SEAL Qualification Course. SQT is the last major hurdle before these BUD/S graduates will be officially designated as Navy

SEALs. The class officers will enter a series of training courses before they begin a future SQT class with the enlisted men of the BUD/S class graduating behind them. There are several reasons for this roll-back of class officers.

The evolution of advanced SEAL training to the current version of SQT has resulted in a lengthy and expensive curriculum. SQT, not BUD/S, is now considered the key training venue in the making of a Navy SEAL. This training asks the students to think and learn, and it demands that the officers and senior petty officers plan and lead. The officers are sent to training courses to help them meet this elevated expectation and to provide them with planning and leadership tools. But there's more to it than that. The bonds formed in BUD/S tend to blur the definitive lines of authority and responsibility between the officers and their men. These time-honored distinctions, while often quite subtle in close-knit special operations units, are essential in the execution of special operations missions. Within the SEAL community, graduates of the same BUD/S class are brothers for life, and nothing will ever change that. All SEALs are brothers, but there is a special tie between those who have shared the attrition and pain that accompanies surviving the basic course together. But it is helpful for the officers to lead and train with men who are perhaps not so close to them as are their BUD/S brothers. And it allows these officers to share a rigorous training experience with yet another group of enlisted men. For the enlisted men, it's a chance to demonstrate their skill and professionalism to another group of officers. The men who share the burdens of BUD/S and SQT as classmates will see and greet each other with a special affection throughout their NSW careers. Those bonds will last well beyond their time in uniform. Mine certainly have. All the while, personal and professional reputations are being formed. In the teams, reputation is everything. A man's reputation begins during BUD/S, and is refined and enhanced in SQT. If a man has struggled during BUD/S, his reputation as a weak trainee can quickly be overcome if he is able to demonstrate that he is a strong SQT student. So for the enlisted, airborne-qualified BUD/S graduates, it's straight to the finishing school; for the officers, it's interim training.

LEADERSHIP

Leadership is taught and expected at all levels of SEAL training from early in BUD/S up through SEAL platoon training and SEAL squadron deployment. A great deal of this leadership is driven by traditional leadership roles within SEAL operational elements as they have evolved over time. Leadership is a part of the SEAL culture. "It pays to be a winner" is replaced with "Here's how we are going to accomplish this mission; follow me." Much of what SEALs do individually and collectively is seeing a task and very quickly, based on their experience and training, taking the action to resolve it. In many traditional military units, officers or senior enlisted men give the orders and the troops follow the orders given. If there are no orders, there is no activity. In the operational SEAL platoons, when there is a job to do, some guidance is usually given, but not always. Often, the individual SEAL will see what needs to be done and then do it. Other times, the command to execute is simply "Okay, guys, make it happen." In an operational SEAL platoon, every man is a leader. This does not happen without a great deal of training and trust among the individual SEAL operators.

Throughout BUD/S, officers and senior petty officers have been held to a higher leadership standard than other members of the class. They have had to perform to standard, but they have also had to see that their squads and boat crews performed as well. After BUD/S graduation, officers will still have to perform to a defined training standard, but they will also be expected to demonstrate responsible, often innovative, leadership. Throughout SQT and into team operational training, there will be an increasingly distinct division of responsibilities. Enlisted men are expected to become subject-matter experts in communications, diving, air operations, weapons, and any number of

SEAL technical specialties. The officers have to focus on mission planning and tactical decision making. All of them have to maintain an elevated standard of professional skill and physical fitness.

The key leadership training venues at the Naval Special Warfare Center are the Junior Officer Training Course and the Senior Petty Officer Training Course (JOTC and SPOTC, respectively). The petty officer course is for team petty officers who have two or more platoon deployments and are being groomed for platoon leading petty officer (LPO) responsibilities or for duty as the platoon chief petty officer. The duties and responsibilities of these two key leadership positions will be discussed in later chapters. Each of these leadership courses at the Center are conducted somewhat differently than the previous one. In some cases, it is because of instructor changes or a different availability of guest speakers. Generally speaking, it is the continuing vision of Naval Special Warfare Center commanding officers to take every opportunity to strengthen the caliber of team officer and petty officer leadership. The officer and petty officer leadership courses have similarities. Since the junior officer course is the one given before the awarding of the Trident, it is treated in this text.

The JOTC is currently a five-week course. The course begins with three weeks that are heavy on scenario-based leadership seminars. There are presentations on NSW history, command relationships, enlisted performance evaluations, and public speaking, and a series of lectures by noted SEALs in the community, active and retired. During these weeks in the classroom, the new BUD/S graduate officers learn about Army and Air Force special operations components. They also learn how the U.S. military fights wars, and the role of NSW in the chain of command when deployed to an operational theater. There are classes on their administrative and legal responsibilities as SEAL officers, and the computer software to help them with these duties.

Each morning the students do group PT followed by a run or a swim. Usually they are led by someone from the teams or the training command, perhaps a platoon officer or a platoon chief petty officer. At least one run during the JOTC courses I observed was led by

Captain Rick Smethers, Commanding Officer of the Center, and Captain Bob Harward, Commander, Naval Special Warfare Group One. The student officers admitted that neither of these senior officers led them on particularly docile runs. When possible, lunches are spent in the company of team commanding officers and command master chiefs. Much time and energy in the JOTC is devoted to getting these new BUD/S officer graduates to spend time with SEAL officers and enlisted leaders in the operating SEAL teams.

The leadership seminars provide case studies of actual events in the teams and platoons, both deployed and at home. They deal with examples of good leadership and the lack of it. Seldom are these case studies black-and-white. The student leaders must wrestle with shades of gray where there is no correct solution or a range of choices, each with negative consequences. All members of the class are expected to speak on prepared subjects and deliver impromptu talks with no advance warning on the topic. The talks are video recorded so the students can learn from their performance. The classes on legal and administrative requirements associated with duty in the teams are the least favorite, but leaders cannot escape these responsibilities. In addition to learning about standard reporting and personal evaluation criteria, the student leaders are made aware of a host of agencies and services available to their men and their families. For many of these young officers, this may be the first time, but certainly not the last, that they are made aware that their duties include the welfare of their men's families. Most of the men in the leadership curriculum I poll say that the guest speakers are the best part of the first three weeks. Most afternoons the JOTC schedules a SEAL combat veteran who speaks about a specific engagement in a conflict. Those conflicts include Vietnam, Grenada, Panama, the Gulf War, Somalia, Bosnia, and Afghanistan. Retired captain Bob Gormley talks about firefights in Vietnam as a young platoon officer and as the commander of SEAL operations in Grenada. Retired lieutenant "Moki" Martin tells of the last SEAL killed in Vietnam and of the struggle to bring his body back from enemy waters. And now there is Iraq. Veterans from

SEAL Team Three, just back from the Middle East, are in to describe their fight with the Republican Guard and the Fedayeen Saddam. The subject matter focuses on leadership under combat conditions and lessons learned under fire.

Invariably, the leadership classes are addressed by "the Admiral," the Commander, Naval Special Warfare Command. During the JOTC for the officers of BUD/S Class 238, Rear Admiral Eric Olson spoke to them twice. His first presentation outlined what he expected of them as junior naval leaders. His remarks were much the same as those he made to the officers of BUD/S Class 228 two years prior when he took over as the Commander:

> *I expect you to lead at the upper levels of your knowledge, skill, and authority. Be a teammate. What's good for the team has priority over what's good for you. Demonstrate professionalism in all that you do. Be sharp, look sharp. Teach, coach, guide, and mentor your force, but don't claim experience you don't have.*
>
> *Never sacrifice what you know is right for what is convenient or expedient. Live the life of a leader—one of values, character, courage, and commitment. What you do and what you tolerate in your presence best demonstrate your standards.*
>
> *Empower your subordinate leaders to work at the full level of their authority. Encourage your subordinate leaders; train them, trust them, hold them to standard. Remember—the prime measure of your performance is the performance of your men.*

The Admiral's second presentation was a firsthand account of the fight in Mogadishu. He was there, and he was not the only SEAL. I have talked with other SEALs who were in that fight, and most seemed to derive a sense of satisfaction that no one seems to know that they were there. Rear Admiral Olson compared his recollections of that terrible battle with Mark Bowden's book *Black Hawk Down* and the movie of the same title. His point was that Bowden's book accurately captured the violence of the day, but the details were only as good as the information he was given by those who wanted to tell their own version of the story. Then he turned the engagement into a series of lessons learned.

"Amid all the heroics and the carnage, and yes, the mistakes, we found out some things that may help us the next time. And these lessons did not come cheap. Two hundred men from Task Force Ranger were involved start to finish. We suffered ninety-nine casualties—sixteen dead. No SEALs were lost, but we did collect some Purple Hearts. So what did we learn?" The Admiral ticked them off on his fingers, and the JOTC students write furiously.

"There are some macro issues, like the lack of armored vehicles and the nonavailability of an AC-130 gunship, but there are times when you simply may not have the assets available you would like to have for a mission or for mission contingencies. We also had a mission statement that focused on capturing a single personality—the warlord General Muhammad Farrah Aideed. Our mission statement in Somalia was to get General Aideed, which meant that we could destroy his infrastructure, nab his top lieutenants, restore global peace, and solve world hunger, but it would still have been mission failure if we didn't capture Aideed. So, although we had many tactical successes, we still didn't get Aideed, so we failed our mission. Aside from those terrible twenty-four hours, since we didn't get him, our mission was a failure in that regard. The lives we lost in Mogadishu drove our national policy regarding the use of the military up until 9/11. That's why we fought the conflict in Bosnia with air power alone from twenty-one thousand feet. No one wanted to accept the political risks of another Mogadishu. A policy that involves a single personality sets you up for failure. Much the same thing could be said in Afghanistan because we did not get bin Laden. However, in Afghanistan, we successfully routed a brutal regime."

"Sir, what should our mission be in these situations?"

"They should be as general as possible. In Somalia, to go after the clan infrastructure that was opposing our humanitarian efforts there. In Afghanistan, it is al-Qaeda and those who support terrorism. I think our failure to find bin Laden cost us something in the eyes of those who oppose our interests in the area. But these are big issues, well above your pay grade and mine.

"Let's talk about things we can do—what you can do as future naval leaders as you train and prepare your platoons for special operations. First of all, you cannot do enough medical preparation and training. Every man in the squad file has to be medically competent. You don't always want to send your corpsmen to drag the wounded out of the line of fire, but the men you do send must have the medical skills to deal immediately with the life-threatening injuries. You have to be prepared to carry on the fight and the mission while you treat your casualties. We had some problems with communications in Mogadishu. We cluttered up the nets when things got hot and didn't use proper call signs. Keep your comms clean and stay with procedure. That said, train for this. In all your scenario-based training, have a man go down; have your radio malfunction. Train for the worst-case scenarios." Admiral Olson began to pace the room. "If it's a daytime mission, plan for what will happen if you have to stay out after dark, and for the reverse as well. In Mogadishu, when we went back in that evening with the relief convoy, it was to be a daylight mission, in and out quickly. We didn't get out until the next morning. One of my SEALs handed me a night-vision optic right before we left. As it worked out, I would have been hard-pressed to do my job without it. Close air support. Know your fire support platforms; know how to use them. Our special operations pilots are the best in the world. We had pilots flying continually for fifteen hours in a very dangerous environment. They were magnificent. Know what they can and they can't do; don't misuse these brave and talented airmen. Body armor. It's heavy and that day it was very hot, but some of those sixteen good men we lost could have been saved if they had worn body armor with ballistic plates. Your SEALs might complain, especially during training on a hot day, but in an urban environment, it's a life saver. You are leaders; do the right thing. Train like you intend to fight. See that you and your men train *exactly* as if you were doing it for real."

Rear Admiral Olson turned and faced his young officers. "This is my last day on the job, and as you know, I will be relieved by Rear Admiral Bert Calland. It's been a great tour. The next battles I fight will be in the Pentagon." He paused a moment before continuing. "One last thought concerning Somalia. In Mogadishu, we put men at risk and remained in harm's way to bring back the bodies of those we could. We have to bring them back; it's part of who we are. It's the right thing to do for ourselves and for the families of our fallen comrades, but it also affects policy. If we are involved, it's a tough mission and we are on the world stage. The bodies of those Americans they dragged through the streets of Mogadishu changed American policy for more than a decade. It will always be a judgment call, risking lives to bring home the remains of our own, but it's something we must do if at all possible. Someday it may be your call. Think about it ahead of time, because if that decision falls on you, it will be in the heat of battle under the worst possible conditions. Good luck to all of you. Take care of your men."

That was Eric Olson's last JOTC address. On 2 August 2002, he was relieved by Rear Admiral Bert Calland, formerly General Tommy Frank's special operations commander in Afghanistan. Bert Calland brings a great deal of special operations experience to his new job as "the Admiral." Vice Admiral Eric Olson is currently the Deputy Commander, U.S. Special Operations Command.

Most of week four is spent in the classroom, learning mission planning, the most recent version of mission-planning software, and the capabilities of the SEAL Mission Support Center (MSC). This mission and operational planning training builds on the basics learned and practiced during BUD/S Third Phase. Mission planning and mission support are something of an exercise in alphabet soup. The current version of mission-planning software is called SOMPE-M, for Special Operations Mission Planning Environment—

Maritime. It is a Windows NT Office 2000 variant that allows special operations planners a secure platform from which to access information, conduct Web chats, have whiteboard sessions, and bring the vast military and special operations databases to the operational and tactical-level planners. There was a different system in place two years ago, and I expect it will be different still when this book goes to press. I have watched these systems develop over the years; as the programs evolve, they become more efficient, more dependable, more user compatible, and more SEAL-operator friendly. The capabilities of the SOMPE-M system are something someone else should write a book about; they are quite amazing.

The Mission Support Center is a new tool to support deployed Naval Special Warfare assets. The MSC provides deployed units with what is called "reachback." It provides task units and task elements with the ability to reach back and interact with rear-echelon support staffs for logistical support and operational information on a real-time basis. SEAL squadrons deploy with a minimum of operational equipment. The MSC coordinates and facilitates their support with forward-deployed logistics and an on-call capability for special requirements or a surge of mission-specific equipment. As for information and intelligence, the MSC is something of a special operations Google-like search engine. While the guys in the field are loading magazines and conducting rehearsals, the MSC staff is downloading and packaging information to support the mission. They cannot as yet tell the SEAL patrol leader in the field what is over the next tree line or berm, but that capability is not far off.

The final week of the JOTC has the new officers back in the field. They are out in the rugged, mountainous terrain at La Posta doing quick-reaction leadership drills. The instructors are armed with artillery simulators and blank ammunition. The students have no live or blank ammo during this FTX period. These are combat patrols that last two to four hours, sometimes longer. They are quick, hard-hitting drills to teach tactical decision making in an operational environment and simulated combat. They begin with a short scenario briefing that outlines the situation and the rules of engagement. Then the student officers become a squad moving in hostile territory. The leadership decisions fall on the point man, the patrol leader, and the assistant patrol leader. The rest of the squad must practice good "followship." Everybody learns. Following an action or engagement, the student leaders circle up for a field critique. Then everyone moves up a notch in the squad file, and they move on to the next drill. They do this for five straight days, breaking only for a quick meal of MRE (meals ready to eat) field rations or a water break. They sleep very little—and when they do, it's in the field.

"This was one of the best things we've done," Lieutenant John Flattery told me. "It was good, for a change, to not have to go through a day or two of planning and briefing and gear prep for a single field operation. This was all tactical decision making and reacting to changing conditions while carrying out the mission."

"I learned an important lesson," Ensign Trent Bollinger said. "When I'm leading a patrol, I'll be a lot better about keeping the guys in the squad informed on the tactical situation. They told us that in BUD/S, but you don't really understand it until you're stumbling along in the patrol file at night, wondering what's going on up front."

To a man, the officers in the JOTC praised their training and felt they were much better prepared to be leaders in training. They can't wait to get to SQT, but there are other schools they have to attend before they get there. They must first complete the Range Safety Officers Course, the Diving Supervisors Course, and SERE (Survival, Evasion, Resistance, and Escape) School.

Range Safety and Dive Supe are both one-week courses of instruction. The courses are designed to comply with Navy and Naval Special Warfare regulations in the safe conduct of shooting and diving. Both courses begin with a heavy dose of regulations that strictly govern these activities. These regulations introduce the officers to the procedures and checklists they must follow prior to, during, and following all shooting and diving training. In the Range Safety Officers Course, the officer students go to different ranges and conduct shooting training. Each in turn acts as the range safety officer under the watchful eye of a qualified instructor RSO. During the Dive Supe course, they dive. Before they qualify, each student diving supervisor must properly set up and supervise a diving evolution, including checking all of "his" divers before they go into the water. As qualified RSOs and Dive Supes, they can now serve in these supervisory capacities during SQT training, although those roles will normally be filled by SQT instructors. While these officers are in training, they will be on the ranges to shoot or in the water as combat divers; they are still students. Their supervisory duties will come when they're qualified SEALs and in their SEAL platoons.

SERE is different. All SEALs must attend SERE school. If, due to SQT convening dates and SERE school scheduling, they cannot complete this school while at the training command, they will have to make time for it once they reach their teams. SERE training is required for SEALs, NSW Special Warfare Combatant Craft crewmen, Marine Corps Force Recon, and all Navy and Marine Corps aircrews—basically anyone who will routinely operate in enemy waters, or on or over enemy-held territory. SERE school is conducted by the naval aviation community at various locations. Most SEALs attend the SERE training facility at Warner Springs, California. SERE trainees spend five days in the classroom learning survival skills and how to assist rescuers in the event they are forced down or caught behind enemy lines. They also learn about the military Code of Conduct and how it relates to a POW's duty to resist during interrogation, exploitation, and indoctrination by the enemy. Then they go into the field for five days of survival and evasion. This field exercise inevitably leads to capture and internment in the SERE prisoner compound. Here the student POWs get a taste of what it may be like if they are ever taken prisoner. This is a psychologically as well as physically demanding experience, even for SEAL trainees who are not unfamiliar with pain and suffering. Most of my aviator friends have stories about their SERE experience; if there were SEALs or SEAL trainees in their SERE class, the best of these tales detail the recalcitrance of their fellow POW trainees who were SEALs.

"They couldn't keep this one SEAL in the slammer," a pilot friend told me, recounting his SERE experience. "Every morning we had roll call and this guy was gone. And the other SEALs got their chops busted because they couldn't quit grinning about it."

When the BUD/S officer graduates have finished their post-BUD/S classes, they are ready to begin SQT with the enlisted men who graduated from BUD/S a class behind them. Before we begin SQT with Class 2-02, it might be helpful to understand how other special operations forces, or SOF, train their officers, both in their basic and advanced military training. It's quite different—and different by way of necessity.

THE OTHER GUYS

The United States Army has two major ground SOF components: the Rangers and the Special Forces (SF), also known as the Green Berets. Both are highly capable special operations organizations with very different primary missions. There is some commonality in their capabilities, but they train differently for different reasons. The Rangers are light, airborne infantry. A veteran Special Forces officer told me that he considers them SOF shock troops. The Seventy-fifth Ranger Regiment is, in my opinion, the finest light infantry in the world. They specialize in airborne assaults and company-size infantry operations. These special warriors are light, mobile, and very professional. If they have to, Rangers can cover long distances on the ground and be ready to fight when they get there. They select their officers from the Army's corps of infantry officers. The Rangers are looking for first lieutenants who are graduates of the basic infantry course with platoon-level experience in the infantry. They also seek captains who are graduates of the advanced infantry course with company-level infantry command experience. In both cases, the Ranger regiment is looking for airborne-qualified officers who have demonstrated superior leadership in a troop command and are Ranger School qualified.

The Special Forces have an entirely different primary mission. They are the SOF experts in the area of counterinsurgency and unconventional warfare. The SF is looking for men who know how to work with other people and other cultures. For new officers, the SF is looking for Army captains with company-level command experience who have had five years' experience as an Army officer. SF officer candidates must be airborne qualified and are carefully screened for their ability to work with the regular and irregular foreign military forces. They are selected for their maturity and their ability to succeed in an ambiguous and hostile environment. The Special Forces doesn't care if a prospect is an infantry officer or an engineer. It does care if he can think on his feet and has good people skills. Special Forces Officer Training lasts twelve to fourteen months. The new SF officer will go to his A-Team as the team OIC (officer in charge) with six years of experience in the Army.

Both the SF and the Rangers are looking for seasoned enlisted men who are volunteers and who have demonstrated superior physical, mental, and motivational qualities. The SF enlisted men train in specialties such as weapons, communications, and medicine—training that can last as long as a year. For Rangers, enlisted and officer, the key school is Ranger School. It is an eight-week ordeal not unlike BUD/S Third Phase. It teaches young men that they can move, fight, and lead even when they've been on the march for several days with no sleep.

The point of all this is that the SEAL teams have no pool of infantry talent from which to draw their officer and enlisted trainees. The Navy is simply not a ground combat-arms service. So Naval Special Warfare must find its prospective SEAL officers in the newly commissioned ensigns from the Naval Academy, the Naval Reserve Officer Training Corps (NROTC), and the Naval Officer Candidate School. Perhaps as many as 15 percent of the officer input comes from the fleet—officers who have two or three years of shipboard experience. These fleet lieutenants understand the workings of the Navy, and they bring proven leadership skills to a BUD/S class; but they're sailors, not soldiers. They bring none of the infantry skills that are so valuable in ground combat operations—even special operations ground combat.

Much the same is true in the enlisted ranks. Both the Rangers and the Special Forces are able to cherry-pick men from a large pool of trained infantrymen, many of whom are on their second or third enlistment. The Rangers and the SF have programs that will take younger men as long as they meet the physical, mental, and psychological requirements for special operations. Most enlisted BUD/S trainees are only a few months out of boot camp, and those who come from the fleet bring a degree of maturity and experience, but they're still sailors.

The Air Force Special Tactics Teams—the Combat Control and Para-Rescue Teams—face the same problems as Naval Special Warfare: They must take airmen and young officers and make special operators out of them. They are the smallest of the SOF ground components, and their approach to their special operations requirements is much like the Navy's.

The SEALs have no choice but to grow their own personnel. This begins in BUD/S. This is why BUD/S training, start to finish, is thirty weeks, and why BUD/S is as much a screening process as a training program. This is also why SQT is so important and so comprehensive. Enlisted men are in the womb of the training command for at least a year, the officers slightly longer. When a new SEAL gets to his team, he faces at least another eighteen months of predeployment training before he begins an operational deployment. The grooming of officers and enlisted petty officers for leadership in the SEAL platoons continues during these predeployment training periods, as well as on operational deployment. In later chapters we will talk more about the training of SEALs and SEAL leaders in the platoon and team environment. But first, let's get to the heart of making a Navy SEAL: SEAL Qualification Training.

CHAPTER 2

The Finishing School

THE ROAD TO THE TRIDENT

Enlisted BUD/S graduates who have completed Army Airborne School, and officers who have completed airborne training and their assigned interim schools, will anxiously await the convening of their SEAL Qualification Training, or SQT. Enlisted men who went straight through BUD/S with no injuries can get to SQT about eight months after they began the Indoctrination Course at BUD/S. Officers will, on average, begin their SQT training some ten months after beginning BUD/S. This again assumes good timing and no injuries.

Just as the immediate needs of amphibious warfare and the debacle at Tarawa spawned Hell Week in the training of a Navy frogman, the current SQT evolved in response to lessons learned in combat. Advanced training in SQT descended from the need to train SEALs for combat duty in Vietnam. During the mid-1960s, when SEALs began regular platoon rotations into the Rung Sat Special Zone in the Mekong Delta, there was no formal Naval Special Warfare–based training for SEALs that met the deployment requirements. BUD/S

Breathe, hold, and squeeze. An SQT instructor coaches a shooter in proper technique from the offhand firing position. *Photo by Dick Couch*

trainees generally went to the Underwater Demolition Teams. The two SEAL teams at the time were manned by veterans from the UDTs. The first deployments to Vietnam were on-the-job training for the new SEALs. The SEAL teams immediately learned that there needed to be additional training for the deploying platoons; experience from the UDTs was simply not enough. So a practice evolved in which veteran SEALs who returned from Vietnam would hold training classes for the soon-to-deploy SEALs. As new basic graduates began coming directly to the SEAL teams from the training command, this form of SEAL training became a requirement for all new men reporting to the teams. It was called Cadre Training—the cadre being all Vietnam combat veterans. This evolved into a formal team training called SEAL Basic Indoctrination, or SBI. The skills taught in Cadre/SBI were hard-won, often bloody lessons learned in battle. In the beginning, one thing and one thing only was taught: how to conduct combat operations in a jungle environment. The training was all about operating and surviving in Vietnam. We learned how to fight in the jungles and the rice paddies, and little else. This was advanced SEAL training—or as advanced as SEAL training got in those early days.

I went through SEAL Cadre Training with SEAL Team Two in 1969 on the East Coast and again when I arrived at SEAL Team One on Coronado in 1970. Harry Humphries, Ed Leisure, and Bo Bohannon were my Cadre instructors. They and men like them were the corporate knowledge in the SEAL teams, and their experience was invaluable. I can honestly say that what they taught us kept me and the other new guys alive in combat. Today, advanced SEAL training is highly formatted and refined. In my time, the instructors made it up as they went along. I can still remember one of them saying, "Now pay attention, 'cause what I'm going to show you can save your life. When I deployed on my first Vietnam tour, we didn't have this knowledge or experience and it cost the life of one of my teammates. This piece of information that I will now share with you was purchased with blood." The lessons that Instructor Bohannon shared with us didn't come from an approved lesson plan, nor were they sugarcoated. I remember him going to great measures to show us how to set a good ambush. "Let's get this in perspective," he told us. "You do this right and it's nothing more than premeditated murder—as quick and as painless as putting down a dog."

On paper and on the surface, advanced SEAL training is kinder and gentler than it was during the late 1960s and early 1970s, but no less effective and perhaps a good deal more professional. Based on my observations during the writing of this book, I believe the formal teaching of military and special operations skills is now much more precise and comprehensive. But I was also encouraged to see that at the end of the training day, students and the advanced training cadre continued to talk at evening chow or over a beer. During breaks in the course of training evolutions, a great deal of learning takes place. Many of the advanced instructors bring combat experience from Afghanistan, Bosnia, the Gulf War, and Panama. Now the experience is coming back from operations in Iraq. When these seasoned warriors talk about their deployment experience and what they learned in combat, the SEAL students listen attentively—just like I did way back when. Some things never change, nor should they. In a small organization like Naval Special Warfare, combat experience and lessons learned can get from the operational components to the training command almost immediately.

The Cadre Training/SBI system of old team guys breaking in new team guys lasted through the mid-1990s, when the Naval Special Warfare Groups assumed this training responsibility. This was a dramatic change in advanced training, as it took the training responsibility away from the individual teams. This advanced training was called SEAL Tactical Training, or STT, and it was conducted by NSW Group Two for the East Coast SEALs and NSW Group One on the West Coast. This group-sponsored approach allowed for a measure of standardization and a more efficient use of training resources. It also freed the individual teams to concentrate on training their platoons for operational deployment. During the STT era, West Coast training took place in the San Diego area and at Camp Billy Machen, the Naval Special Warfare desert warfare training facility just north of the Mexican border near the Chocolate Mountains—a three-hour drive east of San Diego. The East Coast teams trained their STT students in the Little Creek area and at Camp Pickett and Camp A. P. Hill in Virginia. These STT courses lasted twelve to fourteen weeks. The new men left STT for their teams and completed their final training and testing requirements with that team. The team then awarded their new men the Tridents. In 2001, SEAL advanced training was further consolidated into SEAL Qualification Training; STT became SQT. SQT now conducts the SEAL training for all BUD/S graduates and awards the Trident. SQT is a prep school for duty in the SEAL platoons and is currently an eighteen-week course.

The SEAL Qualification Training Course is considered the premier training course in Naval Special Warfare. More time, money, resources, and talent go into this training than any other conducted by Naval Special Warfare. It is high-speed, difficult, and dangerous business. Much public and media attention is focused on BUD/S because of the high attrition rate and the physical misery associated with the basic course. But all the blood and sweat of BUD/S, including post-BUD/S training, does only one thing: It buys a man a seat at the table for SQT. The pace and the professional requirements are elevated several notches at SQT. If a man cannot meet the standards of this course, then he will never become a qualified Navy SEAL, and he will never serve in the Navy SEAL teams. The BUD/S graduates who come to SQT have come a long way. The training cadres at SQT know these students are tough, and they know they are not quitters. But that's not enough. Now, these BUD/S graduates must learn and master-to-standard the minimum professional skills of a SEAL warrior. Most of them will, but not all.

The main body of what follows comes from SQT Class 2-02. Their backgrounds, experiences, trials, and failures in this work are factual; only the names of the trainees and training cadre have been changed to protect their identities. Many of the SEAL students and instructors you will be reading about are currently deployed overseas with operational SEAL platoons. And many of them are veterans of combat duty in Afghanistan and Iraq.

Class 2-02 was the last SQT class before the practice of rolling back BUD/S officer graduates to a future SQT class was started. The officers I observed in Class 2-02 trained in SQT with their BUD/S classmates. All the officers of 2-02 endorse the officer-rollback concept and wished that they had had the leadership base of the JOTC before they began their advanced training. Officers in subsequent SQT classes have had nothing but praise for the scheduling of the leadership course in advance of their SQT training. The SQT training cadres have voiced their strong support for the officer-rollback program as well. Since the graduation of Class 2–02, I have visited specific training venues with subsequent SQT classes. The enlisted men and their new officers train well together; the officers step up to their leadership responsibilities, and they rely on the advice and support of their new petty officers.

Each SQT class, like each BUD/S class, is different and has its own personality. My work at the Naval Special Warfare Center has allowed me to meet a great number of these fine young men. I am often asked to speak to the basic SEAL classes, and many in SQT remember me from presentations I made to their BUD/S class. Along the way, I am continually surprised by the tenacity and character of these young warriors. With Class 4–02, I met a determined young man from BUD/S Class 228. He had completed Hell Week with Class 228 in the fall of 1999, but was too beat up to continue with that class. He came back through BUD/S with Class 240, completed his second Hell Week, and finished BUD/S. He graduated with SQT Class 4–02 and is now in the teams. It's hard to express just how good it is to see one of these terrific young men struggle with this difficult program, overcome adversity, and go on to achieve his goal. It's what this business is all about.

SQT classes are numbered successively within the year; SQT Class 4–02 was the fourth class to begin training in 2002. Depending on scheduling, there are four or five SQT classes per year. The standard

SQT curriculum is fifteen weeks. After the successful completion of this instruction, an aspiring warrior is awarded the Trident; he is now a Navy SEAL. But SQT is not over; the new SEALs immediately face three weeks of cold-weather training. For this training, the SQT class travels up to Kodiak Island, Alaska. The cold-weather component of SEAL training is relatively new—that is, it's new to the Naval Special Warfare Center as a core advanced training course. There was no cold-weather curriculum in SQT prior to Class 4–02. I observed this training with SQT Class 5–02. The training on Kodiak is simply amazing. I live in the mountains in Idaho and thought I knew something about cold weather, but I think differently now. What I found more impressive than the harsh conditions on Kodiak in February was the energy and enthusiasm with which the new SEALs take to this training. But I'm ahead of myself. Let's start at the beginning.

THE BEGINNING

Zero eight hundred, main classroom, the SQT building. Several years ago, this same building on the Naval Amphibious Base, Coronado, was used to house SEAL Delivery Vehicle Team One. SDV Team One is now located in Hawaii to be closer to the submarine forces of the Pacific Fleet. Today, the building, along with the classrooms, the dive locker, the generous equipment bays, and the pier facility, is the home of SEAL Qualification Training. The BUD/S graduates who enter this training are not Navy SEALs. Those who successfully complete this training will be. After their SQT graduation, they will leave wearing the SEAL Trident, the emblem of the Navy SEALs. In the eyes of the Navy and the rest of the world they are Navy SEALs. But in the eyes of their fellow warriors in the teams, they are rookies or new guys— inexperienced and in many ways unprepared as yet for journeyman duty in a SEAL platoon. But the veteran SEALs know these men will bring energy and talent to their platoons. They are the lifeblood and future of the teams. The veterans know it is a part of their job to train and mentor these new SEALs and help them to become fully formed warriors. And make no mistake about it, these new SEALs are ready in all respects to begin the training cycle that will make them combat-ready members of a deploying SEAL platoon. But on day one of SQT, they are students, concerned with the important ordeal in front of them. On this day they are perhaps as apprehensive as they were when they began Indoc, way back during the first days of BUD/S, what must now seem like an eternity ago.

Heading south from the town of Coronado toward Imperial Beach on the U.S.-Mexican border, Highway 75 bisects the Naval Amphibious Base. On the west side of this highway are the West Coast SEAL teams and the Naval Special Warfare Center, where Basic Underwater Demolition/SEAL Training is conducted. On the east side of the highway is the main part of the amphibious base. It is here on the northeast side of the base that SQT is conducted, well away from the Center and BUD/S. Here, the members of SQT Class 2-02 wait to begin the last lap on their journey to the SEAL Trident. The class falls silent as a solid man in his late thirties quietly makes his way to the front of the room.

"Okay, men, I'm going to need your full attention. This is your SEAL Qualification Training indoctrination briefing. This morning I will be putting out some important information about what you will be doing here at SEAL Qualification Training, so I want you to listen up and take notes. My name is Senior Chief Mike Collier. I'm the assistant officer in charge of SQT."

There are fifty-four SQT students in the room. Either Senior Chief Collier or the officer in charge, Chief Warrant Officer Mike Loo, will give each new class its indoctrination briefing. Like all SEAL training, SQT is an evolving course. The SQT for Class 2-02 will be just a little different and a little better than that for Class 1-02. This training is acknowledged within the SEAL community as the most effective yet in preparing BUD/S graduates for duty in SEAL platoons. Many senior SEAL trainers have had a hand in this, but none have been more dedicated to this high-value training than Senior Chief

Mike Collier and Chief Warrant Officer Mike Loo. This course is their creation, and the success of these trainees when they join their operational components reflects on the professional reputation of these two men. They take their responsibility very seriously. Most of SQT Class 2-02 is made up of graduates from BUD/S Class 237. Class 237 was an unusually large one. It began with more than two hundred basic SEAL trainees and graduated fifty-one. Three men in Class 2-02 are Trident holders. Two of them are active-duty SEALs returning from duty away from the teams, and one is a reservist returning to active duty. It's been over two years since I "classed up" with BUD/S Class 228. I, too, feel as if I'm returning to duty for my advanced training.

In the front row, I see a BUD/S graduate I remember from Class 228—the subject of my previous book, *The Warrior Elite*—and stop to say hello. But it's not him; it's his identical twin, who just graduated with Class 237. The brother I knew was a stalwart in Class 228. His look-alike was no less than the Honorman in Class 237, the top graduate of his class. There are four class officers, but none of them are Naval Academy officers, which is a rarity for a BUD/S class. Two are recent graduates from military programs, one from the Virginia Military Institute and the other from the Corps of Cadets at Texas A&M. The third is a Rhodes scholar with a doctorate in political science from Oxford. The fourth officer was a professional surfer before he came to BUD/S. He had graduated from Santa Clara University, having previously attended the Naval Academy for two years. At the Naval Academy, he roomed with the Honorman from Class 228. While attending the BUD/S graduation of his Academy roommate, he decided that he, too, wanted to become a SEAL. His journey from professional surfer to Navy SEAL is fascinating, but then every man's route to the teams is unique.

The enlisted contingent from BUD/S Class 237 is an impressive group. They fall into three general categories. About a third of them have college degrees. Many of those had sought an officer program that would take them to BUD/S, but when that door was closed, they enlisted for a chance to become a Navy SEAL. About a third are fleet sailors who decided they were looking for a different kind of Navy. And a third came to BUD/S right out of high school, or perhaps with a semester or two of college. A few had been on a job that bored them and found themselves in a Navy recruiting office, looking to make a change. Many of these high school graduates are between nineteen and twenty-one years old. They have hard bodies and fresh faces, and are maturing fast. In a matter of months, they will be platoon SEALs. One of them is the son of an active Navy SEAL; his father is currently the command master chief of the Naval Special Warfare Unit in Guam. Another was born in Korea; an orphan, he was adopted by an American family in Los Angeles. He is here because he wants to serve his adoptive country. The leading petty officer is a competent, soft-spoken second class petty officer with several years' duty in the fleet. Prior to becoming a sailor he had been a soldier, having served a tour in the Army. Ethnically, most of the men are white. Four have roots in Latin America, three are of Korean extraction, and there is one African-American. They range in size from six-foot four to five-two. The heaviest student weighs close to 230, while the shortest man has brought his weight up to 125. He graduated from BUD/S at 116, which makes him pound for pound the toughest man in the class. Four men in the SQT class have served in the Marine Corps, but only the one is from the Army. The senior chief again takes charge of the class.

"First of all, let me congratulate the majority of you who recently graduated from BUD/S. For you Trident holders, welcome back and welcome to SQT. You all have a very important fifteen weeks ahead of you, perhaps the most important fifteen weeks of training in your SEAL career. This is the best course in Naval Special Warfare. These are the best instructors in Naval Special Warfare. There are twenty-four of us on staff. We represent almost three hundred years of Naval Special Warfare experience. We are a resource. Use us well." Collier taps the laptop computer on the podium and a blue PowerPoint slide explodes into view behind him.

THE ESSENCE OF NAVAL SPECIAL WARFARE LIES IN THE INTEGRITY OF THE OPERATOR AND THE UNITY OF THE PLATOON.

"This is what it's all about, gentlemen. My responsibility, and the responsibility of every member of this training cadre, is to get you ready to be an effective member of a SEAL platoon. We're here to train you and to mentor you and to do whatever it takes to prepare you for war. You will be very busy while you're here. Fifteen weeks is not a lot of time, and there is some very important material you will have to master. Pay attention and do what's asked of you, and on the third of July, we'll pin a Trident on you. We award the Trident here, and we take that responsibility very seriously. If you haven't shown us that you're ready and that you deserve to be a Navy SEAL, then you won't wear a Trident; you will not become a Navy SEAL. It's as simple as that. We have teammates in combat; we've just lost two SEALs in Afghanistan. This is high-risk, real-world training. Your responsibility is to listen, learn, train safely, and to lock down the skills that you are going to need in a very short time. We expect the same performance and motivation you gave in BUD/S but twice the professionalism. Make a personal commitment to learning and improving your skills. When you get to your platoon, they will expect you to know what to do. Unless you show to us that you know these skills, you will not graduate from this course. This is a big class. We will not shortchange you in any aspect of this training, but we will need your cooperation. Pay attention, ask questions, have your equipment properly prepared and staged, be on time for every training evolution—that means five minutes early with your gear ready. Always have a pencil and a notebook with you.

"You will be tested here. At the end of each phase, there will be a written test and you will be graded in the field. There is a final written exam that will cover all phases of training. More than that, the community will be watching. You guys all know about reputation. Here in SQT you will have an opportunity to build on your reputation. Those in the teams will know if you performed well here. They'll also know if you did just enough to get by. If you're not motivated—if you don't demonstrate a responsible, positive, mature attitude—they'll know that as well. Again, it's your reputation."

Senior Chief Collier slips into high gear with the PowerPoint and pushes quickly through a litany of administrative and logistical items. Whenever he gets to matters pertaining to weapons, demolitions, or safety issues, he slows down.

"On your schedules, you will see PT scheduled most days. Sometimes it's zero six-thirty, sometimes it's zero seven hundred. If we're out working the previous night, it could be as late as zero eight-thirty. We don't have organized PT here like you had at BUD/S. You're on your own. Take care of your equipment; take care of your bodies. Out at Camp Billy Machen you will be rucked up for a hard-ass, thirteen-mile Combat Conditioning Course. You go soft on us and you'll pay the price out there in the desert—perhaps the ultimate price. The Combat Conditioning Course is not some fun run; it's a timed evolution. If you can't make that time, you can't pass this course. Enough said.

"Now, let's talk about attitude. You have to condition yourself mentally as well as physically. We are war fighters; you are preparing yourself for combat. Think about it. If you are not here to prepare for combat then get the hell out. Don't waste our time. This is a school for warriors, and we are training for war. Hey, it's more than that; we're training for the privilege of serving our nation.

"Conduct. I want you to—no, I insist that you—respect our brother warriors from the Special Boat Teams and the aircrews. Treat them with courtesy and professionalism; they deserve it, and you may have to go to war with them. You all know the rules about drinking, driving, and illegal drugs. Drugs are a no-brainer; why do I even mention it? Get a DUI and we'll see that you find another line of work. Here, and in the teams, it's unacceptable.

"Let's talk about integrity. Always behave in a manner that will be respected by everyone. If you're not sure whether it's right or wrong, it's probably wrong. We talked about respect for others, but that includes respect for the cadre and for your classmates here in SQT, as well as for the equipment. Safety—it's a religion with us here in SQT. You show a casual disregard for safety and we'll kick you out of here. If you observe an unsafe condition or you are unsure during a high-risk evolution, then call a training time-out. We respect TTOs here. We're gonna train hard, but we're gonna train safe.

"Maturity. Most of you are not SEALs yet, but you represent the Naval Special Warfare community. You represent me. You represent Captain Couch back there who was in the teams thirty years ago. Conduct yourselves appropriately when you're off duty. When you're here, stay focused. You officers must continually ask yourselves, 'Have I done everything I can to plan and prepare myself to lead my men?' For now, it's training. Sometime in the near future you will be leading men in harm's way. You enlisted men have to study this business; you will be the subject-matter experts in the teams. You must prepare yourself in every way possible to contribute to the success of the mission.

"Teamwork. Commitment to team is very important. Often it is everything. You have to help each other. You cannot feel proud about yourself if a shipmate falls short or is not performing up to standard. We all have weaknesses. Work on them, and help each other to work on them. We'll all be the better for it. It's what teamwork is all about."

The senior chief clips off the PowerPoint and surveys the class. "Remember, we expect you to put out one hundred ten percent, mentally and physically. Demonstrate a positive and constructive attitude. Be a teammate, and work together—support each other. Your lives will depend on it in the teams. Train like you fight, because you will fight like you train. And make no mistake about it, gentlemen, we are in a fight. Our country is in a fight. During the next few months we're going to need your full cooperation and total focus. Both you and my training cadre need to work together. It will take a lot of hard work on everybody's part to get you guys ready for the fight.

"Any questions?" There are none. "Okay, take a quick five-minute break and get back into the classroom. Instructor Thomas will be here waiting for you. SQT begins now. Good luck to all of you, and I hope that I will see every one of you here on the third of July when Class 2-02 is awarded their Tridents."

WARRIORS AND HEALERS

Hospital Corpsman Gordon Thomas has been in the teams for only seven years. He has made two deployments, both with SEAL Team Four, and has been teaching combat medicine at SQT for a year and a half. Thomas is highly animated as he roams the front of the classroom. He's an excellent teacher—very dynamic and explicit, and very comfortable with his subject.

"Okay, guys, here's the deal. You're a member of a twenty-four-man special operations team. You have just inserted by boat and are patrolling to your objective, a cocaine lab in very dense jungle. Everyone's excited; the intelligence you have is first-rate, and there's every reason to expect complete surprise. Estimated enemy strength is fifteen men with automatic weapons. You have a three-mile patrol over difficult terrain to reach your target. You're movin' good— sneakin' an' peekin'—doing everything right. As you approach the objective, your point man trips a booby trap, and there is a loud explosion in the front of the patrol. Your point man is blown off the trail; he has no pulse and no respiration. The patrol leader was second in the file. He has massive trauma to the leg and femoral bleeding. Now you're in heavy fire as the hostiles respond. Your planned extraction is a point on the river a half mile from the target. You are next in command. What do you do?" There is a silence in the classroom. "C'mon," Instructor Thomas says, "give me some help here. You've got teammates dyin' and bleedin' up there. The bad guys are movin' on you. You can hear the rounds snapping overhead." Those who have been in combat talk about the sonic-wave "snap" of a round passing close by. "So, what are you going to do?"

"Find a pressure point to stop the bleeding."

"CPR."

"Treat for shock."

"Get an IV started."

Thomas holds up his hands.

"Look at it this way. You have a medical problem and a tactical problem. We want the best outcome for the man—the men, in this case—and the mission. Good medicine can sometimes be bad tactics. Bad tactics can get everyone killed. You're under heavy fire; you've already got two guns out of the fight. Are you really going to do CPR? Set up an IV? You guys see any problem with doing these things in the middle of a firefight?"

Again there is silence.

"A couple of you guys are EMTs, right?" Two hands go up. "Remember how we were trained in advanced trauma life support techniques—ATLS?" The two men nod in unison. "Right, and we all learned it the same way—the way they treat gunshot wounds in the ER. So what you said was right according to ATLS. But the Rangers in Mogadishu taught us a whole bunch about treating casualties under fire. We don't use ATLS anymore. Those Rangers paid for those lessons with their own blood, and here we put into practice what they learned."

ATLS is the way civilian emergency medics treat trauma victims. This is very methodical treatment in a controlled environment and in a prescribed manner—CPR, cervical-spine immobilization, primary survey, definitive airway, IV fluids, and the like. Military medics followed these same procedures in Vietnam and in subsequent conflicts—until Mogadishu. A careful analysis of ground combat deaths in Vietnam found that almost 60 percent of those came from penetrating head wounds and surgically uncorrectable torso trauma. These men would have been hard to save if they were in the hospital under the very best of conditions. But the rest of those who died might have been saved. Sixty percent of those bled to death from extremity wounds and 30 percent from tension pneumothorax.

"There's a better way, guys. It's called tactical combat casualty care, or TCCC. Basically, we have to treat the casualty, prevent additional casualties, and complete the mission. But the tactical situation dictates everything. First there is care under fire, like in our firefight at the coke lab or the beach scene from *Saving Private Ryan*. The tactical situation will drive what you do. Then there's tactical field care, when you're not under fire and your platoon corpsman can treat the guy, if he's not the guy who just got hit. Then it's up to you. During tactical field care, decisions can be made when the bullets aren't flying. And finally, there's combat evacuation care. That's when you've been picked up and are on the way out. We now call this 'casevac,' for casualty evacuation—not medevac. Medevac is like when you have an ambulance, and a crowd of paramedics hovering about, and all kinds of good gear. On the extraction chopper or the boat, we don't usually have that. Now, we've still got two men down. One's not breathing and the other is bleeding big time. How long does it take a guy to bleed out from a big hole in his femoral artery?"

A hand goes up. "A couple minutes, maybe."

"Maybe, if that. Your teammate needs help, quick. So what do we do?"

Another hand. "Get some rounds out and get the downed guys to some cover."

"Exactly. The best medicine on the battlefield is *fire superiority*. Okay, the boys are on line, and we're getting rounds downrange. The bad guys now think maybe they've tangled with the wrong bunch. You've dragged your patrol leader to some cover. The rounds are still snapping overhead, but you're out of immediate danger. Now what?"

"Stop the bleeding."

"You got it. The number one cause of preventable battlefield deaths is bleeding. He's breathing, so forget the airway. How are we going to stop the bleeding?"

"Tourniquet?"

"That's right, a tourniquet. Under the ATLS method, the use of tourniquets was discouraged. Direct pressure is an option, but are you going to take a gun out of the fight and have someone hold a pressure bandage on this guy's thigh? If a tourniquet can stop the bleeding and he's conscious, maybe the casualty can get his gun back in the fight. If they can, casualties have to return fire. I'm here to tell you, tourniquets are lifesavers. We lost twenty-five thousand guys in Vietnam who had no other wounds than bleeding from an extremity wound. That's twenty-five thousand names on that wall—men that might have been saved if they knew back then what we teach here. So think about it. Okay, about our patrol leader who's bleeding like some stuck pig—do seconds count? You bet. That's why I want that pressure bandage and cravat on your H-gear, and I want everyone to have it in the same place. You don't have time to roll this guy over and do a body search to find his tourniquet. If it's on his H-gear in a standard place, you grab it, slap it in place, and get your own gun back in the fight. You officers, it's your job when you do your pre-mission inspections to make sure your men have their medical gear in a standard location on their H-gear, got that?"

"Hooyah," the ensigns respond. (Hooyah is the universal SEAL response of enthusiasm; recent BUD/S graduates use it liberally.)

Thomas goes on to talk about tension pneumothorax in a way his students can understand. When a bullet enters the torso, it creates a one-way flapper valve in the chest cavity. As the wounded man breathes, it draws air into the chest cavity, which cannot escape on the out-breath. The result is the collapsing of a lung. The treatment is a needle in the side of the chest to decompress the chest cavity. "Sounds hard, I know," Thomas tells them, "but we're gonna show you how to do it. Trust me, you'll know the symptoms for tension pneumothorax and know what to do."

Thomas continues to lecture on care under fire. Win the firefight, stay alive, take cover, protect the casualty. Then he tells them about the BATS protocol—bleeding, airway, tension pneumothorax, and shock.

"So what about our point man; what are we going to do about him? He's your buddy; you went through BUD/S together, and he was in your boat crew—one shit-hot guy. You loaned him half your last paycheck. He's not breathing; he has no pulse." Another silence in the classroom. "This is where it gets hard. There's nothing we can do on the battlefield for this guy—he's dead, no matter what we do. He's dead even if we're not under fire, but then we could try. He's probably dead if he were in an ambulance on the way to the hospital. In Mogadishu, they did CPR on guys that had no chance, and it cost time and it cost lives. You have to think. What can you do for the man who can be saved? What about the mission? You're under fire. Do what you can for those who will benefit from your help; then get your gun back in the fight. In the raid on Entebbe, the mission commander, Lieutenant Colonel Netanyahu—name sound familiar? That's right; the brother of the prime minister—took one in the chest leading the final assault. Did they stop to treat him? Per their orders, his men stormed past him to take the objective—a very important objective—the lives of one hundred six hostages. There was no time to attend to a wounded man.

"Let's talk about care when you're not under fire, or not under effective fire." Thomas again begins with another tactical situation. "You are part of a SOF element and your mission is to interdict a weapons convoy. You parachute into mountainous terrain from an MC-130. You have a four-mile patrol over rocky ground to the objective. Your planned extraction is by helo near the target. One of your men goes into the trees on the way down and sustains an open fracture of his left tibia and fibula." Thomas brings up a full image of a left leg on the screen. It's in color, and you can see the blood and the bones pushing through the skin. "Something like this." Thomas tilts his head one way, then the other, in a professional assessment of the injury. "I've seen one of these. It's just like this in real life. But this is your guy. He's barely conscious, and he's in a ton of pain. What do you do? You're not under fire, but you got a problem. Do you carry him and press on with the mission? That's one option, but you have a big hump ahead of you. Carrying him, can you get there in time? It's going to be tough on him. Think you can keep him from going into shock?" Thomas pauses to study the mangled leg again. The members of Class 2-02 are glued to it. "If he's conscious, he's probably going to do some screaming. If he's unconscious, he'll moan. Can't have that in a tactical situation. Maybe you start an IV and push in some painkiller? That'll ease the pain, but put him out cold—make him complete baggage." Thomas pauses to let the students digest this. "See what I mean; a lot of options, but no single good choice. Or do you call for immediate extraction? That's the best thing for the man, but what about the mission? How many of our guys may die if we don't get those weapons away from hostiles? Is this mission and this intelligence perishable?" Thomas begins to roam the front of the classroom. The blood and the bones are still on the screen. "Or do you leave a man behind to tend to him, maybe your corpsman? Plan B, come back and get him later? I don't want to be the first SEAL to leave men behind—maybe we never see them again. Do you want to be that guy? Each of these options has a negative impact. The mission commander has to make that tactical decision. That's why you officers get paid the big bucks. But any one of us could have to make that call. That guy on the ground could be your officer.

"In mission planning, we give a lot of attention to hitting the target. We talk about tactical 'what ifs'—alternative ways to get to the target or to extract from the objective—different ways to attack. We have to do that in our medical planning, as well. The Rangers in Mogadishu learned that if they had stashed some medical packs and field dressings in the helos and the Humvees, they could have better treated the wounded guys on the way out. We owe those Army guys; they taught us a lot. No one can foresee every medical emergency, but you can plan for the most likely events. We plan and train for unexpected contact. They're called IADs. Think about what might be a likely medical emergency when you plan your mission. If it's a parachute drop in rough country, somebody may get hurt on the jump. If it's a total malfunction, you may have a dead teammate on the ground at the get-go. Think about it; plan for it. Pretend you're a Ranger—hope for the best; plan for the worst.

"That's TCCC—tactical combat casualty care. They don't teach this at medical school. They don't address this in ATLS or in EMT courses. Doctors and civilian medics don't have to fight while they care for the wounded. We do. That's what we'll be doing this week. Later on today you'll draw your medical kits and we'll show you what to do. You're all gonna be experts at this. Pay attention. There will be a written exam. But the real test may come when you save a teammate's life. Or he saves yours. We'll pull all this together on Friday at the combat medical field exercise."

BANG! Through the smoke of the artillery simulator, two members of SQT Class 2-02 race across the beach. They are in light combat gear. Their objective is two men lying on the sand—one is face down and inert, the other is writhing in pain. The two SEAL students take charge of their patients. BANG! Another simulated artillery round. One man grabs his casualty by the collar and begins to drag him to the cover of a sand dune; the other jerks his wounded man up and over his shoulders in a fireman's carry. He also makes for the shelter of the dune.

"C'mon, guys, you gotta move," Instructor Bill Patrick tells them. "You're still under fire." Patrick is a hospital corpsman and new to the SQT staff. Corpsmen in the teams are not just medics, but SEALs trained in medicine. Patrick's previous duty at the training command was instructing in close-quarter battle. Like Thomas, he's a warrior as well as a healer. SEAL corpsmen are trained at the JFK Special Warfare Training Center at Fort Bragg.

They receive the Special Forces Eighteen Delta medical training along with their Army SOF counterparts. It's a twelve-to-thirteen-month course that makes them qualified paramedics and experts in battlefield care. I've visited the school at Fort Bragg. Words cannot describe the quality of this military medical training. If my number comes up on the freeway and I get my choice of the good Samaritan on the scene, I'd choose an Eighteen Delta–trained corpsman over a regular physician. Okay, maybe I'd take a crackerjack emergency-room doctor.

"Move out," Patrick urges them. "Seconds count!"

Once in the lee of the protecting dune, the students tend to their wounded. They move from care-under-fire procedures to tactical field care. The wounded, who are other members of Class 2-02, are well-choreographed casualties. They are smeared with fake blood that appears to ooze from Magic Marker bullet holes. Their clothes are torn, and they are in pain. One is clearly cyanotic—his lips are painted blue—and his downed comrade has a number of Halloween-type paste-on rubber wounds.

"Okay, you're no longer under effective fire," Patrick tells them. "What's next?"

"Tactical field care. BATS," replies one of the students.

"Right. Bleeding, airway, tension pneumothorax, and shock. Go for it."

The student medics go to work while Patrick watches closely, moving from one caregiver to the other. "Tell me what you're doing while you work," Patrick says. It's part of the learning process for the students to talk through their treatment. "And hurry. These guys are in bad shape. Talk to them as well. It'll reassure your downed buddy, and if he's conscious, he can help you learn the extent of his injuries."

The student medics work feverishly—applying tourniquets, prodding and checking their victims for more battlefield damage. The IVs are not simulated; real needles go into the student-victim arms.

"Medevac or casevac?"

"Casevac, Instructor."

"Then let's get 'em ready. And keep talking to them; keep reevaluating their condition. It could change at any time."

On go the splints and more bandages.

Instructor Thomas comes over to observe for a moment but says nothing. These are Bill Patrick's students and wounded SEALs. We watch as the casualties are prepared for transportation from the field. Finally, Patrick tells the wounded students to get cleaned up and get into their operational gear. Then he tells the student SEAL medics to go to the moulage area for makeup so they can serve as the wounded under fire.

"This is really impressive," I tell Thomas. "This setting, the quality of instruction, and the attention to detail. These students seem to really know their stuff. You've brought them a long way in the past week. There was never anything like this in my day—not even close."

"Well, sir," Thomas says, "there's interest in this training from the highest levels. Don't forget, Admiral Olson was in the middle of that firefight in Mogadishu. We had other SEALs wounded in that battle as well."

ACROSS THE LAND

"My name is Henry Dega, and I will be your instructor for the land navigation portion of this training. I've had three deployments with SEAL Team One, and I've been a point man on all three deployments. I've been through the two-month SAS [Special Air Service] tracking school in New Zealand, and I participated in the Eco-Challenge." The Eco-Challenge is a televised team-based orienteering marathon of competition. "The Eco-Challenge was fun, but for you recent BUD/S guys, it was nothing like training or even close to Hell Week. It was more like a vacation with no sleep. I've only been here at SQT a short while." Dega pauses to choose his words. "I'm going to be honest with you guys. I didn't want to come here. I had orders to an operational platoon and a chance to get into the fight. Those orders were changed at the last minute, so here I am. That platoon is now deployed and may be in the thick of it as we speak. I guess that's a lesson in the needs of the Navy coming ahead of your personal desires. But my job is to train you guys, and I know my job. I'm starting to hear back from some of the guys in my previous platoons, guys I trained in land nav. They are now in Afghanistan. I feel pretty good about what they say regarding the training I gave them. They're doing a lot of land navigation there; a lot of map and compass stuff. You guys may soon need this information, real time, so I want you to pay attention."

Dega is a small man, compact and very fit. He has a reputation as one of the best at orienteering in the teams. The class listens closely. Dega's reputation has preceded him from Class 1-02.

"For the next two days, we're going to learn map reading and land navigation techniques. Then we're going up to Frazier Park and put you in the field for three days—do some walking and some map and compass work. Civilians pay good money to do this, and we get to do it as part of the job. Pretty cool, huh? Let's talk about gear. With few exceptions, SEAL operations will call for you to break your equipment into first, second, and third line gear.

"First line gear is what you have on you—cammies, boots, hat, and what you have in your pockets. This should include a pencil and notebook, waterproof penlight, map, compass, pocketknife, strobe light, emergency rations—maybe only a PowerBar or two, and your survival kit. This stuff should be stashed in your cammies. Your rifle and side arm, if you have one, are also part of your first line gear. With this you can run, hide, and get off a few rounds. And if you have to stay out for a few days while you E and E [escape and evade] your way back to friendly territory, you can do it. Remember, your rifle is part of your first line gear. It should never be more than a few feet away from you at all times, even when you're sleeping." Dega gives them a list of helpful tips in preparing their first line gear, like detuning Velcro strips with a lighter so they open more quietly; stashing caffeine, Motrin, and an extra PowerBar in their survival kits; which gloves to use, what fingers to cut out.

"Second line gear. This is all the trash you hang on your H-gear or your vest, however you get set up. Here we will teach and use the standard, Army-issue H-harness. It's just like the one you wore in Third Phase, only this gear you will take with you to the teams when you leave here. Your second line gear is also your operational gear. Here's where you will carry your ammunition and your grenades. You'll also carry your personal medical kit, your PRC-112 survival radio—although you may be able to fit the 112 in with your first line gear—twenty-four hours' worth of rations, and two quarts of water. And there are a number of small items that you may want to fit on your H-gear if you have room: a weapons cleaning kit, insect repellent, water purification tabs or equipment, snap link, IV pouch, and maybe some extra field dressings. Second line gear will vary depending on your area of operations. This is the stuff you're gonna fight with. Your manual says you ought to have a fixed-blade knife. I know some of you will favor those Gucci, eighteen-inch field sabers that look cool, but why? The only thing they're good for is to dig a hole to take a crap. My opinion—a good folding knife is all you need. If you want to hump some extra weight, put in another magazine. It may save your life. Your first line gear is on you. Your second line gear should never be beyond arm's reach. If your helo is going down, try to leave the crash site with your second line gear. You can't fight, or you can't fight long, without it."

Dega holds up a web-vest harness. "This is my H-gear, if you want to call it H-gear. It's a long way from the standard-issue H-harness. I spent a lot of my own money on this gear because I want it right; I can move well in it, and I can fight well in it." Dega's second line setup is as tailored as a Savile Row suit. "The standard-issue gear is good equipment, and you may get your team to pay for some upgrades and customization. Or you may have to come out-of-pocket for it. Just do what it takes to make it right for you. The civilian equipment isn't cheap, so try it out before you buy. The other guys in your platoon can help you with this." He gives them a grin. "That's one definition of a SEAL squad: seven guys dressed differently all doing the same thing."

The SQT students are each issued a standard, basic set of first, second, and third line equipment. It belongs to them. They will work with it and modify it under supervision during SQT, and take it with them when they leave.

"Your third line gear is your rucksack," Dega continues, "sleeping bag, ground pad, rations, water, extra this, extra that. Make sure you tuck in an extra polypro [polypropylene] shirt to sleep in. Good sleep is important. Socks, toilet paper—I like Handi Wipes; just like taking a shower in the bush—and a watch cap. You may also have to hump some operational gear in your ruck—maybe some extra ammo, demo, grenades, whatever. Your rucksack rides over your H-gear. Make sure they are compatible. Go over every piece of all your gear to make sure it's secure and rides properly. Tape all loose straps. When you're all set up, give it a jump test. Jump up and down to make sure nothing's loose and it's quiet. If you have a creaky strap, use WD-40 or some other light oil and it will quiet right down.

"We'll have two days at Frazier Park before the long-range nav problem. This will allow you to shake down your gear. Make sure your boots are comfortable and well broken in. I favor Danners, but you can use what you like so long as the boot is over the ankle. No sneakers. During those two days at Frazier we'll put you through some day and night skills courses—teach you something and give you a chance to make sure all your gear is riding well. Regarding the long-range compass course, start getting yourselves psyched up for this. It's a hump and a good time to learn while you're out there on your own. If we catch you on the roads—and we *will* catch you if you're on the roads—we add thirty-five pounds of rocks to your rucks. More than that, it's cheating, and you're not going to be able to cheat in Afghanistan while picking your way over some mountain range to get to an enemy base camp. No personal GPSs. You will have a sealed GPS with you to be used for emergency purposes only. We catch you with a personal GPS, and you're out of here. Map, compass, and your pace count; these are the skills we want you to learn. In the teams, you'll get all the neat electronic toys—not here. Here, we cover the basics. Pay attention and do it right. Persevere and find the markers at your way points, just like you would persevere and find your target on a real operation. Don't accept failure and don't cheat yourself. Questions?

"Okay, let's take five and get right back in here. Next class is in map reading."

In the vast wastelands of Iraq and Afghanistan, SEALs, like smart bombs, plot their position with GPS, but they must direct their line of march with map and compass. And if their GPS goes down, they will have to find their way entirely with map, compass, and pace count, just like they did in SQT.

Prior to beginning their land navigation week, the members of Class 2-02 spend two days learning about SEAL communications: voice procedures, antenna theory, satellite communications, and encrypted transmissions. They cover seven of the radios currently in the SEAL inventory. During field exercises at SQT, they will use only the AN/PRC-118 man-pack radio. After a day of map symbols and navigation techniques with Henry Dega, the class loads out for the seven-hour drive to Frazier Park.

Frazier Park is a small town on the edge of the Los Padres National Forest. The students set up camp in the forest, well away from the town, and begin a day and a half of field and land nav skill building. By day they work on concealment and pace count, and tune up with short map and compass exercises. At night they practice patrolling skills, building hide sites, and work through a night compass course. On the third day, they begin a three-day, long-range land navigation problem. They work the problem in pairs, going to layup positions (LUPs) by day and walking at night. SEALs work at night and hide by day. Dega and his staff are out checking on them, making sure that they have chosen their LUPs well, and use their ponchos and natural vegetation for concealment. Some pairs from Class 2-02 are easy to find. The better ones are almost invisible, and the SQT cadre almost have to walk over them to find them. Several times each day they observe a communication window and check in with Instructor Dega on their PRC-118 radios. Often they have to maneuver to higher ground to establish comms; it's all part of learning to communicate in the field.

Many in Class 2-02 are city boys. They had a few days in the field during BUD/S, but for some, this is their first extended fieldwork—the first time they have moved long distances at night. During their three-day, three-night excursion, they carry at least fifty-five pounds of equipment. They will walk about thirty miles and negotiate some eight thousand feet of elevation. The class arrives back at the SQT building unshaven and dirty, but little worse for wear. Gear is quickly tossed from the trucks and stowed in the equipment cages. The men have an evening to get cleaned up and grab a night's sleep in a real bed. Tomorrow they will be in to rework their equipment and load weapons for the trip to La Posta.

ROUNDS ON TARGET

The NSW Mountain Warfare Training Facility at La Posta is a 1,078-acre SEAL training facility east of San Diego in the Laguna Mountains. It is where the SQT students become combat shooters. The attitude on the part of the instructor cadre during medical and land navigation was agreeable, but it is more so at La Posta. It is not a relationship one finds among peers, but among fellow professionals. Perhaps this is because they have begun live-fire training.

Part of this atmospheric change could be attributed to the three Trident holders in the class. This is the first time the new BUD/S graduates have trained alongside qualified Navy SEALs. But it's more than that. In BUD/S, pain and harassment were an integral part of the process. BUD/S trainees learned to live with it. The SQT instructors have not lost their ability to come down on one of their students, but it's almost always regarding matters of safety or inattention to detail. For these BUD/S graduates, they are finally full-time students—students of this special brand of warfighting. They seem to feel this as they go about their training duties. I know that I'm feeling the difference from my days following Class 228 through BUD/S.

"You guys did pretty well out there today on your famfire and basic quals." They are in the main classroom at La Posta, and the man at the podium is the lead pistol instructor. "We've still got one or two of you to get qualified, but we'll work on that. Right now, we're going to focus on how to fight with a pistol. Some of you guys are going to think that this is hot-shit, Wild West stuff, but stop and think again.

That pistol on your leg is like your reserve parachute. If you have to go to it, you're already in deep doo-doo. It means that you're out of ammo for your primary weapon, your primary weapon is jammed, or some booger-eater is bearing down on you and you don't have time to reload your primary. You've got to do something fast—kill him before he kills you. So you have to engage him with your pistol."

Class 2-02 spent the day on the range conducting familiarization fire with the Smith & Wesson 686 pistol and the MK23 Mod∅ pistol. Most shot expert with both weapons. The S&W 686 is a stainless-steel revolver that can fire a .38-caliber round or a .357 Magnum. The MK23 is a special .45-caliber pistol made to SOF specifications by Heckler & Koch. Both of these weapons have their advantages, but are of limited use for SEALs. The secondary weapon in the teams, by issue if not by choice, is the Sig Sauer P226, a 9mm pistol. It is a relatively light, safe, and versatile semiautomatic pistol that can put sixteen rounds at the shooter's disposal. Each member of Class 2-02 sitting in the classroom has a Sig P226 strapped to his thigh. As with several blocks of instruction for Class 2-02, only half of the class is present. The other half will train later on. This allows for a better ratio of instructors to student shooters.

"As we get into combat shooting, keep in mind that the mechanics you learned for shooting a basic qualification score are still valid." The SQT handgun instructor is Petty Officer Matt Reilly. He has been in the Navy for fourteen years and has had four platoon deployments at Team Three and Team Five. He has been to several civilian shooting schools, including the John Shaw School and the Chandler Shooting School. He can shoot, and—more to the point—he can teach others how to shoot. He's a highly focused instructor, but there is a twinkle in his eye that says he loves the shooting as well as the teaching.

"In combat shooting, brothers, smooth is fast. So to begin with, I want you guys to concentrate on the basics. Keep it slow; the speed will come later on. What are the most important things in firing a handgun? Sight picture and trigger control, right? When it comes to winning that gunfight, you have to be quick, but it still comes down

to basics. Sight alignment, front sight focus, and a good trigger discipline." Reilly reviews basic shooting mechanics with the class for a
few minutes, then moves on to combat shooting. "In combat shooting, you have to be aggressive. Stance: feet apart, knees bent slightly,
arms straight—roll your shoulders forward, elbows in tight. Put the
tension in your shoulders; keep your arms and grip more relaxed."
He calls the class members to their feet. They draw their weapons
and assume a combat shooter's stance.

"This is the ready position. This is the position from which you
can do the most damage with your secondary weapon—arms
straight, looking out over the top of your weapon, ready to engage.
This is the position you want to get to as fast as possible. There are
two other positions we will teach you to shoot from as you come up
to this position, but here's where you want to be. Everybody sit down
and pay attention." The class sits and all eyes are on Reilly as he
turns ninety degrees from them and holsters his Sig. "Okay, by the
numbers; watch me. I clear the bail from the gun and draw. Notice
I've dropped to my shooting position, knees bent, back straight but
forward; I'm aggressive. As soon as the gun clears the holster, I level
the weapon—draw and rotate; get the barrel level as soon as you
clear. Notice that I haven't taken my eyes from my target. I'm ready
to shoot from the holster position if I have to. If that badass is almost
on me with a baseball bat, I'm gonna start shooting now. From the
holster position, I move to the transition position—the gun in both
hands with a proper grip, centered about belt level. Again, notice that
I've kept the barrel level. And finally up to the ready position, shoulders rolled forward, elbows in tight. Remember, bring the gun to
your eye, not eye to the gun, nice and smooth. Watch again." Reilly
draws again slowly. "Notice that as my gun clears the holster, the
barrel comes level and stays level right up to the ready position." He
faces the class and does it again. "Watch my head and shoulders. My
body does not move, only my gun hand and arm. My eyes never
leave the target. And I'm ready to engage as soon as my gun leaves
the holster. This is what it looks like when you put it all together."

Reilly holds his hands up like he's holding a rifle. "Click! My primary weapon's jammed! Shit, what do I do? Go to my secondary weapon." It's a blur. In a fraction of a second, his pistol is out of the holster, moving through ready position, clicking off rounds all the way up, very smooth and very, very fast.

"That's the way it works. I've done this a time or two," he says with a grin, "but I want you guys to start slow, focus on the mechanics, and be smooth."

For the next hour, Class 2-02 practices drawing their Sigs. The students click off imaginary rounds from the holster position, from the transition position and from the ready position. The SQT instructors roam among them, coaching and correcting.

"Okay, guys, listen up. I want you to practice this and dry fire from these shooting positions for at least a half hour this evening and a half hour before we hit the range tomorrow. And try this. With the gun level at the holster position, put a penny on the front sight of your gun. The penny won't stay on the front sight if the gun isn't level. If you can dry fire the weapon and not drop the penny, the gun's level and you have good trigger discipline. Do this ten times, then go from the holster position to the transition position and squeeze off ten more with the penny on the front sight. Then from the holster position up to the ready position for another ten. What's this do? It keeps you in the habit of keeping your weapon level and forces you to have good trigger discipline. It'll keep you from putting rounds in the dirt on the way up. We don't want to make 'em dance, we want to put holes in 'em. Be slow, be deliberate, be smooth. The speed will come. Practice and more practice. Don't shortchange yourself with these dry-fire drills. They'll pay off on the range."

The next day, Class 2-02 is on the ranges, learning to fight with handguns. It's crawl, walk, run—slow and smooth. Several magazines from the holster position, then the transition position and up to the ready position. Then the class members begin to move. They fire from all three positions, but focus on getting the gun from the holster to the ready position and making a clean, effective shot. Instructors roam the firing line, coaching and encouraging their student shooters. The only harsh words come from a potentially unsafe condition. Range safety procedures are more liberal than at BUD/S, but no less religiously observed. "Big-boy rules, not BUD/S rules," Reilly tells them, "but you have to be safe; you have to think all the time out here."

There are timed qualifications that require hits on ten-inch, knockdown steel plates at fifteen yards. Some of these timed quals require a magazine change or clearing a fouled weapon. By the end of the day, the student shooters are crabbing sideways across the range, engaging multiple targets while on the move. Instructors run behind them, away from their line of fire, jostling them to simulate obstacles—trying to throw off their rhythm. All drills and timed evolutions begin with the shooter facing the target, simulating that his primary weapon has just gone down—draw and shoot, draw and shoot.

"Keep moving . . . Keep shooting . . . Change mags . . . Keep moving . . . Front sight focus!" Magazines are purposely loaded with plastic rounds to simulate a dud or a jammed round. "Tap, rattle, bang—get it fixed; get your gun back in the fight!"

At the end of the day, it's winners and losers. Two shooters stand with their hands at chest level, pretending to hold a rifle.

"And . . . bust 'em," Reilly calls.

The two students draw, snap up to the ready position, and begin to fire.

BANG-ping! BANG-ping! It's a single elimination shoot-off; draw and clear six steel targets. The first one to clear all six is the winner. After each round, the number of contestants is cut in half. Finally, there are two shooters left standing. Petty Officer Dan Nixon from BUD/S Class 237 manages by a fraction of a second to beat Lieutenant Jacob Allen, a Trident holder headed for Team Two. The lieutenant is a good shooter, but he finished second. This is training; in a real gunfight, there is no second place.

"Okay, brothers, pull it in here," Reilly tells them. "Good day of shooting. You guys are coming along. Some more than others, but I like what I see. Remember, when that round goes off, get right back on target. You keep shooting it until that asshole goes down. Engage the most serious threat first. When you've put that sucker down, cover your area of responsibility—big vision, your gun follows your eyes. If you find another target, bring it in—small vision—sight picture and BANG! Pop that sucker." While he talks, Reilly demonstrates. "If he's still there, shoot him again, BANG-BANG! Remember, we teach you to clear and draw fast so you can quickly get that secondary weapon into the fight. We've taught you to shoot with accuracy so you can, if you have to, make that head shot from fifteen feet. Some day a hostage's life may depend on your ability to ring up some scumbag with your first round. You guys clear on that?" The members of Class 2-02 all nod as one.

"That's all I got. Keep up the good work. You guys have shown me a good attitude here on the range. Good attitudes make good shooters." Reilly turns to an instructor standing nearby. "Billy, do you want them in the classroom now?"

"How about right after chow, say 1830."

That evening, Petty Officer Will Gautier is in front of Class 2-02. "Gentlemen, tonight we're going to introduce you to the H&K MP5A. Guys, you're gonna love this submachine gun. It can do a lot of things. In the teams we use it primarily for ship boarding and close-quarter battle."

Petty Officer Third Class Neil Venterello examines his MP5. He is from Chicago and never shot a gun before he joined the Navy and began BUD/S with Class 237. That was a little over a year ago. He began with a previous class but was injured in training. He joined Class 237 in Second Phase. Venterello is not a natural shooter, but he works hard at it. He is average in the class with a pistol and managed to qualify expert with two of the three handguns. Lieutenant Allen easily put him away in the first round of the combat pistol shoot-off.

The submachine gun feels good in his hands, compact and solid. "Maybe," Venterello tells himself, "I do can better with the MP5. Maybe this baby is my weapon." Students don't shoot for score with the MP5, but there will be competitions; everyone will know who's good and who's better with this submachine gun. Under the direction of Instructor Gautier, Venterello begins to disassemble his weapon and lay the parts in an orderly manner in front of him on the table.

The next day, the members of Class 2-02 are back on the range. They have their Sig Sauer pistols strapped to one thigh and magazine pouches strapped to the other; fifteen-round magazines for the Sig and thirty-round magazines for the MP5. After a round of familiarization fire with the MP5, they begin combat shooting drills. They are taught to use the ring-and-hooded sights on the MP5. If the sight picture is there, the rounds go through the target. As with the pistols, they begin with a single target, then begin double-tapping individual targets—two rounds on the same target. Compared to the Sig, the MP5 is easy to use and accurate. The men practice changing magazines on the MP5, then the transition from the submachine gun to the Sig. In the afternoon, they continue on to the stress courses—competitive shooting drills where accuracy and speed both count. The MP5 stress course is run two by two, so the student competitors must be aware of the targets and their shooting partners.

"You two ready?"

"Yes, Instructor," they answer together. One of them is Petty Officer Venterello. The other is a classmate who easily outshot him with the pistol. As they were yesterday during their initial work with the pistol, both of them are wearing their second line gear.

"Okay, bust 'em!"

Venterello and his classmate race up the hill, around a road gate, and back to the range. They then press a full case of 9mm ammo, some thirty-five pounds, over their heads twenty times. After weight lifting, the shooters run to the firing line. They take their submachine guns from the slung position, where they carried them on the run, and swing them up to the firing position. The run and the lift are to get the student shooters breathing hard, like they are in a running firefight, or racing through a building or a ship to get to their objective. Venterello's shooting partner gets to the firing line a few steps ahead of him. First they have to double-tap two of the ten-inch steel plates—two rounds, two *pings* each—with their MP5s.

Venterello rings up his plates first and is now a half second ahead of his shooting partner. He likes the MP5 and it seems to like him. He snaps the submachine gun on safe, swinging it down and to one side as he draws his Sig. The two shooters begin to clear the six steel plates, knocking them down as fast as they can get a sight picture and squeeze. Venterello needs seven shots to get his six to fall; his opponent uses only six. Venterello thumbs the hammer-drop to safe the Sig, and reholsters it. Back to the MP5. The two shooters are dead even.

"Got him," Venterello whispers as he quickly draws a bead on the five-inch steel target fifteen yards downrange.

BANG-ping! Done! Both shooters clear and safe their weapons, then step back from the firing line.

"And we have a winner. Nice shooting, Venterello. You, too, Patterson, but you lost. Take another lap up around the gate."

Venterello and Patterson grin at each other. "Maybe next time, Pat."

"Next time, Neil. Count on it."

The drills go on all day and the next. Where appropriate, there is competition—winners and losers. For the winners, it's a chance to gloat; for the losers, it means a short run or some push-ups. It still pays to be a winner. That much has not changed from BUD/S. Submachine gun to pistol to submachine gun. With the Sig, they practice shooting with the off hand—right-handers must shoot with the left hand and change magazines with one hand to simulate being wounded. Skills with the pistol improve, but everyone loves the MP5. The shooting is done with a full sight picture, but they are only a step away from point-and-shoot with both weapons. Matt Reilly and Will Gautier keep them focused on the basics: good mechanics and a religious observance of safety procedures. But they do a lot of shooting.

The drills become more complex and increasingly competitive. Sometimes the competition is individual, *mano a mano,* and sometimes squad against squad. This isn't BUD/S, so the losers don't have to pay BUD/S prices—but they do have to pay. In SQT, it's becoming a matter of personal and professional pride. That, too, is one of the lessons of this training.

Each day the students shoot a qualification course with one of the handguns. On the last day, the students work with the shotgun. At SQT, it's the Remington 870 twelve-gauge. Most of the shooting is done behind a barricade, but they engage multiple targets. The 870 holds four rounds in the magazine and one in the chamber. The men learn to shoot, and to load and shoot with a round in the chamber. "If there is a lull in the fight," Gautier tells them, "use the time to feed more rounds into the gun. If you can avoid it, don't get down to your last shell." Compared to the 9mm weapons, the 870 is a blaster and a kicker. A few of the students have never before fired a shotgun. The mechanics are the same, but it takes a few rounds to adjust to the bead-type front sight and the kick of the weapon. But it's the same with the shotgun as with the other weapons: the more they shoot, the better they get.

"All right, gang, bring it in." Reilly calls them into a circle. "You guys had a good week of shooting here. You learned a lot, and I can see some real fine shooters in the making. Remember, concentrate on your mechanics—and when you get to your platoons, practice whenever you can. Combat shooting is a learned skill, and it's a perishable skill. A good shooter never stops practicing. Bottom line, brothers, we're gunfighters. Never forget that."

Twenty-eight men—just over half of Class 2-02's members—have their Combat Qualification Course, or CQC, behind them. All fired expert on at least one of the pistols. It took five days, the services of four very talented SQT shooting instructors, and more than fifty-two thousand rounds of ammunition. Of that, more than forty-five thousand were 9mm rounds for the Sig Sauer pistol and MP5 submachine gun. Only once were they allowed to fire the MP5 on fully automatic fire—one magazine in bursts of two to three rounds during famfire.

Those many thousands of rounds went downrange one bullet at a time to teach these BUD/S graduates to shoot like Navy SEALs.

The twenty-eight Class 2–02 combat shooters from La Posta arrive at Camp Pendleton at 0730 on the following Monday morning. The U.S. Marine Corps base at Camp Pendleton is a large coastal military facility some fifty miles north of San Diego. At Pendleton, the SEALs have a rifle range, a pistol range, and a kill house that they have built on property on loan from the Marine Corps. Training at the kill house and the pistol range is used primarily by the SEAL platoons, but the platoons, the SQT students, and the BUD/S trainees all use the rifle range. This morning, the class was up very early to draw weapons and ammunition and make the drive from Coronado to the Marine base. This week there are different conditions, different criteria, and different weapons, but the objective is the same: get the rounds on target. By 0800, the twenty-eight combat shooters are in the classroom. Once again, their shooting instructor is Petty Officer Will Gautier.

"This week it's all about marksmanship. For the next few days we will concentrate on marksmanship, along with some fire-and-movement drills. We're going to build on what you learned at BUD/S in Third Phase. The object is still to get rounds on target, but from various ranges: one hundred, two hundred, three hundred, even five hundred yards. We're going to teach you good shooting habits, and, hopefully, we'll not have to undo any bad habits. I know most of you have shot expert with the rifle, but we'll do it again, by the numbers. When you leave here you're going to be a good marksman, and you will know what you have to do to become a better marksman. By that, you'll know where your bullets go and why they go there."

Gautier has been in the Navy eleven years. He is a sniper instructor and has attended a number of shooting schools. He has three platoon deployments with SEAL Team Five plus a tour of independent duty in Bosnia. Gautier has been at SQT for two years and wants very much to get back to an operational platoon—back to the fight.

"Okay," Gautier continues, "what's *the* most important aspect of good shooting? Somebody? Anybody?"

"Sight alignment."

"Right. And what's second, but also very important?"

"Trigger control."

"Right again. Everything we do and teach is to support those two keys to good shooting. Everything you do—natural point of aim, bone-to-bone support, proper breathing, good cheek weld, good body position—is to help you to attain a proper sight alignment. Then you must control the trigger. Do this properly and it's in black, every time."

Gautier reviews with them the basics of good shooting and the mechanics. They talk about elevation and windage—how to shoot good groups and then bring the groups to the center of the target. Finally, he talks about the weapon of choice of the Navy SEAL Teams. He holds an M4 rifle at arm's length with both hands, as if it were an offering to the gods.

"This is the M4A1 carbine, guys. For my money it's the finest military weapon in the world. A shortened version of this rifle will soon replace the MP5 for close-quarter battle. The M4 is about the same size as the MP5, a little longer with the standard barrel, but it's a lot more accurate and it has a better round. That 5.56mm round is a small round, but it comes out of there haulin' ass—some three thousand feet per second. It can do a lot of damage, and as you're going to see, you can hit someone a long way off with this gun. It's also a versatile weapon. With the rail system you can hang a lot of trash on this rifle— a four-power scope, a laser sight, a laser designator, a flashlight, or an IR sight. This is the gun you guys are going to go to war with. Learn to use it well, and you can put a world of hurt on the bad guys."

That afternoon, the twenty-eight members of Class 2-02 take to the range. They set up their M4s at two hundred yards. In a short while and in a stiff crosswind, the student shooters are shooting six-to-eight-inch groups and adjusting the groups onto the black bull's-eye. These gunsight corrections are called doping the gun. The student shooters note the shooting conditions and wind, and the windage and elevation on their M4s. All SQT students carry small, vest pocket notebooks called wheel books. They enter this individual shooting dope in their wheel books and can refer to this data in the days ahead. The M4 rifles are their personal weapons for the duration of SQT.

The next day, it's more shooting with the M4 at two hundred yards. The groups get tighter and the scores improve. There is no head-to-head competition on the rifle range, but there are a number of side bets on who's the better shooter. The SQT shooting instructors are starting to identify the good shooters and the shooters who need help. Even the good ones need coaching in order to get better, but most of the instructor time goes to those shooting poorly. For SEALs, shooting poorly is anything below expert, the Navy's highest marksman qualification. In the afternoon, they take up the M14 rifle.

"The M14 is an older weapon," Instructor Ted Dimarco tells the class. "Guys in Mister Couch's SEAL platoon used this rifle in Vietnam. We still think it's a pretty good gun. Today, we use it primarily in extremely cold weather and in the desert. It's accurate, rugged, and reliable. There are a lot of SEALs in Afghanistan carrying M14s. Both SEALs and the Marines use it as a backup weapon with their sniper teams. The M14 fires a 7.62mm round, the same as our MK43 machine gun, and it packs a helluva punch. SEALs are the only units who deploy with it as a primary combat weapon, or one of our primary combat weapons."

The M14 and Class 2-02 are together only a short time, about forty rounds per man. The schedule calls for just a familiarization shoot, but it's enough time on the gun for the students to learn that it has a sweet trigger pull, and that the M14 is the most accurate weapon they have fired in their short Navy careers. Later that day, they are back on the line with their M4s. First they sight their weapons in for three hundred yards. Then it's time for rattle-battle drills.

"Ready on the right! Ready on the left! The line is hot. Commence fire!"

Class 2-02 drops to the prone position and rapid fire ripples up and down the line. The targets three hundred yards downrange are no longer twelve-inch bulls, but human silhouettes. The students have thirty-five seconds to get off twenty rounds. Will Gautier walks over and lightly kicks Ensign Julio Garcia's boot. This ensign will be the platoon leader for the first rattle-battle exercise.

"Cease fire!" Ensign Garcia commands.

"CEASE FIRE!" the line of shooters answers.

"Ready, up!" Garcia calls.

"READY, UP!" the line echoes. The men move off the three-hundred-yard berm and charge downrange.

They are in their H-harnesses along with all their second line gear and full canteens. They change magazines while on the run, glancing left and right to stay on line. Any unexpended rounds from their first magazine of twenty will not score. Behind the line of students are a line of instructors, offering encouragement and ensuring that all is safe. I run along behind the instructors. The last time they ran forward on a skirmish line like this with weapons hot was during Third Phase BUD/S training on San Clemente.

"Ready," Garcia yells as he runs to the two-hundred-yard berm.

"READY!" the line of shooters answers.

"Down!"

"DOWN!"

At the two-hundred-yard berm, they drop to one knee and sight in.

"Commence fire!" Garcia yells, and the line opens up. This time they have thirty seconds to dump their twenty-round mags. Again, Gautier taps the ensign's foot.

"Up! . . . Forward!" Garcia roars. The line of shooters repeats the commands and surges forward.

Class 2–02 charges the silhouettes, again changing mags on the run. At one hundred yards, the students stand and fire from the off-hand position. This time they have twenty-five seconds to get off twenty rounds.

Will Gautier gives them sixty seconds to adjust their gear, secure their empty magazines, and reposition the full ones for more shooting. "Okay, Mister Garcia, bust 'em."

"Commence fire!" Garcia calls.

Again, they have twenty-five seconds to get off twenty rounds. Rattle-battle is the first of three shooting drills in which they will shoot at the hundred-yard berm on the Pendleton range. At a hundred yards, the silhouettes look huge in their rear sight rings. These are the easy ones, the ones that have to count for a good score.

"CEASE FIRE!" the command ripples down the line of shooters.

"Ready!" Garcia yells.

"READY!" The line answers.

"Back!"

"BACK!"

The student shooters peel left and right, and run for the two-hundred-yard berm. Again, they change mags on the run. They shoot at two hundred yards while kneeling and a final time at three hundred yards while prone.

"This is to get them ready for training at Camp Billy Machen and the IADs out there," Gautier explains. "We want them to start getting back into the habit of moving and shooting while there are other people moving and shooting. They still have to get the rounds on target, but they also have to be aware of where their teammates are. We step it up out in the desert, and these guys will find that it gets a whole lot faster when they get to their platoons."

After they clear and safe their weapons, Gautier calls them in for a critique. He tells them what they did right and what they did wrong, and what they can do to improve their running and shooting. A minimum score for the rattle-battle drill is 60 hits on the target. Most of them score well over 80. Two from Class 2-02 put close to 100 of their 120 rounds on target.

"Everybody reloaded, six mags, twenty rounds each? Okay, we're going to do it again. You know what's expected now; I want to see those scores come up. Ready on the right! Ready on the left! The line is hot! Okay, Mister Garcia, you just got shot. Where's Petty Officer Jackson?"

"Over here, Will."

"You're in charge, Jackson. Get these guys shooting and moving."

Petty Officer Shawn Jackson quickly moves to the center of the line, and Ensign Garcia takes his place on the flank.

"Ready, down!" Jackson screams. "Commence fire!"

The next morning, there's another Navy standard qualification shoot, more rattle-battle, and then on to snaps and movers. In snaps and movers, the shooters don't move but the targets do. It is a graded drill. At one hundred yards, the men must shoot seven targets—four movers and three snaps—with seven rounds. A mover is a silhouette that moves at a walking pace, left to right or right to left. The target's movement, for some twenty paces, is a silhouette on a stick carried by another member of Class 2-02 in the target butts. At the end of the twenty paces, or when a silhouette takes a bullet, the target comes down. A snap is a silhouette that is lifted up on a stick by a student. At a hundred yards, the snap silhouette is up for only three seconds. The shooter must pop the snap or the mover with a single round. It's the same at two hundred and three hundred yards, only the snap is up for five seconds at two hundred and seven seconds at three hundred. The movers just move.

"They seldom miss at a hundred yards, but it gets harder further back," Instructor Dimarco tells me. "We teach them to shoot center of mass on the movers at one hundred yards. At two hundred and three hundred, we tell them to sight in on the leading edge of the silhouette. The 5.56 round is so fast that they don't have to lead the target much at all. They usually all qualify, unless they start jerking the trigger, thinking they don't have enough time."

All twenty-eight members of Class 2-02 qualify on snaps and movers. They must score fifteen out of a possible twenty-one. Close to half of them score at least twenty, and a half dozen record a perfect score. The last of the M4 qualifications is the lane shoot snaps test. The shooters advance in lanes from the two-hundred-yard to the one-hundred-yard shooting stations. Along the way, they stop and engage the snap-up silhouettes that appear. It's a graded shoot, and they all pass. Some are able to shoot only the minimum or just above it. Others punch the silhouette targets every time. In BUD/S, the men in the class break out by physical abilities: Who are the fastest runners and swimmers? Who have the fastest times on the O-course? In SQT, they break out by professional skill: Who are the best and most consistent shooters? Who are the best with map and compass? The scores are recorded; reputations are being established.

On Thursday, they shoot a final Navy Qualification Course. Only four have failed to shoot expert on the standard Navy course. "They're our problem children," Gordy Thomas explains. He's the duty hospital corpsman for marksmanship training at Camp Pendleton, but he's also sniper qualified and a shooting instructor. "It's simply a matter of time on the gun and confidence. Sometimes we get them all where they need to be. Sometimes there are one or two of them we just can't reach. But they will all leave here knowing exactly where their problems are and what they have to work on to become better shooters. The team COs don't want any of their SEALs not to have expert rifle and pistol ribbons."

What I found interesting was the way in which Gautier, Thomas, and the other SQT shooting instructors work with poor shooters. One of them will study a man while he shoots, then offer instruction. This goes on for a while, then he will step back, confer with another instructor, and move on. The second instructor will watch the student who is shooting poorly for a while, then begin his coaching. Each instructor knows that good shooting comes from good mechanics, but he also knows that he may not be able to solve a student shooter's problem where a fellow instructor can. When it comes to a student experiencing difficulties, they team-teach in an effort to bring his scores up.

On Thursday afternoon, the students fire the M4s a final time. This time it is a famfire at silhouette targets at five hundred yards. This is to show the SEAL students that they can effectively engage a man with an M4 rifle at more than a quarter of a mile. They have doped their guns for three hundred yards. To engage the target at five hundred yards, they have only to crank the BZO, or battle zone offset, knobs on their rear sights from three hundred to five hundred and fire away. Not every round clips the silhouette, but as a class, they get more hits than misses. Some of the better shooters hit it every time—at more than a quarter of a mile!

On Friday, while most of the class cleans the barracks and loads gear for the trip back to the Naval Special Warfare Center, the four shooters who failed to qualify as experts are back on the range. Two of them shoot expert and the other two are very close.

AT CLOSE QUARTERS

"This is the way it looks, guys. It is the foundation of everything you will do this week during your Close Quarter Defense training. Notice Chief Dalton's legs—flexed, ready to quickly move forward or in any direction. His weight is on the balls of his feet, heels out. Note the position of his arms—up, and with the hard edges of his forearms and hands protecting his face and midsection. From this position he can deflect blows, absorb blows, and protect his vital areas. It's called the spring-stance, power-point position. Ready, Chief?"

Dalton nods. Chief Ray Dalton is not a big man, but Instructor Jack Meyers, a hefty first class petty officer, is—about six-two and 215 pounds. He walks around Dalton and delivers a series of vicious kicks to his legs and torso. Then he shoves him a few times and kicks him again. Dalton flexes and shuffles his feet in staccato fashion and absorbs the blows. He pops back to the power-point stance like a spring-loaded snake, coiled, ready to strike. Class 2-02 is glued to the drama.

"The body can take a lot of punishment. Now, the chief here will have a few bruises and welts from all this, but notice he didn't go down; he's still in the fight, ready to project his power. Thanks, Chief." Dalton straightens and steps to one side. "Understand, we're not in the business of taking blows and not reacting to them. No one is going to kick you around like this without some serious payback, but this shows you that you can take some punishment and still be ready to fight. We learn and practice these skills so if you have to fight up close, or some badass is able to get in tight, you can take your hits and still win the fight. We're also going to show you how to be aggressive and control your space. We mix it up here. There's going to be a lot of contact. We're going to show you how and when to dial up the aggression, and when to dial it down. We're going to show you how to fight like a warrior, armed and unarmed, alongside teammates or, if you have to, on your own. All we ask is that you pay attention, stay motivated, and keep up the intensity. You'll learn a lot this week."

The subject matter is Close Quarter Defense, or CQD. Chief Ray Dalton is in charge of Class 2-02's training this week. His instructor cadre also trains platoons during their predeployment preparation. Because Close Quarter Defense training is relatively new to the teams, not everyone in the operational platoons has yet experienced it. One of the BUD/S instructors who is rotating from the training command back to the operational teams joins the class. "I missed this training in my last platoon workup," he tells me. "This is a good chance to pick it up." Ray Dalton has been in the Navy some sixteen years and has five operational deployments with Naval Special Warfare, most of them with SEAL Team Five. The other five CQD instructors working with the class are all veterans of three or more deployments.

The week of Close Quarter Defense training is the most popular block of training at SQT. That's what the student critiques say. There are only a few hours in the classroom at CQD. Most of the time is spent on the mats at the CQD training facility. CQD and other NSW training specialties are located several miles south of the Naval Special Warfare Center, just north of Imperial Beach. The Center recently came into ownership of some eighty acres of an old communications site along with several thousand feet of Pacific frontage. The new acquisition was quickly put to use for SEAL advanced training. The CQD facility is not some sport dojo; the instructors and students work in cammie trousers, T-shirts, and boots. The building was recently used as a machine shop, and the rubber mats are industrial strength. Students first work on their spring-stance, power-point position, the one that allowed Chief Dalton to withstand the assault by Instructor Meyers. They advance and retreat, move side to side, cautiously and quickly. All the while, they maintain this protective-aggressive posture. The CQD instructors are everywhere—making corrections, demonstrating proper technique, pushing and lightly kicking the students to test their mechanics. This is full-contact training—for the instructors as well as the students. The students are told to remove their watches and rings and to trim their fingernails. After a number of drills to challenge the proficiency of their stance, the students run a gauntlet of sorts called the pummel funnel.

"Come to my voice! Come to my voice!"

"Get up! Get to your feet!"

"Elbows in, hands up!"

"Come to my voice!"

Ten students, five on a side, form this gauntlet through which a fellow student must run. The man in the arena wears headgear that resembles a catcher's mask and advances between the line of students. They are armed with stiff hand pads and pummel him as he goes by. He advances with his eyes closed, armed only with his stance and body position. His eyes are closed so he cannot react to the blows, only absorb them. This teaches him the value and utility of his spring-stance and defensive technique. Often a student is knocked to the mat, but the blows keep coming. He has to maintain his composure as well as his posture and regain his feet to complete the ordeal. There is an instructor at the beginning and end of this gauntlet, teaching and coaching—checking the position of the students' hands and the balance of their stances. The men in SQT from BUD/S Class 237 have been in SEAL training for close to nine months. This is the first time they have been hit, or hit hard enough to be knocked down. All of them have welts on their forearms from taking blows, and there are a few cuts. CQD is about delivering force, but most of the first day is devoted to learning to take blows and remain in a position to go on the offensive. As callous as it sounds, it was good to see these SEAL students beat on each other—to take a blow and press on with the job. This was not a fight, but they were getting hit; it gets them to thinking about fighting.

CQD is also about managing aggression. Aggression has its place in a fight, but it has to be channeled and, when appropriate, restrained. At the end of the first day, the class goes into its first Box Drills. In a four-by-eight rectangle taped to the mat, two students enter the small arena with only thin leather gloves and a padded helmet to protect their face. The drill is to drive their opponent from the rectangle using the head strikes they have been taught to deliver from their power-point stance. This is not a face-slapping contest; it's a mini fight, and aggression counts. The blows are delivered with the hard edge of the hands. The two combatants rain blows on each other until one or the other is forced from the rectangle-arena. SEAL students are, by nature and training, competitive. There are no penalties imposed by the cadre for losing, but it still pays to be a winner. If you lose, your classmates get to watch. These are furious, ten- to fifteen-second contests with a lot of shouting from the gallery. For many, except those with formal martial-arts training or a difficult childhood, it's their first real fight. Up to this point in their SEAL careers, and most certainly in SQT, the students have endured a steep learning curve. But this learning has been physical training and formal military training—shooting, diving, small-boat handling. CQD is something of a wake-up call. They are now beginning to learn to fight as well as how to fight if the battle is up close and personal.

Close Quarter Defense is the property and the life work of Duane Dieter. His system of warrior training was introduced to the teams in 1995 and made official in 1997. His Close Quarter Defense School has been training SEALs and SEAL platoons for over five years. The training is a blend of martial artistry, commando-style fighting, and the spiritual requirements of a warrior. SEALs do a lot of things. Any useful close-quarter-fighting technique must be adaptable to the SEAL operational environment. It has to support SEAL combat mission requirements and become an effective tool with a limited amount of training time. Because SEALs must operate effectively in a number of threat environments, SEALs must be able to dial up and dial down the level of aggression. This introduces Class 2-02 to the notion of the inner warrior, the duty and responsibility of every warrior to manage aggression and be responsible for the power he projects. And finally, while it is called Close Quarter Defense, it is by the nature of SEAL operations primarily an offensive skill set. In close-quarter situations, SEALs must have the ability to hurt, maim, or kill—or safely be able to do none of the above. CQD training packages this variable-force skill set to meet SEAL operational requirements. The SEAL CQD instructors that train the SQT students and SEAL platoons are certified by Duane Dieter to teach this material.

CQD is not hand-to-hand fighting, nor is it, of itself, self-defense training. It is all about dominating your space and fighting to win a tactical fight. During the war in Iraq, SEALs boarded an Iraqi freighter in international waters that was steaming at full speed for Iranian territorial waters. The ship was suspected of carrying contraband. The hatches to the bridge were welded shut so the SEALs had to come in through the pilothouse windows. The first man onto the pilothouse was a young SEAL officer, and because of the window entry, he was armed only with his pistol. Suddenly he was confronted by four Iraqis who refused to raise their hands. It was four to one. The young SEAL dropped to a spring-stance and advanced. Knowing he must quickly dominate his space, he dropped one Iraqi with a muzzle strike from his pistol and another with a well-placed hand strike. The other two speedily got their hands up. His CQD training allowed him to control his space using less-than-lethal methods.

The unarmed, seemingly defensive tactics first taught at SQT are just a platform from which a warrior can project the proper level of force in a given situation. On the first day, the students train unarmed so as to learn and practice their basic stance and hand strikes. For the rest of the week, the SQT students are armed with their primary and secondary weapons, much as they were on the La Posta and Camp Pendleton ranges. They carry a partial second line gear load and are armed with M4s and Sig Sauer 9mm pistols. The weapons are integrated with the power-point spring-stance. During the technique sessions, the CQD cadre strikes the students with pads to test for correct posture—to see if they can hold their stance while they hold their weapons, ready to shoot or to strike. Yesterday they did hand strikes; now they move on to strikes with the barrels of their M4s and pistols. A sharply delivered barrel strike with an M4 can be just as lethal as a bullet. They practice transition drills from armed to unarmed positions, always ready to absorb or deflect blows, or to attack.

Each morning CQD training begins with operational PT, or OPT, led by an instructor. He first leads the class through a series of stretches and rotational exercises that warm up each joint. Next, they run in place, bringing their knees up to their chests. Then the hand movements begin—short, precise, violent movements. They practice multiple strikes from the power-point stance, moving forward, back, or to the side, all the while making hand strikes. This is to build power and explosiveness into their movements. Push-ups are done on the knife-edges of their hands or on their fists. Starting from a one-armed push-up position, they rapidly go from the support of one arm to the other—left, right; left, right—delivering a blow with each strike to the mat. They do wheelbarrow races, padding across the mats on the hard edges of their hands. Most of the movements are short, combative strokes, designed to selectively build strength and their ability to project force quickly. "Daily PT is a part of your life as a SEAL," the instructors tell them. "Why not use your PT time to make you a more powerful and effective warrior?"

"This is such great stuff," one of the class officers tells me. "The class has never been happier, and we've never been a tighter group; the guys are eating this stuff up. I think everyone appreciates the concept of the inner warrior that we all have to develop. The idea is to bring the necessary level of aggression to the tactical situation. There is a time to strike and a time to shoot, but once that decision is made, or the bad guy makes it for you, you strike with the proper amount of force or you shoot to kill."

CQD training spends two full days on prisoner control. "Not

everybody needs or deserves to be shot," Instructor Jon Rhodes tells Class 2-02. Rhodes is the leading petty officer for CQD training, and a very talented instructor. He is a soft-spoken man, knowledgeable and highly professional. "Some people are going to give up without a fight or give up after they lose the fight. They will be compliant to one degree or another. The level of compliance determines the level of force. You have to control them while you protect yourself and your teammates. You deliver only the level of violence they deserve. Again, every situation is different, and in every situation you have your three-way test: What is your capability, what is the capability of the guy you are trying to control, and what is the tactical situation? You think the crew of a neutral merchant ship that we board to search for contraband may be different from some al-Qaeda assholes you drag out of a cave in Afghanistan? Are you going to handle them differently? See what I mean? The threat will often dictate the level of force.

"We're going to teach you prisoner control one-on-one, but remember that you will do this with a teammate, perhaps several of your teammates. One of your buddies is going to be locked onto this badass with his primary weapon. But while you control and search this guy, even if he's compliant and doing everything you tell him, you have to be ready to react—take nothing for granted. If he goes off on you, you must be able to dial it up. We're going to show you how to effectively control a prisoner and how to dial up the pain if he decides he's had enough of your program and wants to do something else."

The class learns how to control and manage prisoners. This is called the four Ss: seal, stabilize, secure, and search. Seals—the technique, not the men—are leveraged holds that allow the SEAL operator to control a prisoner and bring a great deal of pain to a noncompliant adversary. They learn several types of seals. A stabilized prisoner is one who is facedown on the ground in a specified position, doing exactly what he is told, and has been sealed by the operator to ensure his compliance. Then the students learn how to properly cuff a prisoner, maintaining control of him while he's secured. Once the prisoner is secured, students learn and practice proper search techniques. At any time during this seal-stabilize-secure-search procedure, a SEAL operator has to be prepared to dial up the pain-aggression level if his prisoner, by his actions, deserves it. Or he must be ready to quickly break away and be prepared to fight if the tactical situation warrants.

"You can't get into a wrestling match with these guys," Rhodes tells them. "If you can't establish a good seal and control him, break away and back out while maintaining an aggressive posture; stay in a good spring-stance and get your weapon on line. Remove yourself from the threat if you can't maintain complete control. If he still thinks he wants to be noncompliant, he's now a candidate for a weapon or hand strike by you or your buddy. If he decides he wants to escalate the situation by pulling a gun or a knife, he's just earned himself a bullet. Always remember that the threat dictates your level of force. If he does what he's told and complies, he's not going to get hurt. It's his choice. But you always have to protect yourself and your teammates."

The student operators and their training partners run one prisoner-control drill after another to practice these skills. They are taught to smoothly go from being gunfighters to prisoner handlers, and on a moment's notice, back to the gunfight. Most of the prisoner-control training is done in training pairs—one student as the SEAL operator and his training partner as the prisoner. The quality of training depends a great deal on the training partner. He has to deliver the proper amount of resistance, and he can also coach the operator. He also serves as the focal point for the aggression and pain in this training. This is serious business, and training partners frequently tap the student operators or call out "Red!" when the pain gets too much.

"Talk to each other," Jon Rhodes tells them. "You operators, check to make sure that your training partner is okay. Training partners, let that operator know how he's doing. You can feel it if he's got a good seal on you. Also let him know if he needs to dial it down a little. We deal in pain and discomfort here; too much pain is bad, but a little discomfort is a good thing."

Dalton and his instructors prowl the mats coaching, demonstrating, mentoring, and, above all, ensuring the safety of this training.

After one-on-one drills, the students practice their prisoner-control techniques working in teams of three or four and deal with noncompliant prisoners. Student prisoners in full hood helmets and body armor don't do what they are told or offer carefully choreographed resistance. Often they have rubber guns or knives hidden on them.

"Lay down on the ground! Face down, on the ground! Do it now!"

There are four of them on line, weapons holding on the prisoner. The student/bad guy drops to his knees.

"On the ground, face down!" He does what he's told.

"Roll over! Roll over again! Cross your legs, hands on the ground above your head! Turn your head away!" This guy is compliant—so far.

The student team closes in. Two provide cover while the other two move in on the prisoner. Before they can establish a good seal, the prisoner goes off on them.

"Break," calls the student with primary prisoner-control duty, and the two operators who were down on the mat with the prisoner spring up and back to the power-point stance. In a matter of seconds, the formerly compliant prisoner scrambles to his feet, but once again there are four guns on him. He advances on one of his tormentors and gets a muzzle strike in his Plexiglas face shield for his trouble. He goes down hard, just as he would if he hadn't had the benefit of the padding and protection. By the numbers, the two operators are back on him. They seal, cuff, and search him, and drag him off.

"End ex," calls Instructor Meyers and the action stops. "You okay?" The student posing as the noncompliant student prisoner pulls his hood helmet off and nods. His face is red from the exertion. It is not easy playing the victim in CQD training. But then it's not supposed to be; good training comes with a little pain and some discomfort.

"Good job," Meyers tells them. "Any question that this guy got what he deserved? Any question that if Daniels here hadn't had the hood on that he would be down for the count and wake up cuffed in some detention area? You prisoner handlers did an excellent job; when he turned on you, you got back away from the threat.

Remember to communicate with each other. Every situation is different. Talk it up; that way you can better work together. Okay, let's swap out and do it again."

A number of times during the prisoner-handling drill, the instructors have to caution them about things they may have seen on TV. Asking a bad guy to kick a gun away or hand you a gun he's carrying with the fingers of his left hand are simply Hollywood stuff. In the real world, it's all about recognizing a threat, minimizing the threat, and controlling the situation.

The final day, they bring it all together. The role players are men waiting for their BUD/S Indoc training to begin. It's not an easy job, and they are all volunteers. They are in full body armor and hood helmets. They wear various clothing over their protection to simulate being merchant seamen or irregular desert fighters. Some are armed, which means they can shoot back, and some aren't. In each situation, the threat is different, which means that the student SEAL operators must react accordingly, per their stated rules of engagement. Some situations call for restraint; others for deadly force. The student SEAL operators are given a scenario and a few moments to study the rules of engagement for this situation. The game starts, although this is far from a game, when the student pairs kick the door in and enter the room. Once in the arena, they have a split second to react: What is the threat? How much force is needed? The level of compliance from the role players ranges from angry protests to pulling a gun and shooting back.

What makes this training so realistic and valuable are Simunitions. The Sim kits consist of Sig Sauer pistols and M4s that have been rechambered and rebarreled to fire 9mm paint rounds. These are not recreational paint guns; they are the same weapons the SEAL students qualified on at La Posta and Camp Pendleton. The cyclic rate of fire and short-range trajectories are the same. The only difference is the lethality of the rounds. The operators wear face shields, but the rounds still sting when they hit a man's torso or arm. The students use all their tools: hand strikes, gun-muzzle strikes, and rounds on target. They must manage and control prisoners in a hostile environment.

And they get shot at; sometimes they get hit. Each of the training scenarios reflects some aspect of a real-world SEAL mission tasking. Each situation is designed to test their skills and reflects all of the disciplines they learned the previous four days. The student operators have to think; and when there is no time to think, they react the way they have been trained. It's combat, and the students are drowning in emotion and adrenaline. By the end of CQD training, each member of Class 2-02 has struck a blow, absorbed a blow, experienced unarmed combat, and now has been in a gunfight. To a man, they say it's the most fun they've had since they joined the Navy.

"You all did a great job here this week," Jon Rhodes tells them. The CQD leading petty officer gives Class 2-02 its final briefing, but Chief Dalton is right there with him. "You've come a long way in a very short time. We covered a lot of material. Think about it and, when you can, practice it. It will take some time and future effort on your part to gain proficiency using these techniques. But you can see that this works, right? When you get into your platoons, you'll be back here for more training. The more you practice at this, the better you will become at using these skills. And you will use them—aboard ship or in some remote village where a bunch of terrorist scumbags conduct their training. Remember, you have to control the situation and minimize the threat. Take charge. Don't let some badass minimize you. Dial it up if you have to, and dial it down when it is appropriate. If you can control the threat, then you may avoid having to kill someone who may not need to die. Don't forget, you are responsible when you send those rounds downrange and turn someone's lights out. And you will have to answer for the action you take. That's a big-time responsibility. With this training, you may have a better option. With this training, you may be able to control a situation and not have to take a life. Make it their choice. But hear me on this one: If a bad guy threatens you or your teammates and won't have it any other way, you shoot him and keep shooting him until he's dead. Don't hesitate. Just like in the scenarios you all just went though. They get what they deserve—no more, no less.

"Chief?"

Chief Dalton addresses the class a final time. "We want you all to take some time with these course critiques. Be specific. We read them, and we learn from them. If there is some way we can make this training better, then the next class will benefit from what you have to say. Good luck during the rest of SQT and good luck in the teams."

Friday afternoon, after the men of Class 2-02 cleans weapons and the CQD training facility, they return to the SQT building and begin their load-out for training at Camp Billy Machen.

INTO THE DESERT

"You guys are going to like Bill Machen," Henry Dega tells Class 2-02 as it prepares for training in the desert. "It's just like Camp Al Huey out on San Clemente Island, where you trained during BUD/S Third Phase. Everything is there for SEAL training and none of the distractions you get here on the Strand. The ranges are close by, and there is unlimited terrain for shooting, patrolling, and demolitions." Dega gives them a list of what they are to carry on their first, second, and third line gear, and additional equipment they will need for their three-week block of training at Camp Machen. "You don't have to worry about chow at the camp," Dega tells them. "We eat like kings out there."

Camp Billy Machen, the Naval Special Warfare Desert Training Facility, is located some 135 miles east of San Diego. The facility is part of the Chocolate Mountain Aerial Gunnery Range. Just the SEAL portion includes close to sixty-five square miles of desert and mountainous terrain. It is dry, desolate country, completely uninhabited except for a few wild burros and an occasional illegal scrapper. The SEALs try to avoid shooting both. The burros eke out an existence in the scrub and dry washes of the desert. The scrappers are desert rats of the human variety who ignore the warning signs and sneak onto the well-posted government reservation to gather metal from the surplus and wrecked vehicles that are used as targets. The terrain is not unlike that in central and southern Afghanistan and central Iraq, and with the Chocolate Mountains as a backdrop, it looks very similar to any number of desert nations of the Middle East and central Asia.

The camp is named for Petty Officer Billy Machen, the first SEAL to be killed in combat in Vietnam, which makes him the first Navy SEAL killed in action. SEALs have been coming here to train since 1966. I brought my platoon from SEAL Team One here to train prior to our deployment to Vietnam in 1970. Back then, the camp, yet to be named in honor of Machen, was a series of surplus single-wide mobile homes that served as weapon lockups and sleeping quarters. They were little better than sleeping out on the open ground, especially in the summer, when temperatures soar to 110 degrees on a regular basis. We generally trained at night and sat in the shade by day, trying to stay cool. There was no air-conditioning back then. It's much different today—the facility, not the outside temperature.

Camp Billy Machen has come a long way since the Vietnam days and rusted-out old trailers. It has a modern fifty-thousand-square-foot building with dormitory space, classrooms, weapons storage vaults, and a cafeteria. Surrounding the main building is a weapons cleaning shed, a demolition preparation area, and a dedicated, climate-controlled ammunition storage building. It's like a little junior college where they teach lethal disciplines for special operations warriors. For the members of Class 2-02, the tuition is steep. Here they will train fourteen to sixteen hours a day, seven days a week under some very difficult conditions. But when they come off the ranges or in from the field problems, they will have air-conditioned quarters, hot chow, and a good place to sleep. SEAL platoons from both coasts train at Camp Billy Machen, but it is primarily a training ground for the West Coast teams and SEAL Tactical Training. With the current focus on Afghanistan, Iraq, and the harsh terrain where members of al-Qaeda have been known to hide, it is a very busy facility.

This three-week block of training at the desert training site is a key event in SQT and the road to the Trident. It will challenge the students individually and as a class, and require them to demonstrate good judgment, teamwork, and physical stamina. Previous classes have passed along the word; you will have more fun and work harder at Camp Billy Machen than in any previous training to date. Fifty-two men arrive at the camp for training of SQT Class 2-02, down two from the beginning of training. One man broke his thumb during CQD training and another broke his arm on the O-course. Both are in casts and both will be recycled with SQT Class 3-02.

The first week at Camp Billy Machen, Class 2-02 takes to the range for weapons training. The first thing the students do is to sight in their M4 rifles. They will do this again and again when they get to their operational platoons. A number of things can affect the sighting of a weapon: for example, jostling during transit, as well as the temperature, altitude, and humidity of the operational area. In their SEAL platoons, they will also have to dial in their laser and optical sights as well as the iron sights. A SEAL cannot aim, he is told again and again—he must hit. A SEAL is never really comfortable unless he knows that his rifle is doped and that he can get his rounds on target. Whenever possible, he will take time to sight in and calibrate his rifle. With their primary weapons zeroed in, the students begin a series of classes and familiarization fire with the M79 and M203 grenade launchers, the AK-47 rifle, and the .50-caliber machine gun. The M79 and M203 can deliver 40mm grenades up to three hundred yards, which adds firepower and versatility to a SEAL element. Grenadiers can choose from high-explosive, fléchette, CS gas, and illumination rounds. The M79 is a grenade-only weapon, while the M203 is mated to the M4 rifle, which means that a rifleman can also be a grenadier. SEALs consider the M4/M203 as a combined weapons system. They can engage a target directly with the M4 or indirectly with the 203. The AK-47, with its distinctive banana magazine and wooden fore and butt stocks, is the most widely produced light automatic weapon in the world. It's a favorite of al-Qaeda and mountain tribes throughout central Asia. And the rugged .50-caliber machine gun is perhaps the most deadly static-defense, area-fire weapon in the world. These weapons have been around for a long time—the .50 caliber since about 1926! The SEALs of my generation used all of them in Vietnam. Weapons like the big .50-caliber machine gun and the AK-47 are not carried in the SEAL inventory, but they are found on many battlefields. The students not only fire them but must also be able to disassemble, clean, and reassemble these weapons.

The MK43 and MK46 machine guns are newer additions to the SEAL weapons inventory. Both are fully automatic, area-fire weapons. A SEAL element will often consist of an eight-man squad. Two of those SEALs may be designated as automatic-weapons (AW) men. Depending on the mission, the AW men will carry a mix of the two weapons. The MK43 traces its roots to the venerable M60 machine gun. The M60 was designed as a two-man weapon, with a gunner and an assistant gunner. In Vietnam, SEALs took the standard Army-issue M60 and modified it for SEAL work. I remember my "60" gunners modifying their standard-issue weapons, removing the buttstocks, shortening the barrels, and shaving metal from the frame to cut down on weight. They did this so that one man in a patrol file could carry and fire the weapon. And they did all this for one reason: the 7.62 NATO standard round. The lighter 5.56 round of the M4 is to the 7.62 round what a Boeing 737 is to a 747. As in the E. F. Hutton commercial, when the M60 talks, everyone in the firefight listens. The MK43 is what the old SEALs wanted the M60 to be. It is relatively light—just over twenty-eight pounds—with one hundred rounds of ammunition; it is belt fed and shoulder fired, and it deals out those marvelous 7.62 rounds at six hundred rounds per minute. The MK46, the SEAL version of the Army's squad assault weapon, or SAW, also had its ancestor in Vietnam: the fabled Stoner Rifle. Both the MK46 and the Stoner are belt fed—disintegrating link fed, to be precise—and fire the lighter 5.56 rounds. It is the same round as that of the M4 rifle, but the SAW gunner does not have to change magazines. The SAW, as the SEALs call the MK46, weighs nineteen and a half pounds with a two-hundred-round load, compared to the seven-and-a-half-pound weight of a loaded M4. And the SAW is far more reliable than the old Stoner submachine gun. I carried a Stoner Rifle and it never let me down, but many SEALs of my generation still talk about the sickening feeling of a Stoner bolt going home and nothing happening.

The class rotates through the weapons stations, and each man gets to try his hand at each weapon. There is an SQT instructor at each station to ensure safety and to offer advice. This familiarization fire gets the men in Class 2-02 talking about what they may want to carry when they get to their platoons.

"I'm going to want to carry the pig," one of them tells me; his goal is to carry the MK43. The man with the MK43 is still called a 60 gunner, and the weapon is called the pig. "It's a load, but it's the most important weapon in the squad."

"I like the SAW," says another. "It's a sweet, light machine gun—very steady. You can hold it on center of mass with two- and three-round bursts. It'll be my weapon of choice." The SQT instructors know that these men will join their platoons as rookie SEALs and that their duties and choice of weapons will be dictated by the needs of the platoon and the weapons selection of the veteran SEALs. But the cadre says nothing of this, allowing them to enjoy the moment. Yet many of these SQT students will in fact carry the SAW and the pig on their first deployment and perhaps in their first firefight.

After three days with the area-fire and heavy-caliber weapons and the AK-47, the class again takes up their M4s, but with blank ammunition. It's time for more medical training. In ten-man squads, they patrol near the camp and are ambushed by blank-firing instructors. Corpsman Gordon Thomas is there with the students and designates one of the students as a "man down." The student SEALs must then return fire and begin their man-down drills. They withdraw into the old corrugated metal buildings that once served as barracks at Camp Billy Machen. Here the squad has to treat the wounded while the instructors assault the buildings with Simunitions and artillery simulators—lots of noise and smoke. This creates a surprisingly authentic *ping-ping* of bullets and the crump of mortar rounds. It's as real as it gets without live rounds and real mortar fire. The effect, if not the danger, is what the Rangers experienced at Mogadishu. The student squad must then move the wounded man from the buildings to the camp helo pad for extraction. Along the way, the instructors again attack. It's a vehicular assault—a drive-by shooting with blank automatic-weapons fire. The SQT cadre is in the back of a Toyota pickup and having great sport with this, as if the instructors were a bunch of Somali "technical" irregulars. This results in another man down. Now the squad has to deal with two casualties and continue to return fire as it fights its way to the extraction site. The men extract in pickup trucks that substitute for helos, but the caregivers have to treat and stabilize their wounded men, including giving IVs, while bouncing around in the back of a truck.

The man-down drill is an extension of the training Thomas gave them during their first week in SQT. This exercise could be taken from a page in the fight in Mogadishu or on the road to Baghdad, but it could be any third-world situation where it's hot, dusty, and things happen fast. It gets the SEAL students to thinking about fighting, moving, and caring for wounded, all at the same time. On Friday morning, Class 2-02 has its first graded evolution, the stress course.

"Stand by . . . Bust 'em!"

The first student charges across the desert with his M4 at high port. He is dressed in his first and second line gear, ready for battle. At the first station, he fires five rounds at the standing position, then he's off at a run, changing magazines. He fires five rounds kneeling at station two and five at station three, both times from behind a barricade. Again on the run, he changes mags. With weapon slung, he runs along logs stacked in a Z-shaped formation, then pulls a weighted tractor tire for fifteen yards. Then he runs up a hill to station four, where he kneels and cranks off five more rounds. Next, he runs down to a dry wash, around a marker, and back up the hill to station five, where he loads and fires a 40mm round from an M79. Then it's on the run again. Station six, another shooting station, is reached by crawling under a wall to the firing position. Next, it's back under the wall, under a barbed-wire obstacle to station seven, where he must throw a practice grenade at a target. Station eight, the final M4 shooting station, is a short run from the grenade toss, then a sprint to the finish.

The stress course is a timed evolution, with time deductions for M4 target misses, grenades out of the kill radius, and unsafe or improper practices. Procedure counts; all weapons must be safe after each firing sequence, and clear and safe after the final shooting station. It's almost automatic now for the SQT students, but in their haste for a good score, there is an occasional infraction. Ensign Garcia has the fastest time until Petty Officer Jason Betters beats him by nine full seconds. The times are posted outside the mess hall.

The stress course brings a lot of disciplines to bear. A man has to run, shoot, and think. Jason Betters is breaking out as the best shot in the class. He was among the top shooters on the qualification courses, but he is clearly the best combat shooter with a rifle.

"I grew up in central Pennsylvania on a horse ranch, and I did a lot of hunting. I've been shooting since I was nine years old." Betters will be heading back East to SEAL Team Two when he finishes SQT. He came into the Navy right out of high school. "I can't wait to get to the teams," he says. "I just love this stuff."

Betters also has an interesting part-time job. He's a bronc rider. In high school, he was on the local rodeo circuit and did quite well. On the drive back to Coronado from Army Airborne Training at Fort Benning, he entered two rodeos and placed twice. "Three hundred dollars for eight minutes' work is pretty good pay." I ask him if he plans to continue moonlighting when he gets to Team Two. "We'll see. I'd like to keep my hand in the game, but my goal is to be a good platoon SEAL. The teams and my platoon come first."

Friday afternoon is taken with instinctive-fire drills and the point-man course. They begin with live-fire drills that emphasize reactive, point-and-shoot techniques—both eyes open, getting rounds in the direction of the target. This is an extension of what they learned at the combat shooting course at La Posta. Big vision while looking for a target; small vision when a target presents itself. On target is better, but get the rounds off fast. The idea is that if your squad is the ambushee rather than the ambusher, you have to get rounds out as quickly as possible. The point-man course is another individual gauntlet of sorts. One at a time, each student walks along a trail through desert scrub and tangles with an instructor several paces behind him. Along the way, he must negotiate danger areas—small clearings, fallen trees. The man in the arena is armed with an M4 with Simunitions. Contact is initiated when he gets shot or, if he's lucky and very observant, sees the aggressors and shoots first. The aggressors are fellow students, waiting in ambush with M4 Simunitions. The drill is to react to the contact and quickly return fire. A point man's timely reaction could save his squad and perhaps his own life—if he can effectively engage the enemy and allow his teammates to get their guns into the fight. This course also gives the students some perspective of what it's like to be the man on point as well as to be on the wrong end of an ambush.

Again, one student breaks out from the others. Those hiding in ambush have a distinct advantage, but a single student is able to see his aggressors and fire first. He is a solid performer, but an undistinguished one until the point-man course. I found Petty Officer Mika Kahala cleaning his weapon after training and asked him about it.

"I dunno, sir, I guess I was just lucky."

"You do any hunting before you came into the Navy?"

"Yeah, I hunted a lot with my dad and my uncles."

"Deer? Birds?"

"No, sir. Pigs."

"Pigs?"

"Yeah. I grew up on the Big Island of Hawaii," he says. Kahala speaks with the melody in his voice of someone who spoke native Hawaiian in the home. "Big family. We eat a lot of pork so we hunt a lot of pigs. When you're out in the bush hunting pigs, it's very important you see them before they see you. I've been charged by a wild pig, and it's not any fun."

"You join the Navy right out of high school?"

"Naw, I hung out for almost a year, but I was getting into trouble so I joined the Navy to be a SEAL."

"Are you going to SDV Team One?" SDV One is located on Ford Island in Pearl Harbor.

"No," Kahala replies. "My mama said I should see the world, so I'm going to Team Two on the East Coast. I was never off the Big Island till I joined the Navy."

Over the weekend, the class has its first night shooting exercise and is introduced to laser night sights and night optics. They also conduct a night reconnaissance and surveillance practical. It's long days in the classroom and then night training evolutions. On Monday, they are back on the ranges for rattle-battle. They did this at Camp Pendleton with full first and second line gear. Here at Camp Billy Machen, they will do the same thing, but with the addition of third line gear in the form of a thirty-five-pound ruck. Like at Camp Pendleton, each fire-and-movement drill consists of 120 rounds of timed fire from between one hundred and three hundred yards. Running between shooting stations in the desert heat with a rucksack is hard work. So is shooting with rucks, especially in the prone position. The students learn to dump the ruck off to one side to keep from being top-heavy while shooting and to use the weight of the ruck for stability. Nonetheless, any student with less than eighty hits on the target owes the cadre a minimum of forty push-ups. The deficient shooter is made to lay his M4 across the tops of his hands in the push-up position, and crank them out while apologizing to his rifle: "I am sorry, M4, for having let you down—one; I am sorry, M4, for having let you down—two . . ." The push-ups are done with full first, second, and third line gear—some sixty pounds of additional weight to push away from the desert floor. The men in Class 2-02 continue to break out by skill and toughness. Two in the class put more than a hundred rounds on their rattle-battle targets; one of them is Jason Betters.

The beginning of week two at Camp Billy Machen has the class out patrolling in the desert at night, practicing hand and arm signals.

During the land navigation exercise at Frazier Park, they worked in pairs. Now they patrol in squads, with ten or eleven men per squad due to the size of the class. Individually, they are now a little tighter with their first, second, and third line gear. It's becoming a part of them. Each time they gear up on the ranges or walk on patrol fully loaded, they make some small adjustment to a strap or shift a piece of equipment this way or that. Many in the class wear pads on their knees and elbows, like Rollerbladers. Now when they go down to shoot or to a security position from the squad file, they can better handle the desert hardpan. I walked with Class 228 on night patrols on San Clemente Island during their Third Phase BUD/S training. SQT Class 2-02 is more skilled, and their noise discipline is much better. It should be. Land-warfare training in BUD/S comes during week twenty-two in the formal training of a Navy SEAL. Land warfare in SQT is, on average, about week thirty-eight.

At Camp Billy Machen, Class 2-02 gets a day of rockets. There are three shoulder-fired rockets in the SEAL inventory. One is the Carl Gustaf M3 system, a highly accurate 84mm, variable-purpose rocket launcher. Due to the weight of the rockets and the bulkiness of the launcher, it is normally used by SEALs only on a direct-action mission in which the Carl Gustaf is central to the objectives of the mission. The AT4 rocket is also an 84mm weapon carried in a single-use launcher; it's less accurate and less powerful than the Carl Gustaf, but at eighteen pounds, it's half the weight. One or two AT4s might be carried by a squad of SEALs on a mission where they could expect to encounter an armored vehicle. The third and most versatile of the rockets is the LAAW, which stands for light antiarmor weapon. This 66mm weapon weighs only five pounds, but it can penetrate nearly twelve inches of armor. The LAAW hasn't the range, accuracy, or punch of the AT4 or Carl Gustaf, but its portability makes it a favorite in the platoons. On almost any operation, a mission planner can hang a LAAW or two on one of his SEALs—just in case. It's an older weapon, identical with the LAAWs carried by SEAL platoons in Vietnam, but with a much improved sight. My platoon carried them, and we found them to be ideal weapons to initiate an ambush or to take out a Vietcong bunker.

Wednesday marks the midpoint in Class 2-02's stay at Camp Billy Machen; they are also a little more than halfway through their SQT training. This is celebrated by the Combat Conditioning Course, a thirteen-mile run with full gear and weapons. The men have been working up to this run with four- and six-mile rucksack humps, but this is the big one. The students take to the course at 0300 to stay ahead of the heat of the day, although the temperature is still seventy-five degrees. It's not just a fun run; they have work to do along the way. The evening before the scheduled run, the class meets in the large SQT classroom at Camp Billy Machen.

"Okay, guys, this will be your briefing for the Combat Conditioning Course. Gentlemen, this *is* a race. You are trying to beat the time of your classmates. Beyond that, there is a cutoff time, and if you don't make that time, you'll be out there the next morning. Fail it a second time and your next duty station will be aboard an outbound Navy ship. So we want you to throw yourselves into this and give it your best shot. Why do we do this?"

Instructor Jim Bell surveys the students crowded into the classroom. There are now fifty-one of them. One man picked up one too many safety violations and has just been sent back to the Center on Coronado. He will be counseled and perhaps become a member of SQT Class 3-02. Safety violations and a man's ability to train safely with a weapon are taken very seriously. Eight SQT instructors line the back of the classroom. This is Bell's evolution and his course brief. Before coming to SQT as an instructor, he completed four platoon deployments with SEAL Team Five.

"You probably think that because we all had to do this, now you have to do it as well. Well, that may be part of it, and it is a bit of a gut check, but the platoons do courses like this to get ready for deployment. We do it here because it allows us to evaluate you—see if you can perform after you've been humping down the trail a while. It's also a personal learning experience for you. You will know a lot more about your gear after you hump it around this course. When you get back, make adjustments; change things. You want to go into your platoons with all your gear exactly right. And like with all tough evolutions, you can learn something about yourself. It's a ball buster; it will test your skills and your stamina. Alright, a couple of things before I brief the course. No sunglasses and no low-cut shoes; this is a tactical evolution. Everyone will be in over-the-ankle boots. You will begin the run with a minimum of four quarts of water. That's a minimum, and there will be none for you on the course. I recommend that you take more and maybe a couple of PowerBars as well. Your ammo load will be seven magazines with five rounds, one mag with ten, and an empty mag in your weapon. No slung weapons; I want you to carry your guns unslung, just like you would if you were in hostile territory. And finally, no walking. This is a race, and you will run it all the way. Any questions so far? Okay, before we go over the course, let's talk about safety. At all times you will observe proper weapons safety protocol. After each shooting station, you will clear and safe your weapon before continuing on the course. Safety violations, depending on the severity, will be charged against your time on the course or get you sent back to the Strand. You gotta be thinking out there.

"There's also the matter of medical safety. Don't forget you're rucked up and running in the desert. Hydrate before you begin the run and keep drinking water while you're on the course. Heat exhaustion and even heatstroke are things you need to be on the lookout for. Much of the course is along the irrigation canal, so if you find yourself in trouble, get yourself into the water. There will be an instructor cadre on the course and in vehicles checking up on you. If you have a problem, we want to know about it. Otherwise, drive on. This is a max-effort evolution. Class leader?"

"Right here, Instructor." Ensign Rob Tanner is senior ensign among the four officers.

"Has everyone weighed their rucks?"

"Yes, Instructor."

"And all of them are at least thirty-five pounds?"

"Yes, Instructor."

"Okay, guys. Good luck to you. Make it happen."

At 0300 the following morning, the first two men set off at a jog from the start-finish line. Every two minutes, another two men leave. One of the cadre is there to see that every man is in complete first, second, and third line gear with at least four full canteens. With weapon and ammo, that comes to about sixty-five pounds of gear. I pair up with the sixth man off the line, one of the class officers, and run with him. We have a five-mile run to the first station. I *am* wearing low-cut shoes, Nike hiking boots, and carrying only a Camelback with sixty ounces of water, a camera, and a few PowerBars. We arrive at the first station in about fifty minutes. Here, the students must dump their rucks and fire at a silhouette target: first, they shoot five rounds at one hundred yards while standing, then five rounds while kneeling at two hundred yards, and finally five more rounds at three hundred yards while prone. Each miss adds two minutes to their time. I shoot only pictures. Eight men in the class score a perfect fifteen hits at the first station. These guys can shoot! My student pulls on his ruck, and we run on for two more miles to the MK43 station. On a wooden plank is a disassembled MK43 machine gun. Each man has to assemble the 43, clip in a belt of ten rounds, and put a burst downrange—all in less than three minutes and with the proper safety precautions. A failure to do this in the allotted time adds two minutes to their total time. Another run, another station. This one is the AT4 rocket launcher with a 9mm practice round. Here the students must set up the weapon and hit a steel silhouette at one hundred yards. The penalties: two minutes for improper procedures and two minutes for missing the target. Another run to station four, the stress course. This is an abbreviated version of the course they had run earlier. Here they dump their final four five-round magazines and fire the M79 grenade launcher. Each miss: two minutes added. No one in the class hits all the targets, but several have only one miss. On the run again, students are almost back to the camp compound, but they have to take a two-mile detour out to the grenade range.

Again with the M79, they have to hit a tank at one hundred yards with two of their three high-explosive rounds. Now they have only one more mile to go and one more station. Back at the small-arms range next to the main camp building, they shoot their final mag of ten rounds at a steel silhouette from three hundred yards. Eight of them hit with all ten rounds. Then it's a two-hundred-yard sprint to the finish.

The honors for the individual champion in the Combat Conditioning Course were hotly contested. Based on the shorter ruck-run times, there were two clear favorites: Ensign John Miller and Petty Officer Carl Wilchinski. Wilchinski is a big man, six-one and close to 220 pounds. Prior to joining the Navy, he was a timber faller and made a living setting chokers in the woods in Oregon. When he wasn't setting chokers, he was spending time in the tattoo parlor. Wilchinski is outgoing, capable, and a bull of man. Ensign Miller is a quiet, solid, twenty-eight-year-old ensign with a Ph.D. from Oxford. The big ruck run was seen by the members of Class 2-02 as a contest between the Rhodes scholar and the logger. Jason Betters was given an outside chance because of his shooting skills, but most of the betting was on Miller and Wilchinski. All three men finished well, but Petty Officer Eric Robertson, a solid performer from Omaha, managed to run fast enough and shoot well enough to post the fastest time. Robertson had finished two years at the University of Nebraska when he became bored with college. He wanted more of a challenge, so he enlisted in the Navy for SEAL training. From what I've seen of him, he's going to make a great platoon SEAL.

All make it within the four-and-a-half-hour adjusted cutoff time. The fastest time is two hours and fifty-three minutes, but they're all winners—they're all a step closer to their SEAL qualification. As the last of the students straggle in from the final shooting station, the rest of Class 2-02 cheers them on. The sun is well up, so a few of the final entrants are near heat exhaustion, which creates another training opportunity. While Instructor Thomas watches, the earlier finishers give IVs to those who feel light-headed, as well as to many who don't.

It's a good evolution for the class. SEAL students, like herding dogs, are happiest when they've been worked hard. After the run, I borrow an M4, rucksack, and second line gear from one of the students and saddle up. Then I shuffle-trot around the building. Fifty-five plus pounds of gear (the canteens were empty) and a seven-pound rifle is a lot to carry—I barely make it a hundred yards. How did they do it? Thirteen miles with this load, in boots over soft sand and desert hard-pan! Another day in the life of an almost Navy SEAL. And think about the smaller men; namely, the class little guy at 125 pounds. SEAL training does not index combat load for size. He just ran a half marathon in the dirt carrying half his body weight. Simply amazing.

The next several days at Camp Billy Machen are devoted to demolitions. At BUD/S, Class 237 had ten days of basic demolition training; SQT Class 2-02 will get four. Military demolitions is all about procedure and safety. The students have had the basics. At SQT, they will review the basic safety and handling procedures they learned during Third Phase of BUD/S and build from there. Much of this will be repetition, but doing it again and again is very important. They have to handle explosives and be comfortable with them. Safety is a function of repetition and procedure.

"We're going to bring the tempo down a little during the next four days," Instructor Larry Andrews tells them. "Most of what we do here at SQT is dangerous, but explosives, if you don't handle them properly, can get a whole bunch of people hurt. You have to respect demo, but you can't be afraid of it, either. Ask questions; if something's not clear, let us know. The only stupid question is the one you don't ask. We're going to handle a lot of different types of explosives over the next few days, and we're going to do it safely. Basic demolitions, what you've learned in BUD/S and what we're going to review here, is very important. The team guys in Afghanistan are still finding a lot of ordnance and are blowing it up. They're using the same skills and procedures that we use here. And we'll cover a few new things that you didn't get to in BUD/S. Now, we won't be going into any advanced work, like with breaching charges; you'll get that when you get to your platoons. But the basic procedures are the same. During the next few days, we're going to practice the basics, develop good habits in handling explosives, be safe, and have a helluva lot of fun. Blowing up things is great fun, and we get paid to do it."

In Afghanistan, SEALs found and blew up tens of thousands of pounds of Taliban weaponry and ammunition. They are still finding and blowing up these munitions. Caches of weapons and ammunition were not nearly so numerous in Iraq, but those that were hidden served the Fedayeen Saddam. These, too, were destroyed using standard demo procedures learned in BUD/S and refined in SQT.

As with BUD/S, it's crawl and walk. There is no running on the demo ranges. The class first takes up claymore mines. A claymore is a particularly nasty explosive charge that sends some seven hundred steel pellets downrange in a directional, lethal blast. The students work from patrol formation, setting up claymore ambushes by day and then by night. They also work with Mk-57 explosive kit sections capable of providing cut-to-size, claymore-like results. The second day is like the first: early morning classroom work, late-morning charge preparation. The students do a shot in the afternoon and then go back at night for a second shot. The second-day demolitions include Mk-75 hose, bangalore torpedoes, and shaped charges. The night shots are done from patrol formation with the students conducting brief, walk-through rehearsals before going into the field. The drill is to move in a tactical patrol formation, and to get quickly in and out of the target area. Already they are beginning to think about their TOT—time on target. During the first two days, the demolitions are initiated nonelectrically. This means with time fuse and blasting caps, the way most tactical field demolitions are primed. Electrical priming is most often used in an administrative setting.

On the third day, the class members move on to electrically initiated explosives and something they did not see in BUD/S: radio firing devices, or RFDs. This allows a demolitioneer to place a charge, in either an administrative setting or a tactical situation, and fire it remotely on command. It's like a long-range TV channel clicker, only there's a big bang on the other end. They are also introduced to electronic clocks that can be set for a few minutes or a few days to initiate a charge.

"And just so you can do it if you have to," Instructor Andrews tells them, "we're going to shoot a few caps using a firing reel and a portable blasting machine. This is dark-ages stuff, but you could find yourself in some third-world situation, and this is all you have to work with."

This makes me feel more than a little dated. When I was in training, we did all our electric shots with firing reels and blasting machines.

During the third-day demo, they build a number of different charges using most of the demolitions they will or could see in their platoons: cutting charges, shaped charges, cratering charges, satchel charges, sheet charges—the list goes on and on. But the firing assemblies they build do change, getting smaller and more portable. There are publications and procedures that drive much of this training, but there is a host of small things that only the instructors can teach them. Like how to build a shockproof container from a grenade packing canister to carry blasting caps on a SEAL mission. Or how to build a det cord slip-tie that can quickly be tied into a trunk line at night. Or something as simple as when to use electrical tape and when to use duct tape in the building of a sheet charge. These are among the little things, the "do betters," that Andrews and his demo instructors pass along to the members of Class 2-02. On the last day of demo, the featured lesson is in improvised explosives. The class spends the day learning to make dangerous explosives a little more lethal, and expending any unused demolitions from the previous three days' work.

The demolition instruction is scheduled right after the Combat Conditioning Course because many in the class need a few days to get their legs back under them. The hours are long but the pace is slower. Following demo, the pace picks back up as the class goes into IAD training. SEALs practice immediate-action drills in the event they find themselves in inadvertent contact. The tactic may be used to assault a target, but usually it's done to break contact. The men must react quickly to the unexpected threat, follow commands, and maneuver while shooting. This is dangerous training; they will first crawl, then walk, and finally run—with live ammo and at night. They did this during BUD/S, but the SQT instructors will dial it up a notch.

The SQT students practice two of the IADs they learned during BUD/S: the leapfrog and the center peel. During the basic leapfrog, a squad is on a skirmish line when contact is initiated. The men go down and return fire. On command, one element lays down a base of fire while the second element of the squad rises and runs to a position away from the contact to a new firing position. Then the first element withdraws while the second covers its dash, with the first element running past the second to its new position. The two elements fire and maneuver away from the danger in leapfrog fashion. With practice, the maneuvering elements can leapfrog left or right. Again, this tactic can also be used to assault a target, but more often it will be employed as a defensive measure to break contact. The center peel is used when a squad is patrolling in an extended formation, generally in closed terrain, with the squad in two files. It is initiated when the point man makes contact and initiates the center peel. He drains his magazine and bolts between the two files of his teammates. The two files then alternate, one at a time laying down a base of fire and running back between the files. In this manner, the squad continues to "peel" away from the threat. In both the leapfrog and the center peel, the student SEALs are on the run, changing magazines as they move—different drill, same mechanics.

The new maneuver that the students learn at SQT is the strong left or strong right IAD. From a single-file patrol formation, the squad leader gives the command "Strong right [or left]!" and the IAD is begun. In the strong right, the leading element in the file swings right in a gatelike movement with the point man as the hinge. This gets half the squad's guns quickly on line. The second element file also swings around to the right, but this element drops back and to the right. Now they are in a basic "leapt frog" position. While the second element moves, the leading element, which has the patrol leader in it, lays down a base of fire. Then, on command, the lead element leapfrogs back under the covering fire of the second element. Sound easy? In a manner of speaking, it is; but add darkness and live rounds, and it becomes very dangerous business.

Class 2-02 is broken into four ten-man squads and one eleven-man squad. They work in their first and second line gear. Each man knows his position in his squad, whether patrolling in a single file or an expanded formation, and to which element he is assigned in the squad. They begin with walk-through drills in the parking lot, then move on to walk-through drills with blank ammunition. They are like ballet dancers under the direction of a choreographer who wants them to practice the steps and know the movements before increasing the tempo. At night, they are back out in the desert with blank ammo. The second day it's live ammo. The squad does a walk-through in the daylight before running through the IAD drill. And then they do it again at night—walk, then run.

"A guy can get through SQT for the most part by putting out and following the lead of the guy next to him," Warrant Officer Mike Loo tells me. "But in IADs, he has to think for himself and move the right way at the right time. He has to know when to pivot to the left, not to the right, in a given IAD, because if he turns the wrong way, he runs into someone, or he sweeps his teammate with the muzzle of his rifle. It's not hard, but each man has to think and do it right. We have a lot of instructors on the ranges during night IADs."

"Are you on the range for IADs?" I ask him.

"You bet I am. This is high-speed stuff, and it will get faster and more intense when they get to their platoons. Our job here is to get them ready for platoon training, so these student squads will do these drills again and again until we are satisfied they have the basics down pat."

After IAD training, another man is sent back to the Strand. He will not be recycled through with Class 3-02. It's not his professional skill or his physical ability; both are up to standard. It's his attitude. He has a smart mouth, and he often takes his classmates for granted. He has demonstrated on more than one occasion that he is not a team player, and he shows no sign that he will change. With his SEAL qualification barely five weeks away, he is gone. And he is absolutely devastated to find himself no longer in training. But he was counseled repeatedly and given every chance to succeed. The stakes are simply too high to risk sending to a SEAL platoon a man who is not committed to the team.

Time on target is a very important consideration in a SEAL mission. In preparation for its FTX, Class 2-02 learns about TOT in the classroom, then takes this information into the field. Basically, these drills or rehearsals are designed to impress on the students that time on target is usually the time of the greatest danger for them. The less time that they are on target, the better chance for mission success and the more likely that they will get off target safely and get everyone back home. Surprise, quickly achieving the mission objectives, and a safe getaway all relate to time on target. Because of this, they spend a full day with TOT drills, or TOTs, and with the TOTs they have another opportunity for a night IAD.

Following TOTs, the helos come for a day and the students get to use the fast rope from an airborne platform. The fast rope is a thick, feltlike rope that serves almost like a fireman's pole from helo to ground. They all did this at BUD/S from a tower, but it is different from a hovering helo amid the noise and dust. And it's different still with a combat load. Without a load, the students can drop to the desert floor using only their hands to grip the line. With a load, most of them will run the line through their legs and feet. The helos stay late that evening for a combat search and rescue, or CSAR, practical.

CSAR is a very important mission for the deployed SEAL platoons. Combat pilots, like the ones who flew strikes over Afghanistan and Iraq, know that if they have to bail out over hostile territory, some very dedicated and capable people will be trying to rescue them. SEALs conducted successful pilot rescues during the first Gulf War and were able to recover the remains of a pilot during recent operations in Iraq. Approaching, authenticating, and recovering a downed pilot is a very disciplined skill set. And very dangerous for the rescuers if the pilot is compromised. There is a whole protocol for making an approach to a downed airman and safely bringing him out. Once the SEAL students have their pilot, the stage is set for more training—first-aid training and moving a wounded man in a tactical situation under fire. Air Force para-rescue teams have this mission as a primary duty—the only Department of Defense special operations force so tasked—but all SEAL platoons deploy with the ability to conduct CSAR missions, at sea and on land.

With the completion of a night CSAR practical with the helos, the class nears their final days at Camp Billy Machen. All that remains is range cleanup, camp cleanup, and the FTX. The men in SQT Class 2-02 are getting tired. The long days in the desert are starting to wear the class down; they're wearing on the instructor staff as well. The instructors work as hard as the students and often have longer hours. But the staff and students do have time off. The interaction between student SEALs and SQT cadre is important. Questions get answered that didn't get asked in class, or ones for which the student wanted a one-on-one answer. They talk about the teams and the platoons: who saw action in Afghanistan; what's the latest from the platoons deployed in theater. Occasionally, a student learns that one of his BUD/S instructors will be reporting to the team to which he has been assigned; they will be teammates, perhaps even in the same platoon. One of the SQT shooting instructors who just worked with them at La Posta has orders to SEAL Team Five. Six men in Class 2-02 are going to Team Seven, nine to Team Ten. Both teams are just beginning their predeployment training. Most of the others are assigned to Teams One and Two, the teams that are currently deployed. It's starting to get real. There are several weeks of hard work ahead, but the SEAL teams and their first SEAL platoon now seem within reach.

The students do have a few hours of down time each day. Camp Billy Machen is a great place to run, but they have to dodge the heat of the day and fit it around their classroom and range time. As at most SEAL facilities, there is a good weight room. Most off-duty camp life centers around the chow hall and the adjacent lounge. The students mostly sit, talk, and drink Gatorade. There is a large-screen TV with a good stock of current movies on DVD. For some reason, Class 2-02 seems content to watch the classic *Das Boot* again and again. There is a pool table, usually with two players and six to eight kibitzers. Left-overs from meals are kept in a ready-service pantry, so the students can snack when they come off the ranges at night. Like BUD/S students, SQT students burn from five to seven thousand calories a day. They can eat constantly. No longer so for an older SEAL who is now a writer. I tried to stay out of the food pantry at Camp Billy Machen, but I was not always successful. One night a student found a scorpion and brought it in for inspection. Then another promptly went out and cap-tured a black widow spider. One of the galley serving trays was pressed into service as an arena, and the two contestants were sent into battle. It was not much of a contest; the black widow won easily, and quickly. The students drifted back to the pool table and *Das Boot*.

The last three days at Camp Billy Machen are devoted to the final mission problem, or field training exercise. Much as they were on San Clemente Island during their BUD/S Third Phase land-warfare train-ing, the days are long and so are the nights. The students use much of what they've learned in BUD/S and SQT. The squads receive their mission taskings, and begin their target analysis and mission plan-ning. When it becomes clear what they have to do and how they will do it, there are demolitions to prepare, weapons and equipment to stage, and rehearsals. In Afghanistan, SEALs were sent in on a host of nonmaritime targets because their training had prepared them to quickly work through the target-analysis, mission-planning, equipment-staging, and rehearsal aspects of a special operations mission. Sometimes this amounted to the platoon leader's dropping to one knee and drawing up his attack plan in the dirt. Then the platoon climbed aboard the insertion helo—locked and loaded. The SEALs got these missions because they were good to go in a very short time. In the platoons, these soon-to-be SEALs will do these training missions again and again, so they can react rapidly and proficiently when they do it for real.

The SQT staff all work very hard during the FTX as well, and they've been laboring in advance to prepare for it. There are three targets; two terrorist training camps and a command-and-control center. Corpsman/Instructor Gordon Thomas, with his ingenuity and flair for authentic training, has been preparing these targets. There is only so much one can do with sandbags, plywood sheeting, fifty-five-gallon oil drums, old truck tires, camouflage netting, and scrap lumber, but he's a very creative guy. The training camps have shooting ranges, obstacle courses, guard towers, even caves. At the command-and-control target, an old aircraft fuel tank has sprouted cardboard wings and is now a Scud surface-to-surface missile. There are bunkers, fuel storage areas, and POW holding facilities. In the daylight, they look pretty tacky; but at night, they look very much like the real thing, and at almost no cost to the taxpayer. The rigor with which Thomas and the other SQT cadre members work to create these realistic training targets is a testament to their commitment to this training. They care a great deal, and it shows.

Regarding the POW holding facilities at two of the FTX targets, SEALS are trained early on to be on the alert for, and in the handling of, POWs. I can't speak to the SQT-level training of the SEALs who brought out Private Jessica Lynch in Iraq, but their first practice rescue operation could well have taken place when they were in training, just like the members of Class 2-02. During operations in Iraq, SEALs were able to disable Iraqi Scud missiles. Again, the training wheels for those real-world operations could well have been a mock-up missile site at Camp Billy Machen.

In the classrooms, the three patrol leaders do their mission planning. The FTX calls for a reconnaissance and surveillance mission with a follow-on direct-action strike on each target—three days of planning and two nights in the field. The officers and petty officers learn something each time they go through the mission-planning process. They get a little better at estimating time on target, finding a good route to and from the target, and what they can and cannot get and use in the way of intelligence and support for their mission. Those busy preparing weather and environmental data to support the mission are becoming more adept at it. The mission-planning software is becoming a little less intimidating.

The three squads patrol into the desert on the first night to recon their target. The recon missions are very important; they represent a key SEAL mission of special reconnaissance. In Afghanistan and Iraq, Navy SEALs spent many long days and nights in hostile territory on special reconnaissance missions. In SQT, as in Afghanistan and Iraq, information the students bring back after a night of eyes on the target helps them to prepare their weapons and demolitions for a follow-on direct-action mission. These direct-action missions are full-on, live-fire exercises. They attack their targets with combinations of small-arms fire, rockets, and demolitions. Their tactics and actions on target are in keeping with SEAL methods and standard operating procedures. Within the constraints of safety and range protocol, the FTX missions are made as real as possible. A single instructor, called a lane grader, walks with each squad as a safety observer and to evaluate the men's performance. The objective is a stealthy approach to the target and a tactically proficient attack. On the way in, one squad has to "go admin" after an encounter with a rattlesnake. The rattler hit one of the students, but a quick inspection revealed that it hadn't penetrated his boot. The squad file quietly presses on to its target. For the FTX problems, the student squads are armed with their M4 rifles plus MK43 machine guns, grenades, and rockets.

All three squads get to their respective targets within their target windows. The three squads are in radio contact, so on a prearranged signal, they make a coordinated attack. Their success in destroying their targets will be measured in the number of hours it will take Gordy Thomas and his fellow instructors to rebuild them for the next class. Near the command-and-control center target, two dark figures watch the action through night-vision goggles. The taller one straightens and turns to his companion.

"Nice job, Mike. I like what I see," says Captain Rick Smethers, the Commanding Officer of the Naval Special Warfare Center. He's on hand to observe this important part of Class 2-02's training. "You've brought them a long way in a very short time. And you did it with a big class. Very well done."

"Thanks, Captain," Warrant Officer Loo replies. "I think we're about ready to take them back to the Strand and get them wet." The two men climb into their truck and move to where they can watch one of the squads finish the FTX.

On the way out, the student squads are challenged with various scenarios. Instructor Larry Andrews sat in on their patrol briefings and knows how they will come out. He has set up charges that the instructor lane graders can set off with an RFD to simulate an enemy ambush. In addition to attacking their targets and a break-contact drill on the way out, each squad will encounter and have to deal with either a man down, a POW, or a wounded pilot. The SQT staff takes every opportunity to present tactical challenges to its students. Each of these challenges is a chance to drill the student squads on first aid, CSAR, IADs, and basic night patrol disciplines. The FTX shows they are learning their craft. The students can work as a team, and they are able to successfully attack and destroy a remote target at night with a mixed bag of weapons. And when they are confronted with danger, they can respond to command and are able to maneuver and shoot at night. They are well on their way to becoming platoon SEALs.

The land-warfare portion of SQT at Camp Billy Machen is a Rubicon of sorts for every class. The long days of combat shooting, the Combat Conditioning Course, and the FTXs force the class members to work as a team. In their class subgroups, they train much as they will in their SEAL platoons. They are learning military skills and the attention to detail that is required during continuous weeks of hazardous training evolutions. They're learning that when they are tired and short of sleep, they still have to perform in a dangerous environment. This is what BUD/S prepared them for—to take their game to the next level. They are also learning to focus, day in and day out, on fulfilling their role as a member of a combat team in situations where the safety and lives of their teammates demand that they do their job well. This is not inexpensive training. In addition to the efforts of a large and very talented cadre, Class 2-02 expended the following amounts of ordnance and ammunition at Camp Billy Machen:

210,000 rounds of 5.56 ammunition for the M4 rifle
11,000 rounds of 5.56 linked ammunition for the MK46 machine gun
180,000 rounds of 7.62 linked ammunition for the MK43 machine gun
5,000 rounds of .50-caliber linked ammunition for the heavy machine gun
4,000 rounds of 7.67 short ammunition for the AK-47
8,000 rounds of 40mm grenade ammunition, all types
250 hand grenades
50 Carl Gustaf rockets, various types
60 LAAWs
180 claymore mines
6,000 pounds of demolitions

Land warfare and weapons proficiency are just two disciplines in the skill set of an accomplished SEAL operator. No regular U.S. military or other SOF component that I know of can afford this much time, attention, and expense in their advanced training venues to develop this level of skill. Yet when the members of Class 2-02 graduate from SQT, they will be qualified SEALs, but far from achieving the status of an operational, deployable SEAL warrior. That will require another eighteen months of training.

After the FTX debriefing and a few hours of sleep, the members of Class 2-02 clean their barracks and weapons, stow their gear, and head back to Coronado. Their number stands at fifty: forty-seven men from Class 237 and the three Trident holders.

UNDER THE SEA

The men from Class 2-02 have just had time to stow their gear after returning from Camp Billy Machen when they find themselves back in the classroom again. They are about to begin their two-week Combat Swimmer Course, or CSC. The change in environment could not be more dramatic. During land-warfare training, many days got close to 110 degrees. Now they are preparing for 60-degree water in San Diego Bay. It's a mental transition as well as a physical one. Many aspects of their combat shooting and land-warfare training were new. There were challenging shooting drills and exciting night direct-action missions with live rounds. Combat-swimmer training is cold, demanding, procedure-driven work that is often repetitious and always requires attention to detail. In land warfare, the men operated in squads and used all their senses; in the CSC, they will move through a silent world in swim pairs. Much of the current work of deployed SEALs is land warfare. SEALs are on the ground in the Middle East, the Philippine Islands, Malaysia, and Central America. Yet the business of being a naval commando means that SEALs must be prepared to come from, and operate in, the sea.

"This is what sets us apart from all other special operations forces," Chief John Tortorici tells Class 2-02. "With the skills you're going to learn and practice over the next few weeks, you will be able to conduct clandestine ship attacks and harbor penetrations. There are going to be some long days and long cold nights, but that's what you signed on for, right? I want you guys to work hard and stay focused. The SEAL platoons on deployment right now currently have and must maintain the ability to conduct combat-swimmer operations. At any time, you may be called on to perform an underwater attack on a ship or a harbor installation. You may have a special reconnaissance mission that requires you to make a clandestine, underwater approach to a shore facility or an enemy coastline. It's an important part of the SEAL skill set."

Chief Tortorici is in charge of the Combat Swimmer Course at SQT. He has a broad range of experience in SEAL and SDV operations, including two platoon deployments with SDV Team Two. Before coming to SQT, he was an instructor at the SDV School in Panama City, Florida. In addition to conducting this training, he is responsible for supervising the SQT dive locker and organizing the logistics that support diver training at SQT.

"This is a very important block of training," Chief Tortorici tells me after he briefs the class. "We have to bring their skills up to a pretty high level so they can conduct combat-swimmer operations in their platoons and not hold back the more experienced operators. And nine of the men in this class will be going to SDV teams. At the SEAL Delivery Vehicle teams, many of their operational mission profiles will be conducted entirely underwater. Each man who leaves here has to be trained to a standard as a combat swimmer. If they cannot meet those standards, they will not receive their SEAL qualification. Most of them readily take to this business. Others we'll need to watch closely, and a few will require some special attention to get them through this part of the training. And that's okay. If they have the right attitude and are willing to work hard, we can teach them these skills and get them up to that standard."

In many ways, the SQT Combat Swimmer Course is an extension of the training the students received in BUD/S. But not entirely. The BUD/S Second Phase, or dive phase, instructors and the SQT CSC instructors work together. Chief Tortorici knows exactly what his SQT students accomplished while they were at BUD/S. If any of them had problems in Second Phase, he will know that as well. When Class 228 went through BUD/S Second Phase, they spent a week on open-circuit scuba and quickly moved on to the tactical LAR V, closed-circuit scuba, or the Draeger, as it is called in the teams. The final weeks of 228's training during Second Phase consisted of tactical ship-attack problems and harbor penetrations. Recently, the SQT instructors have asked the BUD/S instructors to focus on the basics of underwater navigation, and leave the tactical, combat-swimmer skills to SQT. The idea is that with a firmer grounding in basic Draeger orientation, buoyancy control, pace count, and underwater navigation, the CSC can more quickly and effectively develop a proficient combat swimmer. The SQT students from Class 237 are among the first to arrive at SQT from BUD/S with the emphasis on these basic underwater skills.

The first day involves classroom and administrative work devoted to a review of what they learned at BUD/S, equipment issue, and an introduction to the practice limpet mines they will use in their training. They also begin to study the characteristics and vulnerabilities of the underwater portion of a ship's hull. In a class on the history of the combat swimmer, one of the students takes on the role of instructor. Petty Officer Gene Fouts, one of the three Trident holders in Class 2-02, was a "new guy" at SEAL Team Four during Operation Just Cause in Panama in 1989. SEAL combat swimmers destroyed two Panamanian patrol boats. Fouts was not in the water when the two patrol craft were attacked, but he helped to support the operation, and gave a firsthand account of the mission planning and conduct of this operation.

"One minute the gunboats were tied up pierside and a threat," Fouts tells his classmates, "the next they were two smoldering hulks sitting on the bottom. This kind of an attack can send a very powerful message to those who think their ships are safe in port. It was a textbook operation, and the doctrine we used came from the mission profiles we conducted during platoon predeployment training. What you learned in BUD/S and are going to put into use here in SQT are what we used on the Panamanian gunboats."

I have spoken with the man who conducted this attack, and he told me it came off *exactly* as it had been briefed and rehearsed. He said for the SEALs toting in the charges and placing them on the hulls, it might well have been just another training exercise—easier perhaps because the water was warm. To my knowledge, this is the only successful combat-swimmer attack conducted by Navy SEALs— or at least the only one that has been made public.

The students' first dive is a pool dive in the combat training tank on the Naval Amphibious Base. During this dive, the students reacquaint themselves with the Draeger. This is a review of the preparation and in-water procedures of this closed-circuit, 100 percent oxygen scuba. The Draeger is a small, compact rig, worn on the combat swimmer's chest. It emits no telltale bubbles and has an endurance of up to four hours. For training in SQT, dives are limited to three hours. During these skill dives, the men will check their buoyancy and review their safety procedures, diver-rescue techniques, and basic hand signals. It's a procedural, back-in-the-water familiarization. The SQT students have brought with them their newly made custom wet suits and personal diving gear from BUD/S. While in BUD/S, they trained without additional operational gear. As student combat swimmers in SQT, this will change. In addition to mission-specific equipment, which in most cases will be a limpet mine, the students will carry two canteens of water and a pistol on their belt. If their mission were one that would take them ashore, they would wear cammies over their wet suits or perhaps a simple black jumpsuit for close-quarter battle.

The first open-water dives are devoted to underwater skill build-ing and navigation. Just as in their land navigation training, the combat-swimmer students focus on two key elements: direction and pace. During these dives, each swim pair is armed with an attack board—a rigid, flat-plastic, pie-plate-sized device with handles. Strapped to the attack board is a compass, a depth gauge, and a div-ing watch. One man, the driver, swims with the attack board and is tasked with the direction of travel. The driver will time each leg of their underwater journey, as well as gauge how much distance they've traveled by counting his leg kicks. His swim buddy "flies" above him and to one side. He may assist with the pace count, but his main job is to look for underwater features and obstacles. As when traveling on land, they must know their direction of travel and how far they have traveled in any given period of time. But underwater, they often must account for the effects of tides and currents. They have to make adjustments for the load they are carrying, which may include a limpet mine or a satchel charge. These are relatively simple tasks, but they can only be perfected and made usable in a tactical environment with lots of practice. So the SQT students spend hour upon hour boring holes in San Diego Bay. The driver is glued to his attack board, keeping the swim pair on course and at a constant depth for a given period of time. At the end of one underwater leg of travel, he will take up a new heading and continue on to the target.

Other navigational skills include establishing their error boxes. In planning their dive, a swim pair must know what they will or should see if they are left or right of their intended track. They must also be aware of the bottom contour so they can use depth and bottom characteristics to assist in their underwater navigation, much as they would use contour lines in land navigation. They practice box drills, which is how they are taught to search for a target when they reach the end of their navigational run. During the first week of the CSC, Chief Tortorici and his staff plan the dives and brief the student combat swimmers. Each of the first five dives is designed to introduce a new navigation or attack-swimmer skill, and to refine those previously learned. The dives are basic, and each skill builds on the preceding one. It is repetitive and exacting. All that will change during the second week of the CSC.

The instructor staff presents the students with a tactical problem, and each dive pair must plan their attack. This is a change from their diver training in BUD/S. In dive phase during the basic course, there was no dive or mission planning done by the BUD/S trainees. Two by two, the SQT student combat swimmers meet with an instructor and brief their dive plans in what is called a "dirt dive." A dirt dive is one in which the dive pair talks through, and in some cases walks through, each aspect of the dive from start to finish—on land. Dirt dive is also a favored expression in the teams, and is a euphemism for "Have you thought this through carefully and planned well?" When a SEAL decides to get married, his teammates will often ask, "Have you dirt dived her?" Prior to each of the tactical dives, one of the officers or petty officers briefs the class on the problem, but each dive pair will dive their own plan.

The final four dives are tactical problems in which the student combat swimmers must develop a plan of attack as well as plan the dive. Early each morning, the class is presented with a mission package. The dive pairs have to pull the pertinent intelligence from this package, as well as from various nautical publications, to plan their dive around a simulated target. The days are taken with planning, rehearsals, briefings, gear preparation, equipment inspections, and personnel inspections. At night they dive. Days begin at 0800, and often the post-dive briefing is not concluded until well after 0200. It isn't Hell Week, but SQT Class 2-02 does not get a great deal of sleep during the second week of the CSC.

The standard for the Combat Swimmer Course in SQT requires that a dive pair swim into a harbor, attack two ships with limpet mines, and exfiltrate to a pickup point—all without being detected from the surface. And they must do this at night. There are other reconnaissance and harbor-attack missions for which SEALs may be called upon, but if they can successfully attack two waterborne targets, they can handle most other combat-swimmer taskings. Unlike previous BUD/S graduates in SQT, the men from Class 237 have never been under a ship; all their combat-swimmer training has been in basic navigation and classroom work. Now they must take this theory from the classroom, along with their practical navigation training, and develop a combat dive plan. For the first time, the student combat swimmers will use the Mk 1 practice limpet mine. It's a dummy charge with strong magnets for attaching the device to the hull of a ship. The men carry the circular-shaped limpet on their backs. With their wet suits, canteen belts, canteens, pistols, and the LAR V Draegers on their chests, they look like armadillos entering the water. On their first attack dive, 80 percent are successful in placing their mine on the first ship and just over half find and place their second limpet. Some have their underwater navigation and search skills well in hand, and are able to quickly find their targets. Others are still struggling. And each night, the targets and mission profiles become a little more difficult. But on each dive, they learn. Mistakes made on one dive are not made the succeeding night.

"The big ships are a lot easier," Petty Officer John Franklin tells me. "You can hear them and feel the vibration in the water when you get close. It's dark the whole way in, but once you get under a big hull, it really gets black. It's a rush; working your way along this huge black hull. Last night we hit a destroyer and a helicopter carrier, a big LHA. They seem so much bigger underwater than walking beside them down the pier. First, you have to make sure you're on the right ship and then get your limpet to the right place on the hull. You want the charge where it will do the most damage. You may not be able to sink a big ship, but if you can damage one of the propeller shafts or flood out an engine room, the ship will have to be dry-docked for repair."

Following the second attack dive, the instructors have a surprise waiting for the student combat swimmers when they crawl aboard the recovery boats. One of the students is designated the victim of an air-gas embolism, or AGE. He and his dive buddy are rushed to the recompression chamber and taken back to depth for treatment. The class observes while they are treated in the chamber as if it were the real thing. An AGE is caused by gas expansion in the lungs if a diver should come up too quickly from depth while holding his breath. The condition is serious and life threatening. Back in the classroom after the casualty-treatment drill, the class begins a debrief of the dive. Each pair gives a quick overview of their dive: the run in, their actions on target, and their extraction. Then one of the students, this one a Trident holder, tells the lead instructor that he is not feeling well. Soon, he begins to cough up blood. Both are symptoms of an AGE. He is rushed to the chamber, and this time the recompression treatment tables are for real. He gets relief from the symptoms, and is carefully decompressed under the supervision of a medical officer. This is yet another reminder to student SEALs and instructors alike that this is high-risk training. Nothing can be taken for granted. The class casualty is taken off dive status until his condition, and what brought it on, can be more fully investigated. Since he has his Trident, the training is not critical to his SEAL qualification, but the class becomes one man smaller.

Thursday night of the second week is the last dive of the Combat Swimmer Course. The students are dragging, but with this last dive, they will be one step closer to the SEAL qualification. I ask Petty Officer Phil Kim how he is going to conduct tonight's attack. He takes out a chart of San Diego Bay that show the approaches to Glorietta Bay at Coronado and the piers at the Naval Amphibious Base.

"We'll enter the water here"—he marks a point well out in the channel—"about twenty-one hundred, just after dark. From there we will turtleback to about here." Turtlebacking refers to swimming on the surface. On the surface, SEALs swim with their faces blackened and face masks down around their neck to prevent telltale reflections from the faceplates. This allows the attacking swimmers to save their underwater time until they get close to the target. Also, there are visual references on the surface that allow for more precise navigation than when they transit underwater. When they reach the outer boundaries of harbor security, the attackers submerge for the underwater assault. Petty Officer Kim and his dive buddy will turtleback on the surface for a mile and a quarter before they turn on their Draegers, and "go on bag."

"We'll then go on bag about here and make our attack," he continues. "We have a seven-hundred-yard run into our first target, a one-hundred-seventy-foot patrol craft. Our course in to the piers will be two zero five. From there we have a one-hundred-fifty-yard transit to the second target, an LCU. Landing craft are difficult as they present a flat, shallow, square-bottom profile, and you want to make sure you get the right one." He traces their planned underwater route on the chart. "After we plant our second limpet, we will come straight out from the LCU. Under a steel hull, you can't ride your compass away from the ship—too much metal. So you tack away from the ship for thirty yards or so, then take a compass heading out. We'll come out on nearly the reciprocal we went in on, zero two zero, for a thousand yards. From there, we'll turtleback on zero nine zero for another thousand yards to the pickup point."

"Good luck," I offer.

"No sweat, sir," he replies. "We got this stuff down."

Kim and his dive partner enter the water just after 2100 and arrive back at the pickup point just after midnight.

"How'd you do?" I ask after they report in to Chief Tortorici and are back aboard the recovery boat.

"Got 'em both," Petty Officer Kim reports. "We had a little trouble getting on the second target. We went into a box search and it took us about fifteen minutes to find it. But we got good placement on both hulls. If this were a real op, both of those boats would be history."

Almost all the other dive pairs do as well—almost. Three men are having problems and have yet to achieve a successful two-ship attack while they were driving the dive pair. On Friday, most of the class perform a final maintenance of their Draegers and CSC support equipment. They are now ready to move on to the final course of instruction in their SEAL Qualification Training—maritime operations, or MAROPS. Others are not so lucky.

Over the weekend, two CSC instructors will be in to work with the three men who are having trouble. They are given new mission taskings and begin to work up their attack plans. A makeup dive is scheduled for the following Monday night. This will involve six SQT students because the three deficient combat swimmers cannot dive alone. The three men on the bubble will have to perform to standard and complete a two-ship attack at night, or they will not be allowed to continue in SQT. For these three members of Class 2-02, it is not a very restful weekend. They still have to perform to standard.

The following Monday, after the first day of MAROPS, most of the class heads for the barracks and on to the evening meal. Six of the men from 2-02 begin to predive their Draegers. Shortly after dark, three dive pairs slip over the side of the support boat at ten-minute intervals and begin their attack. They turtleback for close to two thousand yards, then submerge for their run into the target—two small craft moored at the NAB piers. Two of the formerly deficient drivers hit both targets. One of them does not. He has been given every chance to succeed, but he still cannot meet the standard. He is performing well in all other aspects of SQT training, so he will be rolled back to the next SQT class. Class 2-02 now stands at forty-eight men.

OVER THE BEACH

The whiteboard taped to the door of the classroom above the SQT equipment bay reads:

Gear and kit bag inspection:	1300
Load-out and load-out inspection:	1330
Muster in cammies for PLO, rubber optional:	1430

It's 1430. Thirteen of the students from Class 2-02 are seated in the classroom to prepare for the maritime operations FTX. They, along with the other members of the class, returned to the SQT building about 0330 this morning from last night's exercise and OTB rehearsal. After a few hours sleep, they were back in the SQT bay to clean equipment and prepare for tonight's FTX. This FTX is their final field evolution in the MAROPS phase and their final field problem in SQT. After tonight, all that stands between them and the coveted SEAL Trident is the MAROPS exam, the SQT final exam, a combat equipment jump, and a water jump. They're almost qualified SEALs— almost. If all goes well, in a week's time they will be awarded their

Tridents. Then they will have earned the esteemed title "new guy" in the Navy SEAL teams—rookies in very elite company.

One of them leaves his seat and faces the class. "Alright guys, listen up. My name is Ensign Dave Tanner, and I will be the patrol leader and mission commander this evening. Our three action elements are designated as Task Unit Ka-bar. Our group here is Task Element Alpha. Okay, security has been set; all members of the operation are present?" The boat-crew leaders roger up with a full count. "Good. Let's get started. This will constitute your PLO [Patrol Leader Order] for tonight's mission. Now, we'll do a time hack." There's a rustling as everyone pushes back rubber and cammie sleeves to get to their wristwatches. "It's fourteen thirty-two in fifteen seconds . . . ten seconds . . . five, four, three, two, one, mark . . . fourteen thirty-two."

He turns to the screen behind him and his first PowerPoint slide drops into place. It's a matrix of names and special operations equipment. "Here are the assignments for load-out and the special equipment. All the gear should be ready and staged; any problems with this equipment?" No one speaks, so apparently not. "Then let's move on to the mission scenario." An overhead photo of the California coastline south of the Naval Special Warfare Center comes into view. The most prominent feature is a large circular structure that is a disused antenna array, referred to as the elephant cage. It's a huge structure and could even be a dinosaur cage. This section of coastline is Navy property located several miles south of the Naval Special Warfare Center. The last time Class 2-02 visited here it was for Close Quarter Defense training. This time they will enter this facility quite differently and with a totally different training objective.

"Mission scenario. The primary mission this evening is to rescue three American airmen who have bailed out from a B-1 bomber in hostile territory. All three have gone to ground and are alive but wounded. They are in radio contact, and their survival gear is intact. However, they are close to an Iraqi command center and there are regular patrols in the area. Enemy troop concentrations are not precise, but are suspected to be company-sized units in the area armed with light automatic weapons and RPGs. There are no friendly forces in the area. Our secondary mission is to gather any intelligence along the way to pass along to higher command. We will transition from the parent craft into our CRRCs [Combat Rubber Raiding Craft] at approximately nineteen hundred, just after dark at a position here, some thirty-four miles off the coast." He taps the screen with a pointer, indicating a spot well out to sea west of San Diego. "Our three boats in Task Element Alpha will leave first, followed at twenty-minute intervals by the boats from Task Elements Bravo and Charlie." In the other classrooms, two other ensigns are briefing Task Elements Bravo and Charlie. "We will transit to a rendezvous point here about a mile and a half from our beach landing site. Once off the BLS, we will prepare to deploy the scout swimmers. When the scout swimmers are ready, the three boats will idle into the beach, perhaps as close as a half mile, depending on the moon. We have a big moon out there tonight, but we'll get some help from the cloud cover. Once in close, we'll put the scout swimmers in over the seaward side of the CRRCs and move back out of visual range of the beach. Scout swimmers will come in, cross the beach, and do a quick cloverleaf recon of the hinterland. Then they will try to make contact with a friendly agent who should be visible on the beach between twenty-two thirty and zero thirty. They will exchange bona fides and receive any additional intelligence. The scout swimmers will then attempt radio contact with the pilot we are assigned to bring out. The three pilots are on different frequencies, so each task unit will contact its pilot on their designated frequency. When contact is established, and our pilot reports in that he is still uncompromised, the scout swimmers will bring in the rest of the platoon. Once the rest of us cross the beach and link up, we'll patrol to the location of the downed pilot. Standard procedures and precautions are in effect approaching the pilot—we assume nothing, just like the CSAR drills out in the desert. Once the pilot is confirmed friendly, we will secure him, provide medical treatment as needed, and prepare to travel. We'll go out the way we came in—scout swimmers, then the pilot and his two handlers, then the rest of the squad. The boats will come back in to get us by prearranged signal. Once we're aboard and we have a good head count, we will idle back out to the rendezvous point off the BLS. Then we rig for transit and haul ass for home. That's our job tonight. Any questions so far?" Again, there are none.

"Okay then, let's get in, get our package, and get the hell out. These are our guys in there, so let's stay focused and do the job right. Now, let's get to the details." A slide with columns of data and times replaces the chart. "These are our launch-time windows, way points, times at the BLS, time on target, no-earlier-thans, no-later-thans, and drop-dead times." It looks like a metro bus schedule for a large American city. "Can everyone read this? Boat-crew leaders, I know you have this information from the workup, but take a minute to make sure this data checks with what you have on your nav boards."

The mission scenario or overview is the portion of the Patrol Leader Order where the patrol leader tells his men, in his words, what they will be doing and how they will do it. And why. The rest of the briefing is highly formatted, exhaustive, and contains sensitive information as it relates to the specifics of a maritime special operation. It goes on for close to two hours. There are various "actions": actions to and from the target and at the objective area, actions at way points, actions at the rendezvous points, actions at the BLS, actions crossing the beach. There are specific duties assigned to individuals for when they reach the downed pilot and when they get the pilot moving back to the water. There are the "what ifs": What if they get separated in transit? What if they cannot contact the agent on the beach? What if they cannot establish radio contact with the pilot or, once they have it, they lose it? What if they make contact coming through the surf, on the beach, on the way in, and on the way out? What do they do if the pilot is compromised and it's a trap? The list goes on. One member of the platoon briefs them on the weather conditions, sea state, and environmental dangers—sharks, stingrays, and sixty-degree water. Another man briefs them on the rules of engagement—when and how deadly force can be used and exactly who this deadly force can be visited on. There are frequencies for the various radios—primary, secondary, and tertiary. The comm plan is thoroughly briefed. This briefing covers where the communication plan is carried on the radio operator's person so a teammate can get to the comm plan if he goes down. If the devil is in the details, then the devil is a member of a well-briefed special operations element.

There is the mission ashore to rescue the pilot and the piece of navigation to get them there and back to the rendezvous point offshore. They've learned and practiced both. But a key ingredient of this mission is the over-the-beach operation. The OTB is one of the core skills of the Navy SEAL Teams, just like combat-swimmer operations. SEALs do a lot of things well, but no SOF unit does this one better. It's the soul of the naval commando. There are obviously no beaches to go over in Afghanistan, but SEALs did in fact conduct OTBs in support of maritime special operations in Iraq.

The problem last night was similar, but did not involve an actual target. And the distances over the water were much less. But on the previous FTX, they had to do a complete change out. For this exercise, they swam in with full rucks and crossed the beach in full rubber, simulating an OTB in much colder water to much colder land. Once ashore, they changed into dry cammies, unless they improperly prepared their waterproof kit bags—in which case they put on wet clothes and patrolled away from the insertion site, ready for cold-weather battle. This full change out after an OTB has to be practiced again and again, in simulated tactical conditions at night. For the final FTX, they will not change out, and the students wear what rubber they feel they will need to be able to swim in, cross the beach, and find their downed pilot. Most wear only shorty wet suits under their cammies so they can move better on patrol, but the water is still a very chilly sixty degrees.

For most of the previous week, the class learned about boats, motors, and the basics of small-boat navigation. During BUD/S, the students all had familiarization with boats, but nowhere near the in-depth training they receive at SQT. Their first full day of their MAROPS training was spent in the classroom. They studied and worked with nautical charts and publications. They learned the mechanics of dead reckoning, plotting courses, and performing time-speed-distance calculations. Then they factored in tide, wind, and current data while plotting dead-reckoning tracks. On the second day, they were out in the SQT building learning about the CRRC, a fifteen-foot Zodiac designed for maritime special operations, and the standard 55hp OMC outboard engine. The CRRC is a 265-pound rubber boat with interlocking aluminum floorboards. It can carry four to six fully armed SEALs. The outboards are easy to operate and very reliable, but the students are taught the tricks and ploys of coaxing a recalcitrant engine to life and to make minor underway repairs. A CRRC with an OMC 55 can make up to thirty knots in calm water, depending on the load, and up to fifteen knots in a state two sea, again depending on load. These are the largest craft in the SEAL inventory; the larger Naval Special Warfare Combatant Craft are the province of the NSW Special Boat Teams.

In the sheltered waters of Glorietta Bay near the Naval Amphibious Base, the SQT students get the feel of running fast across water in an inflatable boat. The first day on the water involves familiarization and orientation. There is a measured mile set up just off the base, and the student SEAL boaters calibrate the speed of their craft under loaded conditions and learn to trim their outboards. Then misfortune strikes; two CRRCs have a head-on collision. They were running flat-out with their bows high in the air, and neither coxswain saw the other boat. Gear and SQT students are everywhere. All but one avoid serious injury. Petty Officer Mark Calnan, the class leading petty officer, suffers torn ligaments in his knee. Calnan, the former Army man and fleet sailor, was hoping to finish SQT as soon as possible and return to his wife and two daughters on the East Coast. He has orders to SEAL Team Two. He was the enlisted leader of BUD/S Class 237 and SQT Class 2-02. The next day he is in a full cast. He watches from the shore as his former classmates load their CRRCs and head back out to San Diego Bay for more open-water drills. He will have to wait for Class 3-02 or, depending on how slowly he heals, Class 4-02 to complete SQT and earn his Trident. The SQT cadre members are concerned about this accident; Calnan was a good leader and a solid performer. As penalty for their inattention to duty, the two coxswains running the boats are made to give a presentation on boating safety and rules of the road to the class. SQT Class 2-02 is down to forty-seven men.

For several days, the students practice their dead reckoning, first in San Diego Bay and then in the ocean. *Dead reckoning* is a term that applies to navigating with only chart, compass, and the known speed of your boat—no radar, Fathometer, or GPS. They lay down dead-reckoning tracts and plot their way points along the route. They navigate these tracts, first by day and then at night. Along the way they take compass bearings to establish fixes and navigate using basic piloting skills. In the teams they will have GPS and electronic navigation aids, but in SQT it's the basics—map and compass. And if the electronic nav aids fail on some future combat mission, the SEALs will still have to get to the target, so they all must know how to do it the old-fashioned way. Class 2-02 spends hours banging through the chop off San Diego, practicing basic small-boat navigation. It's cold, tiring, monotonous, uncomfortable work, but it has to be learned. The students make a game of it, and success or failure become a matter of bragging rights and perhaps a side bet. The student coxswains and navigators run their tracks through a series of way points. From each way point, they alter course and run at a given speed for a specified length of time to get to their next way point. The end game is to arrive at their RV, or rendezvous point, on time. When they arrive at where they think they should be at the appointed time, they radio one of the instructors in a support boat. An instructor with a GPS comes over and tells the student crew, within a matter of a few yards, how close they came to their objective. It's a contest and, of course, it pays to be a winner. The winning boat crews gloat; losing crews clean the classrooms and the SQT equipment bay.

At 2215, I'm on the beach with Warrant Officer Mike Loo waiting for Task Element Alpha. Later on, the other student task units will approach the beach a few hundred yards away in search of their pilots. There is a dull blanket of light overhead from the moon above the clouds. The surf is moderate—three to five feet—and the air is chilly for San Diego, fifty-five degrees. This evolution taxes the full complement of the SQT staff. There are nine CRRCs on the water and forty-seven students. There have to be safety boats along the route and off the beach. There is also a matter of the actors: the role players who serve as friendly agents and downed pilots, plus roving sentries—some of them on four-wheelers—patrolling the beach.

"This is a hard evolution for them," Mike tells me, "not so much technically difficult, but they're getting tired. They don't get a lot of sleep this week, and because it's training, the mission timeline is compressed. We want them on the water or in the water. There's a lot packed into this week. And they didn't get a whole lot of sleep during their Combat Swimmer Course, either."

Following the PLO briefing, the student downed-pilot rescuers loaded their boats onto a landing craft for the long transit out to sea to begin the FTX. Each boat, including motor and gear, weighs in at something over five hundred pounds. The students had to manhandle them aboard the landing craft and then, after a three-hour transit, launch them in a seaway well offshore. Many hours later, after the students have been cold and wet most of the night, they will have to haul the boats back aboard the landing craft for the trip home.

"And, they're mentally tired. Out at Camp Billy Machen they were shooting and blowing things up and learning all kinds of new things. There were new challenges for them during Combat Swimmer, but even in the CSC they can only have so much bottom time each day. In the MAROPS course we try to challenge them with a variety of nav problems and different mission scenarios, but it's still cold, wet, miserable work. Yet it has to be done. And they'll do it again and again when they get to the teams." We watch as four dark forms tumble one by one from the surf some fifty meters up the beach. They form a four-man file and scurry across the sand into the beach grass and ice plant. "Excuse me," Mike says, "but I better get to work. I'm the friendly agent for this task element."

Warrant Officer Loo strolls up the beach between the breakers and the berm line. He's wearing a wool overcoat and a baseball cap. Cautiously, two forms approach while the others wait out of sight. The three confer on the beach for a few moments. Loo is taller than the two students, and I can see him pointing with his arm. He walks away, and the two raiders fade back into sparse vegetation. Almost a half hour later, nine more men spill in with the surf, form a ragged file, and cross the beach. Loo and I move to a position to watch the student element. We now wear lime-green Chemlites around our necks to identify us and the lane graders. Our presence is to be ignored by the students as they continue with the problem. The squad file slips under a hole in the fence along the beach and sets off in search of its downed pilot. He's reportedly hiding in scrub bushes a hundred meters off the beach. We follow a short distance back and observe with night-observation scopes. With a combination of radio checks and various recognition signals, they find the pilot and authenticate him. He's cold, scared, and injured. The pilot/SQT instructor is well in character, wearing a flight suit and a full kit of combat-pilot survival gear. The student element sets security and begins the casualty procedure. The pilot has a sprained ankle that needs to be immobilized and has some deep cuts that need attention. When he's ready for travel, two men help him move while the squad heads back to the beach.

The student element returns to the sea in much the same way as it arrived: cautiously, methodically, moving low and quick, signaling to the elements offshore. The students wait in the beach grass while an enemy four-wheeler on beach patrol rolls past their position. The pilot is still being assisted on either side by two handlers, but now they have him in an exposure suit that they brought along on the mission for him. He's still hurt and pretending to be scared, but he's no longer cold. The coxswains in the CRRCs maneuver in closer to pick up their swimmers. I can't see the CRRCs, only the men on the beach, but they all look very smooth and professional.

"They look pretty good," I comment as we watch the last of them duck back into the surf.

"Well, yes and no," Mike Loo says with a smile. "They did a lot of things right, but there's still room for improvement."

"Oh?"

The smile deepens. "There's always room for improvement. When they came in and when they went back out, one or two hopped over a wave instead of ducking under it. After the patrol came ashore and set their security, their perimeter was too exposed and in the open. They didn't use the sand dunes close to them, which afforded better cover and concealment. And when they were in patrol file, they could have chosen a better route, one that would have kept them off the berm and high points of the dunes. Too much silhouette. This was the point man's job, but the patrol leader should have noticed this and corrected it. Individually, they weren't bad, but a few of them didn't make a smooth transition from the water to land travel. They need to stow their fins quickly and securely so they can better field their weapon and more easily get to their ammo to change out magazines. They did a pretty good job in handling the pilot, and I especially liked the way they moved from a patrol file to a skirmish line to search for him. Their hand and arm signals were good. But they made too much noise. They'll probably always make too much noise for me." He grins again, then turns serious.

"You see, that's the difference between a veteran—a two-platoon guy—and one of these guys who is just learning the business. It's the little things. Moving properly through the surf. Making a quick transition from swim gear to rig for land travel. Having all your gear in place so you can move quickly and quietly—and not lose anything! Moving well within the patrol. Finding a good field of fire while at the rally points. Looking for the enemy while being aware of what everyone else is doing in the patrol; being able to do anyone else's job if you have to. Y'see, a veteran will do all this—all the time, every time. All a new guy has to do to be a veteran, in my opinion, is pay attention to detail and focus on doing the little things well. We do some very complex and high-speed things here, but wait until you see some of the platoon training. You'll be amazed. The guys we get in SQT now are smart and talented. They'll learn the hard stuff and do just fine. But for my money, it's the little things that count—the boring, repetitive things that you have to do well, even when you're cold, wet, and haven't slept for a couple of days."

Back at the SQT building, it's early morning. This will be another night with little sleep for Class 2-02. Immediately on their return, the students head for the classroom. The debrief and critiques go on for an hour and a half. Mike Loo tells them what they did right and what they did wrong. Then he moves on to a list of "do-betters."

"Sir, you gave a good briefing, but remember that your mission scenario is just for your troops. Forget about any brass that may be in the back of the room. Most of the time there will be some there, but as far as you're concerned, it's just you and your men. And on the actions at rally points, draw it up; use lots of Xs and Os. I couldn't see your approach in the CRRCs to drop off the swimmers, but make sure you come straight in and straight out. Don't tack in or run parallel to the beach. You're exposing yourself unnecessarily. When you splinted the pilot's ankle, you used duct tape, and I could hear you ripping it from the roll. Use cravats or make up tie-ties ahead of time. And duct tape is shiny, even the dark-green kind." Loo pauses to flip through his wheel book. "Watch for bioluminescence in the water. If it's known to be in the area, brief it during the PLO—brief it anyway. It may materialize once you get close to shore. There was none out there tonight, but we get some from time to time, so be on the lookout for it. You don't want to look like giant Chemlites out there in the water. You boat coxswains, be sure to be at idle speed when you come in to pick up or drop off swimmers. Don't kick it up until you're well offshore, especially if there's an onshore wind. The enemy may not see you, but he could hear you. And always take care with your individual movements in patrol. Forget that you're cold, wet, and sandy. Focus on moving well and doing what it takes to accomplish your mission.

"Overall, you guys did pretty well out there tonight. Now, you

Warriors and healers. Under simulated battle conditions, an SQT student gives an IV to a fellow student. They will soon trade places, and the casualty will become the healer. *Photo by Dick Couch*

Rounds on target. On the range at La Posta, a student from SQT Class 2-02 receives careful instruction from shooting instructor Matt Reilly. *Photo by Dick Couch*

Sight alignment and trigger squeeze. A student shooter demonstrates good form with the Sig Sauer 9mm pistol. *Photo by Dick Couch*

Draw and shoot. Combat shooting sometimes means that the round must go downrange quickly, before the shooter can get to a preferred shooting stance. *Photo by Dick Couch*

On the SEAL range at Camp Pendleton. Instructor Will Gautier coaches an SQT student on the SEAL weapon of choice, the M4 rifle. *Photo by Dick Couch*

On the Pendleton range with the M14 rifle. SEALs are one of the last military combat units to use this weapon. *Photo by Dick Couch*

Rattle-battle. SQT students in full battle dress change magazines on the run. Here they move from the one-hundred-yard shooting station back to the two-hundred-yard station. *Photo by Dick Couch*

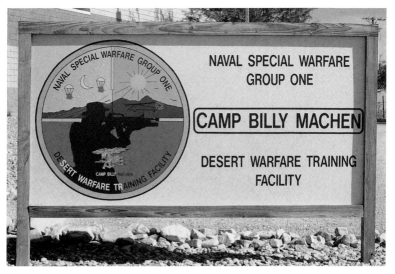

SEALs have been training at the NSW Desert Warfare Training Facility since the mid-1960s. Billy Machen was the first Navy SEAL killed in Vietnam. *Photo by Dick Couch*

On the firing line at Camp Billy Machen. Under the watchful eye of their shooting coaches, SQT students from Class 2-02 prepare for more rattle-battle. *Photo by Dick Couch*

Team shooting with the M4 rifle. From the prone firing position, the student SEALs are expected to hit a silhouette target at three hundred yards. *Photo by Dick Couch*

It pays to be a winner. A student from Class 2-02 fires from a barrier during the Combat Stress Course. Run and shoot; elapsed time and fewest misses determine the winner. *Photo by Dick Couch*

At Camp Billy Machen, SEAL students conduct shooting drills with a full pack and combat load. Here a shooter clears a jam from his M4 and keeps firing. *Photo by Dick Couch*

Old warriors mentor the new. Chief Warrant Officer Mike Loo coaches a shooter from SQT Class 2-02. *Photo by Dick Couch*

Shooting and more shooting. Students from Class 2-02 take a break from their M4s for some work with the MK43, the standard machine gun in the SEAL teams. *Photo by Dick Couch*

Combat Swimmer Course. Two SQT students place their charges on the hull of a ship. Note the LAR V scuba on the chest of the diver and the limpet mine on his back. *Official Navy Photo*

Boat drills. SEALs come from the sea, often in Combat Rubber Raiding Craft, or CRRCs. SQT students prepare their CRRCs for infiltration and over-the-beach exercises. *Photo by Dick Couch*

Into the cold. Training is never over, as new SEALs quickly learn. After students get their SEAL Trident, they immediately go to Kodiak Island for cold-weather training. *Photo by Dick Couch*

Rewarming drill. SEALs from SQT Class 5-02 in Chiniak Bay. After a dip in the glacier-fed water, they must scramble ashore and get warm—or perish! *Photo by Dick Couch*

Home sweet home. Following the immersion drill, a student goes to ground, dry and warm and with a hot meal in his belly. Life is good. *Photo by Dick Couch*

From the sea. Not all coastlines are sandy beaches. Here SQT students from Class 5-02 climb a coastal cliff. After a cold swim and a tough climb, they move inland to complete the mission. *Photo by Dick Couch*

The cold waters off Kodiak Island. First in the daylight, then at night, the new SEALs practice cold-water insertions. *Photo by Dick Couch*

A leap and a swim. Students from Class 5-02 debark from an eleven-meter RHIB and begin their swim to shore. There they will strip off their dry suits and prepare for land travel. *Photo by Dick Couch*

Across the snow. SQT Class 5-02 traversing the northwest face of Raymond Peak, Kodiak Island. For a few in the class, this was the first time they had ever seen snow. *Photo by Steve Howe*

Climbing into the sun—with a load. Kodiak students carry upwards of eighty pounds of gear. Backpacks are rigged to carry snowshoes on one side, swim fins on the other! *Photo by Steve Howe*

Shoot to kill. A SEAL from Echo Platoon, SEAL Team Five, coaches his platoon mate. The weapon is an M4 with a ten-inch barrel for close-quarter shooting. *Photo by Dick Couch*

Warming up. SEALs from Foxtrot Platoon, SEAL Team Five, practice before entering the SEAL kill house at Camp Pendleton. *Photo by Dick Couch*

Knock-knock. Team Five SEALs make an entrance. The multiroom Pendleton kill house can be configured in a number of ways to challenge SEALs during close-quarter shooting. *Photo by Dick Couch*

More shooting drills. A SEAL from Team Five holds a target in his sights. Drills begin with blanks, then move on to full-on scenarios with live rounds. *Photo by Dick Couch*

And more drills. If a door is locked, it has to be opened. Note the breaching tools on the back of this shooter from SEAL Team Five. *Photo by Dick Couch*

From the air. SEALs from SEAL Team Three exit the rear of a C-130 for a free-fall parachute to the water. Note that the jumpers are wearing swim fins. *Official Navy Photo*

Airborne recovery. A CH-46 pulls SEALs from SEAL Team One from San Diego
Bay after a combat-swimmer training evolution. *Official Navy Photo*

have your MAROPS final tomorrow afternoon—or rather, this afternoon, right?" Class 2-02 nods. "Well, good luck then. One more week and you'll be on your way. Stay focused and keep your head in the game. That Trident pin is just a few days away."

That afternoon, Class 2-02 is back in the classroom for its maritime operations exam. There are forty-five questions and a final page with two columns of latitudes and longitudes—six sets of coordinates in all. Each student has to plot the coordinates of these way points and lay down his tracts between them. Then, for a given speed, and accounting for set and drift, he has to calculate his courses, time, and distance to the objective.

Fourteen weeks down, one to go.

THE TRIDENT

It's graduation week—a week of administrative chores and a few operational matters. Well over half of Class 2-02 will leave Coronado for the East Coast SEAL teams and for the SDV teams. SEAL Teams One and Two will draw most of these new SEALs. While SQT Class 2-02 was in training, Team One, based in Coronado, and Team Two, based in Little Creek, Virginia, were overseas on operational deployment. The new SEALs will join these teams on their Stateside return and begin the eighteen-month workup for the next operational deployment. A few will go to Teams Seven and Ten, which have just begun their eighteen-month predeployment workup. En route to their new teams, some of the men from 2-02 will be attending advanced schools or language training. All will have to pack up their personal diving and field gear. No matter what the route, they will finally join an operational team. They will be platoon SEALs. For a Navy SEAL, training is never over, but these men will no longer be in the womb of the training command. There are formal SEAL training courses in their future, but for the most part, they will be in the company of teammates and platoon mates. To one degree or another, they will always be students, but after SQT, they will be SEAL students—not student SEALs.

The SQT written final is rigorous, but routine. They've learned a great deal in the past fourteen weeks, and they are well prepared for their final exam. The parachute jumps are almost routine. The first is an equipment jump. They launch from North Island and drop onto Brown Field east of San Diego. All of them made an equipment jump at Army Airborne School, but perhaps not with this much gear. They parachute in with their standard second line combat load and a forty-five-pound ruck, along with their personal weapons. It's how they would be loaded on a combat drop for a long special reconnaissance or direct-action mission. The second jump is a water jump, the first they will make as Navy SEALs. They carry no equipment on this jump; that will come later in the teams. They do, however, wear life jackets and have their fins taped to their legs. The only difference is the landing. There are straps and buckles that have to be released in the air just as their feet hit the water. Then they swim from the harness and help the recovery boats with the wet parachute. San Diego Bay is still chilly. Some of them wear a rubber shorty under their cammies, others don't.

"How was it?" I asked as my boat hauls a wet jumper aboard.

"Fantastic! Sweet! Can't wait to do it again!"

SEAL Qualification Training graduation is held in the bay of the SQT building. The American flag behind the podium is much smaller than at a BUD/S graduation, as is the crowd—a smattering of instructors and active-duty friends of the new SEALs. Also present are several team COs and command master chiefs. SQT graduation and the awarding of the SEAL Trident is an in-house ceremony. The speeches are shorter but no less important. It's less of a graduation than a recognition of warrior status. They've earned the right to call themselves Navy SEALs. There are three speakers, all SEAL operators and all with important words for the newest Navy SEALs. The first is Chief Warrant Officer Mike Loo.

"Good morning, everyone, and welcome to the graduation of SEAL Qualification Training. The purpose of this brief ceremony is to recognize these men for completing fifteen weeks of SEAL Qualification Training and to award the Naval Special Warfare SEAL insignia, the Trident. BUD/S was the first step; now you men have successfully completed SQT. You now have the skill set needed to integrate into an operational SEAL platoon; you are prepared to go in harm's way as an operational SEAL." Loo sweeps his eyes over the ranks of students. They are paraded in front of the podium in starched cammies and spit-shined boots. "This course has laid the foundation of warfighting knowledge and skills you will use during your entire SEAL career. Mastering these skills should be your primary goal. Your mission and the lives of your teammates depend on it.

"Never forget that the teams are the number one maritime special operations force in the world. You must do everything in your power to be worthy of this. The Trident does not make you invincible; only teamwork and professionalism can gain you the victory.

"Handling the many tasks and difficult challenges given to SEALs requires great effort, dedication, and persistence. When you get to your team, you must be ready to work extremely hard to ready yourselves for real-world operations. You won't get a second chance to make a good impression. You must be physically and mentally prepared to win the gunfight and accomplish the mission.

"As a new member of our community, you enjoy a reputation that was earned by the sweat, blood, and hard work of those who have gone before you. You haven't earned this; you inherited it. But you have earned the right to carry this legacy forward and add the next chapter. This is a sacred trust. Never let the teams down and never leave a teammate.

"Stay focused, train hard, be professional. Always maintain your personal integrity and the integrity of the teams. Congratulations and good luck.

"Finally, I'd like to recognize my instructor cadre, at least those who are here. Many of them are out on training evolutions with

Class 3-02. They work incredibly hard and are very passionate about their job. They do whatever it takes to train men like you to the highest standards. Thanks, guys. And now, Lieutenant Commander Ballentine will tell us about the Trident you men will soon wear."

Lieutenant Commander Roger Ballentine, the advanced training officer at the Naval Special Warfare Center, steps to the podium. SQT is one of his direct responsibilities.

"The Trident has been the badge of the Navy SEALs since 1970. It is the only warfare specialty pin that is the same for officers and enlisted. It symbolizes that we are brothers in arms—that we train together and we fight together. There are four parts to the Trident. Each one symbolizes an important facet of our warfare community.

"The anchor symbolizes the Navy, our parent service, the premier force for power projection on the face of the planet and the guarantor of world peace. However, it is an old anchor, which reminds us that our roots lie in the valiant accomplishments of the Naval Combat Demolition Units and Underwater Demolition Teams.

"The trident, the scepter of Neptune, or Poseidon, king of the oceans, symbolizes a SEAL's connection to the sea. The ocean is the hardest element for any warrior to operate in—it is the one in which SEALs find themselves the most comfortable.

"The pistol represents the SEAL's capabilities on land—whether direct action or special reconnaissance. If you look closely, it is cocked and ready to fire and should serve as a constant reminder that you, too, must be ready at all times.

"The eagle, our nation's emblem of freedom, symbolizes the SEAL's ability to swiftly insert from the air. It reminds us that we fly higher in standards than any other force. Normally, the eagle is placed on military decorations with its head held high. On our insignia, the eagle's head is lowered to remind each of us that humility is the true measure of a warrior's strength.

"You share a unique badge and an honorable tradition. The Tridents that you will be awarded today have been dedicated to the legacy of Naval Special Warfare. On each diploma, there will be a name other than your own. That name is the name of a teammate who was killed in action—a fallen brother. Although you should be proud today of your personal accomplishment in joining the SEAL ranks, you are remiss if you do not take a moment to reflect on and pay homage to the legacy of those who have gone before. Do nothing that will tarnish the reputation and tradition that you inherit. Always carry them both forward with honor and integrity. Welcome to the brotherhood. Welcome to the teams!"

When I came into the teams in 1969, there was no SEAL pin. We wore our gold Navy and Marine Corps jump wings, but we wore nothing else that singled us out as Navy SEALs. When it was determined that as a warfare specialty we needed a pin, the designers in Washington went to work. But the design needed the approval of a Navy board, and the naval aviators on the board wanted nothing that resembled their wings. Finally, a larger-than-life design was approved, and they were issued to us. We started calling them "Budweisers" because they resembled the manufacturer's trademark on the side of the company's beer can. It was a large pin when compared with other warfare specialty badges. There was talk in the early days of shrinking the device, but it never happened. The Trident that is about to be awarded to the new SEALs in Class 2-02 is indistinguishable from the one that was waiting for me at SEAL Team One when I returned home from a tour in Vietnam in 1971.

"I want to wish each of you success and good hunting as you join your platoon," Ballentine concludes. "And now Commander Byron Raines will present your Tridents."

"Congratulations, men. It is now my privilege to award your Navy SEAL pins. I want you to wear them with honor and pride." Commander Raines is standing in for Captain Rick Smethers, Commanding Officer of the Naval Special Warfare Center, who is attending the funeral of a SEAL killed in a training accident. Raines was an all–Pac Ten lineman, and he towers over the podium. "I charge you officers with leading the best-equipped, best-trained, best-briefed warriors in the world. As you prepare your men for combat, leave no stone unturned as you prepare to lead them in harm's way. You have an immense responsibility. You must accomplish your mission and bring these fine men back home. You enlisted men must become experts in your warfare skills. The business of Naval Special Warfare is a full-time, lifetime commitment. You are the subject-matter experts, not the officers. For all of you, there is hard work and sacrifice ahead. But you are entering an honorable and very rewarding profession."

One by one the names are called. Raines pins a gold Trident over each man's left breast pocket. The three Trident holders in the class remain in ranks. Commander Raines has a few words for each of the new men, and I'm close enough to hear a few of them. For the enlisted men:

"Congratulations."

"Well done."

"Good luck."

"Welcome to the teams."

For the officers:

"Take care of your men."

"Be a leader and set an example."

"Don't take shortcuts; do it right."

"Always lead from the front."

When the men are back in ranks, they all wear the Trident. They are Navy SEALs. Commander Raines addresses them a final time. "Congratulations and welcome to the brotherhood."

The new SEALs then do what Navy SEALs do; they head for the sea. The members of Class 2-02 file from the SQT building on a dead run, race out onto the pier, and leap into San Diego Bay. But this is just the beginning. They crawl out and quickly strip off their wet cammies, depositing them in a pile on the floating dock. Underneath their uniforms they all wear swim trunks. Then they're back in the water swimming across the mouth of Glorietta Bay to the Coronado Golf Course. It's only a quarter mile from one side to the other, and they swim without fins. The safety boat nudges into Coronado, where the new SEALs collect their boots, socks, and T-shirts. They quickly pull them on and set off on a run around Coronado—just over six miles. The class finishes at Gator Beach on the Pacific Ocean side of the Naval Amphibious Base. There the SQT instructors have a barbecue waiting for them with steaks, a keg of beer, and a tub full of soft drinks. A surprising number of them go for the soft drinks. They are now SEALs, officially members of this very exclusive club. For the forty-five members of BUD/S Class 237, this is the last time they will celebrate as a class. Most of them have been together for more than a year. When they finish their three weeks of winter training, or "postgraduate work," they will scatter to the operational teams—no longer classmates. Their future will be one of platoon mates and teammates.

In many ways it is difficult for SEALs of my generation to understand just how far these new men have come. The quality of current training by the standards of that day are an order of magnitude more challenging and more professional. Truth be told, and with respects to my old teammates, they make them a lot better today than they used to. Back then, a man went to a team and into a platoon right after BUD /S. If it was an Underwater Demolition Team platoon, he might deploy immediately. If his orders took him to a SEAL team, which happened much less than half the time, his SEAL Basic Indoctrination *and* platoon training might last only four months. The new SEALs from Class 2-02 will face *at least* eighteen more months of intensive training before they will make an operational deployment. But before they even begin the eighteen months of training at their team, they face three cold weeks at Kodiak, Alaska.

CHAPTER 3

Postgraduate Training

THE HEADMASTER'S RULES

During times of conflict and crisis, great strides are made in the technologies and tactics that relate to the art of war. You have only to witness the dramatic advances in aviation during the world wars and even the regional conflicts like Vietnam and Korea. The technology has a way of accelerating; look at what happened in the decade between the two regional Gulf wars. The emergence of special operations in contemporary conflicts has also brought changes to Navy SEAL operational tasking and responsibilities. And that drives Navy SEAL training. I have watched as SEAL training has evolved not only to address changing operational requirements, but to achieve a new level of professionalism; the guys keep getting better. Every admiral, group commander, commanding officer, command master chief, platoon officer, platoon chief, and platoon leading petty officer wants to do his job better—better than it was done last year, and better than the last man who held their job. But it's more than

---

Climb the cliff, then bring up the equipment. SEALs rig a makeshift highline to hoist their packs up from the shoreline of a coastal cliff. *Photo by Dick Couch*

that. From SEAL commander to seaman, the benchmark is themselves: How can I be more effective? How can I improve? How can I become a better warrior? During the period between the Gulf conflicts, duty in the teams meant preparing for war with little chance of actually having to go downrange. Those days are over. Navy SEALs now feel that at some point in time they will be doing it for real—in harm's way. Since 11 September 2001, that has proved to be the case.

SEAL operations are not often regarded as high-tech ventures; indeed, senior SEAL leaders are quick to point out that people—specifically SEAL operators—are our most important resource. But technology can help. The early reports from Iraq suggest that recent advances in communications and the rapid dissemination of intelligence were critical to the SEAL missions there. The rescue of Jessica Lynch was a fairly complex operation; there were a number of moving parts and supporting components backing up the SEALs who made the rescue. The ability to rapidly process and disseminate critical operational intelligence and securely communicate with a number of units simultaneously all made this operation possible. Yet, technology aside, for my money, it's the guns in the fight that count most.

As I observed SEAL Qualification Training, I was continually amazed at the caliber of training and the high standards that are now expected of today's Navy SEALs. I have been close to SEAL training for the last four years, and every year it seems to get a little better, a little more refined. And a little longer. A great deal of time, attention, and money goes into making these modern special warriors. BUD/S Class 237 was trained a little differently and a little better than BUD/S Class 228—"my guys" from *The Warrior Elite*. The it's-never-good-enough philosophy allows the teams to maintain their edge. SQT Class 2-02 was just a little different—a little better—than Class 1-02. Once again, I was able to recognize those subtle improvements in Class 5-02 as I observed their combat-swimmer and winter training.

In my day, we pretty much did things the way our instructors did it and theirs did before them. The SEAL Cadre Training and SEAL Basic Indoctrination was in-house, informal instruction that the veterans

conducted for us new guys. For ten years after the commissioning of
SEAL Teams One and Two, the enemy was the Vietcong, and an occasional main force of North Vietnamese Army (NVA) regulars if you
were really unlucky. Our area of operations was the jungles, rice paddies, and mangrove swamps of Southeast Asia. While the focus in
recent years has been the Middle East and central Asia, modern SEALs
have to be prepared to conduct special operations in a number of environments. When I was in the teams, we did very little diving and/or
parachuting. There was certainly no such thing as winter training. It
was a game of rifles and radios; SEALs had to shoot and communicate,
and we got pretty good at beating the Vietcong at their own game.
Every deployment was a combat deployment; every operation a combat operation. Today, SEAL training is comprehensive and changes
continually, always seeking a higher standard and greater degree of
standardization of the basic skills. And with respect to the warriors of
my era, the SEALs today are smarter, better trained, more lethal, and
(just a little bit) tougher than in my day. I'm very proud of them. But
the training of SEALs is more than just a matter of extended training
days and more training dollars. There is also a great deal of personal
capital that has gone into this training. The basic and advanced training cadres work very hard, often harder than their students. This level
of training is not accomplished without dedication and passion on the
part of the trainers. Before we leave the basic SQT curriculum and
move on to graduate work on Kodiak Island, it might be good to take
a closer look at the man most responsible for SEAL Qualification
Training, Chief Warrant Officer Mike Loo.

Mike grew up in Seattle, joined the Navy in 1979, and graduated
with BUD/S Class 115. He is a veteran of five operational deployments and is the leading community subject-matter expert on air
operations. Mike coauthored the operational bible for SEAL air operations. He is a quiet, powerfully built six-footer with a stern look and
a soft manner—one of those men who think before they speak and
choose their words carefully. In 1998, he was assigned as the officer
in charge of SEAL Tactical Training for Naval Special Warfare Group

One. STT was then conducted separately on each coast. At that time, STT provided advanced training for SEALs, but the individual teams awarded the Trident. In 2000, the decision was made to consolidate advanced training into a single entity *and* to charge this consolidated training with awarding the Trident. The first SQT classes began in 2001. At that time, BUD/S graduates were expected to complete STT and serve a six-month probationary period with their team before they could wear the Trident. So this was a dramatic step. The groups surrendered the advanced training of their SEALs to the Naval Special Warfare Center, and the teams gave up their role as the final judge of who could and could not be a Navy SEAL. The Naval Special Warfare community is a tradition-bound organization and can be very resistant to change, especially concerning critical issues like advanced training and SEAL qualification. Under the new arrangement, SQT became "the finishing school" and the final arbiter of who would and would not become a Navy SEAL; SQT in effect became the final gatekeeper. To make this difficult and controversial transition, the community needed a man of stature and ability. The community turned to Mike Loo.

Mike made it happen. He took the best of the two STTs and consolidated them into SQT. This merger of the advanced training venues under the control of the Naval Special Warfare Center was greeted with skepticism and outright resistance, especially when it came to awarding the Trident. Navy SEALs can be exceptionally creative and think outside the box in tactical situations, but when it comes to organizational change, they can be very hidebound. "What's wrong with the way they did it when I came through training?" I heard this a lot. But Mike Loo quietly went about creating his vision of SQT training. He then let his students do the talking. When the first new SQT-trained SEALs began arriving at the teams for platoon duty, the team veterans quickly learned that these new SEALs were capable, motivated, and well grounded in SEAL operational tactics. What they lacked in experience they made up for in attitude and sound basic tactical skills. Platoon chief petty officers and leading petty officers still sort through the classes like it was the NFL draft, but the reality is that the SQT graduates are uniformly trained to standard and ready to train in the platoons with SEAL veterans. Naturally, in the competitive cauldron that is SEAL training, some new men break out better than others; all of them have strong and not-so-strong aspects of their SEAL skill set. This is to be expected, and it will continue as they begin to train with their platoons for operational deployment.

But all these men leave SQT certified by Mike Loo as ready for SEAL platoon duty. Mike also sees that each new SEAL has a personal copy of his training philosophy. At SQT, Mike is referred to simply as The Warrant. I heard one new SEAL call Mike's philosophy The Warrant's Manifesto. I thought it important enough to include it in its entirety.

> FROM: CWO2 MIKE LOO (SQT OIC)
> TO: SQT GRADUATES
> SUBJ: RULES TO LIVE BY IN NAVAL SPECIAL WARFARE

1. Congratulations. You guys have completed a major milestone in your Special Warfare career. Here at the Naval Special Warfare Center you have completed BUD/S, Army airborne training, and SQT, and you have been awarded the NSW SEAL insignia, the Trident. SQT has taught you the SEAL tactics, techniques, and procedures required to successfully integrate into a SEAL platoon. You are now prepared to go in "harm's way" as an operational SEAL. This course laid the foundation of warfighting knowledge and skills you will use for your entire Special Warfare career. Mastering these skills should be your primary mission. Your lives and the lives of your teammates depend on it.

2. Don't forget that Special Warfare is the number one maritime Special Operations Force in the world and arguably the number one Special Operations Force in the

world. Being number one in the world in anything means *paying a very high price*. You have to be more focused, smarter, work harder, and have more desire than anyone else in other SOF units. Accomplishing the many tasks and difficult assignments that are thrown our way requires great effort, dedication, and persistence.

3. When you get to your team you need to work extremely hard to prepare yourselves for real-world operations. You must be physically and mentally prepared—trained to win the gunfight and accomplish the mission. Stay focused, train hard, and be the professionals we expect you to be. Always maintain your own integrity and the integrity of the teams. This handout contains, in no particular order, a list of lessons learned and rules to live by in Naval Special Warfare. Some of these are my personal rules for success and others are from great leaders in NSW who have been mentors and role models in my life. Keep this handout! Refer to it now and then. Never forget that you are the future of Naval Special Warfare. Talk is cheap; action is everything. Put out the effort and take the action needed to keep our force the best in the world.

A. Master the basics and you will be a good operator. Take care of your equipment and always have your operating gear complete, in good working order, and ready to go into the field. Forgetting a flashlight or having a dead battery in your strobe may cost lives and/or the mission. Pay attention to the basics, in training and real-world. Be the consummate professional whether in the water, in the air, or on land. Practice good noise discipline and situational awareness—360-degree security. Know your duties and responsibilities.

B. Never make the same mistake twice. You are your best critic! When you make a mistake or do something wrong, take it onboard and take it seriously. Be hard on yourselves. Do what you have to in order to not make the same mistake twice.

C. Strive for perfection. You'll never get there; perfection doesn't exist for SEALs, but we can ALWAYS do better. Being number one in the world is a heavy burden. You will often feel that you are not ready—that you haven't trained enough in a certain area or you're not in top physical shape or there are shortfalls in your gear. Take action. At anytime you could have to risk your life on a dangerous, real-world mission. Knowing this will happen in advance, like right now as you read this, will make you train that much harder to get to the highest possible level of readiness. Put out 110 percent in every endeavor. Identify your weak points, tackle them aggressively, and make them your strong points.

D. The SEAL work ethic. Our job is not eight to five. You cannot be number one in the world and not put in the extra hours. Don't be lazy; it is infectious. If some part of your platoon's training is not working, perhaps it's a matter of command and control or a gear problem or a tactical maneuver; fix it now! Don't let it go or put it off to the next training day. As a new guy in the platoon you have the right to speak up and take action on issues like this.

As a new guy, you'll find the learning curve steep and difficult. You will be required to know and perform a number of tasks to a high operational standard. You will have to master specific assigned duties in the platoon organization. This means working overtime to get the job done. This will not end, even when you have a deployment or two under your belt. It is the SEAL work ethic.

E. Responsibility/Accountability. Ultimately, you have a responsibility to the chain of command and to this country to be prepared to risk your life and the lives of your teammates as you go in harm's way to successfully complete the mission. You are accountable to do what is necessary to make this happen. This is the big picture. On a smaller scale, take your responsibilities seriously and be accountable for your actions.

F. Be a subject-matter expert in your field. We are a small community and we rely on in-house subject-matter experts in communications, ordnance, air operations, diving operations, intelligence, etc., to accomplish our missions. Strive to be the "go to" guy in your field—the one they come to for the right answer. Know all the references, know what other services/units are doing in your field; strive to know everything there is about your department or area of expertise.

G. Train as you would fight. An old Army saying but a good one. When possible, train with all the gear you will use in real combat. Train as hard and as realistically as possible. That means don't cut corners. During your platoon training, if you accomplish everything successfully, then the training needs to be more challenging. Never say, "If this was real, I'd have this piece of gear with me, or we'd do it this way." Train as you would fight. Use Simunitions as much as possible in urban, CQC, VBSS, and land-warfare training. Whenever possible use role players and other SEALs to oppose you. You may learn that tactics you used for shooting paper targets or bullet traps in the kill house may have to be changed or modified.

H. Don't get cocky; stay humble. Remember the disadvantages we always face:

- Fighting in an unfamiliar foreign country—someone's backyard.
- Bad guys who are highly trained. They may have a lot more real-world combat experience than you do, have top-of-the-line gear, and may know our tactics.
- Bad guys who are passionate about their cause and want to kill you in the worst way.

- Remember, wearing a Trident doesn't make you invincible.

I. Think ahead and stay organized.

J. When you have a good idea that benefits your platoon/team, share it with other teams.

K. Officers and petty officers need to be administratively savvy; be proficient with awards and evaluations; take care of your men.

L. Look out for your buddies on and off duty.

M. Stay physically fit; be just as smart as you are tough.

N. You are an ambassador of NSW wherever you go. You enjoy a reputation that was earned by the blood, sweat, and toil of the true frogmen of old. You haven't earned this; you have inherited it, based on the good faith that you will further the tradition. Do nothing to tarnish something you haven't earned by thought, word, or deed.

O. If you don't know or didn't understand, ASK! It's your responsibility to find out. Research; demonstrate an unquenchable desire to know everything about your job.

P. If something is broken or not right, take the initiative to fix it or make it right! Don't wait for someone else to take action.

Q. Always check your equipment again before going into the field. Make sure you have everything and that it's serviceable. LPO and CPO inspections are to make sure this happens.

R. Listen and take notes during all Patrol Leader Order. Prior to going into the field, know the minimum:

- Routes in and out. Have a map and compass.
- Rally points.
- Basic communications plan, call signs, and frequencies.
- Actions at the objective.

- Your platoon's medical plan.
- Your E&E plan.

S. ALWAYS Rehearse/Dirt Dive everything. Plan the dive (operation). Dive the plan.

T. Mobility. Take only what you absolutely need in the field. When the shit hits the fan, you want to be as light as possible and fast on your feet. You need energy and mobility to win and survive.

U. There is no second place in a gunfight. Winners kill, losers get killed. Fight to win. Train to live.

V. All encounters during a mission are a threat to your team. Never drop your security and always expect contact. Never turn your back on a threat.

W. It takes a shooter to lead a shooter.

X. The easy way out may not be the safest way out.

Y. If the enemy is in range, so are YOU!

Z. Tracers work both ways.

Conclusion: You are a U.S. Navy SEAL, feared by the enemy and respected as the best maritime warrior in the world. Others envy your iron willpower and superior physical toughness. Countless men have dreamed they would become SEALs. Thousands have tried, but only a select few ever earn the right to wear the Trident. Wherever you go, whatever you do, whomever you meet, remember this: you are responsible for your actions. You must protect and defend your country to the best of your ability and uphold the honor of the U.S. Navy and the Navy SEAL Teams. There is no "I" in SEAL team.

You exist to serve the mission. No one owes you anything. You are always on duty, every moment of your career. Your responsibility to be fit and ready to fight never ceases. A crisis will not wait until you complete your next training cycle or recover from a hangover. A warrior's responsibility to be ready for combat never goes on liberty or leave. Think positive mission accomplishment at all times. Synchronize and train your mind and your will just as you train your body. Discipline yourself. Study tactical and leadership material daily. It is only a matter of time before you will engage the enemy in a gunfight. SEAL operations mean you may have to stand toe to toe with an enemy. For those who want to win, there is never enough time to train. Aggressively seek any knowledge that will assure mission accomplishment and make you a survivor and a winner. Never lose the desire to find a new tactic or technique that will make the difference for you and your teammates.

Be openly patriotic. You pay for that right. Wear your uniform proudly and with the same precision and quality with which you would execute a mission.

Live the legend of the teams every day. NCDUs, UDTs, and SEALs have been decorated for incredible acts of valor and accomplished seemingly impossible feats in combat. You are responsible for carrying the SEAL reputation above and beyond your predecessors. Carry yourself with SEAL confidence and professionalism. Leave all who come in contact with you with a positive sense of your combat skills, your loyalty, and your tactical savvy. Make the Trident stand out as the most select special operations insignia in the world.

Be passionate in the pursuit of excellence. Be cautious when working with those who are not. Never allow another man's attitude to jeopardize the mission of your teammates' lives. Look for the best in your teammates, not the worst. There are plenty of flaws within each of us. Look for the positive; help and assist those with weaknesses. Openly build and cultivate the close esprit-de-corps that has made the teams famous.

Never show weakness or dissension to anyone outside the teams. When you speak, you learn nothing; you learn only by listening. Listen, then speak, and speak from the heart. Take only those actions that make you a stronger SEAL or strengthen the teams. Think before you act. If an action does not make you or the team better, then don't take it. You must use every precious moment of training to move forward and prepare for combat. You must always be aware that your every action affects the reputation of the team. Never lose the physical and mental courage that you discovered in yourself in BUD/S. You will fail at many things as an individual during your career but you will always face combat as a member of a team. Never be a loner; never leave a teammate alone. Rely on your teammates and never let them down. You are a member of the Naval Special Warfare community; you are the teams.

Looking back on the good times, the bad times, and the hard times in my career in the teams, it has been challenging, rewarding, and fun. If I had to do it all over again, I would relive my career in the teams. The experiences and the lifetime friends I have made are priceless.

Have fun, train hard, and when the time comes, kick ass. It was great working with you.

Many in Naval Special Warfare, including myself, consider CWO2 Mike Loo the architect of modern advanced SEAL training.

INTO THE COLD

"Good morning, gentlemen, and welcome to Kodiak Island. And for all you new SEALs, congratulations on earning the Trident and welcome to the brotherhood. The teams need you and your country needs you. After this block of training, you will be off to your operational teams. You've been told for the last year or so that training is never over. Well, you now wear the Trident, and for the next three weeks we're going to work your butts off. You're all going to train hard while you're here. We're going to teach you how to survive and operate in some very harsh and difficult conditions, and we're gonna have some fun. This training is important. I want you to pay attention to what my cadre puts out here because it could save your life, and it could enable you to complete your mission. Some of our brothers had problems when they got up into the mountains of Afghanistan. They got the job done, but they had to fight the elements every step of the way. Here, for this training, the enemy is the weather and the terrain. We're going to teach you how to be winners when the weather gets really nasty. You're gonna love it out there."

Master Chief Scott Williams is the Kodiak Detachment Officer in Charge—the Det OIC. He grew up in Maine, and his wife is from Newfoundland. He's spent twenty-three of his forty-one years in the Navy. Williams made chief petty officer in eight years, and a short time after that he achieved the top enlisted rank of master chief petty officer. He completed four operational tours with the East Coast SEAL teams. Scott Williams's expertise and passion are in cold-weather operations. Scott is to cold-weather training what Mike Loo is to SQT. When it really gets nasty outside, he's grinning from ear to ear. Considered one of the leading experts in military cold-weather operations, he has participated in extreme competitions such as the Eco-Challenge and many military cold-weather endurance tests. He is now tasked with training all new Navy SEALs in cold-weather operations. They call it cold-weather training, but from what I saw of the training in Kodiak, it was more like nasty-weather training. I observed this training with the new SEALs from SQT Class 5-02.

Kodiak is both a town and an island. The town is a fishing village in the Gulf of Alaska and has a large Coast Guard base nearby. The island is the largest one in the United States outside of the Hawaiian Islands. There are more eagles than seagulls. The SEAL training compound is located on Cape Spruce, a scenic spit of land that is home to the Naval Special Warfare Detachment, Kodiak. The compound consists of two metal buildings that house sleeping facilities, classrooms, equipment bays, a galley, and a small clinic. There is a third building that serves as a boat barn and indoor climbing facility and a smaller equipment-storage shed. During the winters, which last a long time, Kodiak is cold, wet, and windy. For all its harshness, it is a land of contrast and dramatic beauty, with deserted islands, steep cliffs that rise from rocky beaches, and snow-covered mountains—all within a short distance of the SEAL training compound. This means that Scott Williams can get his SEAL students from the classroom to the cold water and snow very quickly.

Officially, the students at Kodiak are still SQT Class 5-02, so designated since they were the fifth, and last, class to begin SQT in 2002. Of the forty-two in this Kodiak class, forty are new SEALs—the officers are from BUD/S Class 239 and the enlisted from Class 240. One is an officer returning to the teams after completing his college degree. Ensign Brad Taylor graduated from BUD/S with Class 202, completed a single deployment with SEAL Team Eight on the East Coast, and was on his second operational workup when he suddenly became a college student. He qualified for the Navy's Seaman to Admiral Program, which sends enlisted men to college to earn their degrees and then commissions them as naval officers. With no previous college experience, Brad Taylor earned a degree in business administration from the University of San Diego in three years. Taylor is not a new SEAL, but he is a new ensign. He joined SQT Class 5-02 on his way to SEAL Team Three in Coronado. He went through SEAL Tactical Training on the East Coast in 1996.

"My STT training was a great deal like SQT," the new SEAL ensign told me, "but not nearly as comprehensive. The current advanced training is a little longer, and the land-warfare training is more extensive than the old STT. And back then, we had no CQD training. Here on the West Coast we had to deal with the Pacific surf during the OTBs. And back then, East and West Coast STT courses were different. With the current SQT, all new SEALs are trained to the same standard and take this uniform standard of training to the platoons."

"Did you get any cold-weather training on the East Coast?" I ask.

"We had a great cold-weather program at Group Two, but it was training for designated platoons deploying to northern Europe. My platoon did not get cold-weather training. Now with this training here in Kodiak, cold-weather training is another standard skill set that all SEALs receive."

"Glad to be heading back to the teams?"

"I can't wait. USD was great, but I missed the camaraderie of the teams. This will be my first West Coast platoon, and I'm looking forward to operational deployment. I got sniper qualified before I left Team Eight. I hope I go directly to a platoon, but if not, perhaps I'll get assigned to the team sniper cell."

The other veteran SEAL in the Kodiak class is an SQT instructor. Not all of the SQT cadre have had this cold-weather training, or their training is dated, so Mike Loo is cycling these instructors through this course. Training is never over, not even for the trainers. The first several days at Kodiak are spent in the classroom. In addition to medical, nutritional, and environmental briefings, the students have to learn about their cold-weather gear issue. They learn how to use it and how to care for it. There is a clothing issue and a field-equipment issue.

The cold-weather garment issue is a clothing system officially called the protective combat uniform, or PCU. It consists of multiple layers of special fabric and shell materials to protect the SEAL operator in temperatures that range as low as fifty degrees below zero Fahrenheit. The system has seven layers so that the operator can mix and match to achieve the right balance of thermal protection and mobility for a given task and given conditions. Under the guidance of Scott Williams, the best available civilian climbing and outdoor wear has been modified and adapted for the SEAL PCU system. The layers are variously constructed of Thinsulate, knit polyester, encapsulated nylon microfiber, and various other fabric blends to achieve the desired degree of water repellence, waterproofing, insulation, and breathability. Each layer is ergonomically suitable to allow the SEAL operator to function in combat.

The field equipment issue is called PEPSE, short for personal environmental protection and survival equipment. Each new SEAL receives a sleeping bag, a sleeping shelter, boots, balaclavas, ground pads, cooking utensils, water bottles, a portable stove system, several hats, and some six different pairs of gloves and mittens. The kit also includes a water-filtration system, a pack shovel, a folding saw, and a climbing harness. To get around, the new SEALs are issued snowshoes, crampons, and folding ski poles.

"Our backpack is one of the best, designed specifically for our needs and what we have to take into the field." Master Chief Williams adds with a grin, "The manufacturer's eyes got real big when I told them we needed to be able to strap snowshoes on one side of the pack and swim fins on the other."

The final item is the military assault suit, or MAS, as it is called. This is a lightweight dry suit designed for surface swimming. It has latex wrist and neck seals and a waterproof zipper. The feet are built into the suit so the user can wear boots or sneakers over the suit. When it is not in use, the suit rolls compactly into a stuff bag and is stored in the backpack. During OTBs in SQT and BUD/S, the trainees would wear wet suits. After they crossed the beach, they would have to change into cammies as they transitioned to land travel. With the MAS, the SEALs can wear their combat uniform and some of their first line gear under their dry suits.

This is not an inexpensive gear issue. If it were purchased retail, the PCU, PEPSE, and MAS together would cost close to $10,000. But working closely with the manufacturers and purchasing in quantity, the teams were able to get the cost down to less than half of that.

After a few days in the classroom, the new SEALs and their new equipment take to the field. The first outing lasts three days and two nights. The objective is equipment familiarization and appreciation. The days are taken with movement and navigation drills in the low mountains not far from the town of Kodiak. The students learn to use altimeters along with a contour map and a compass to find their way in the rugged terrain. They are carrying sixty-five pounds of gear, and for this first field exercise, no operational gear or weapons.

They spend the first night close to sea level. It's not cold enough to snow, but it rains most of the night. The second night is spent at fifteen hundred feet and in the snow, with a final movement up over a twenty-one-hundred-foot ridgeline. The class is divided up into four squads, with an instructor with each squad. Throughout the drills and night encampments, the squads practice noise discipline and tactical movement. At night, each squad will rotate two men on guard duty at all times, just as if they were on operational patrol. There is little wind during these first days in the field, so the nights are relatively comfortable. On the third day, they come off the mountain and down to one of the many bays near the town of Kodiak. Now it is time for equipment appreciation—the rewarming exercise.

On the beach, the trainees strip to their skivvy shorts and wade out into the water. It's been an unusually mild winter in Kodiak, but the water is still forty-two degrees. They remain in neck-deep water for ten minutes. One of the cadre corpsmen roams the shoreline to make sure they are cold but not hypothermic. The objective is to take their core temperature down several degrees. This is not harassment; it is training.

"Alright," the corpsman shouts to the shivering line of heads in the water, "everyone out of the pool!"

The class members wade back to the shore and recover their gear. Then they head into the brush and behind a small hill to get out of a stiff wind that's blowing off the bay.

"They have about six minutes to get warm," Chief Hospital Corpsman Shawn Beach tells me. "We call it the six golden minutes. Their core temperature is low and will go lower as they begin to work their gear and the blood starts to flow into their fingers. They have to get dry and get warm, and they have to do it fast."

I watch as the students work in pairs. They quickly dry off with one of their base layers and pull on another. Both of them pull on balaclavas and stocking caps. One man gets a stove going and begins to heat water while his buddy erects a sleeping shelter. Both men slip into their sleeping bags, then into the shelter and shiver while the water warms. The drill is to get warm liquid down and get a hot meal prepared. Master Chief Williams, Chief Beach, and the other Kodiak cadre are wandering among the students, keeping a close eye on them.

"This teaches them to trust their gear and their training," Beach tells me, "and exactly what must be done to get a man warm if he falls in the water or through the ice while on patrol. It's life and death, especially if there's a wind. You can teach this in the classroom, and we do. But until you're out here trying to fire up a stove with your hands shaking so badly that you can't hold a match, you don't understand what cold can do and how fast it can do it. Those six golden minutes go by very quickly."

I notice that one of the Kodiak instructors who was with a student squad also went in the water with the class, and had to do the rewarming drill when he came out.

"We never ask the students to do something we don't do on a regular basis," Scott Williams says. "We want an instructor in the water who has been out with them in the field—to have the same demands on him that we place on the students. That way we can make it challenging, but keep it safe and in perspective. It's no picnic being in that water for ten minutes, even if you came out here from a warm bed and a hot breakfast. It's very important that we do this exactly like the students on a regular basis. I have a good crew here. One of the guys always volunteers."

"That include you, Master Chief?"

"Oh, yeah," Williams says with a gleam in his eye. "I take my turn; I also lead the local polar bear club for the New Year's Day plunge." I've come to know Scott Williams during my stay at Kodiak. I don't find this hard to believe at all.

After a day off to reassemble and repack equipment, the trainees are back in the classroom the following morning. Class 5-02 learns about its new climbing harnesses and how to scale cliffs. There is a climbing wall in the boat barn where the students are able to set up and test their climbing gear. This is not recreational sport climbing; this is the basics of how warriors move themselves and their operational gear over vertical rock walls as a part of a mission. That afternoon, the students are out on the cape for some more survival instruction. The class learns how to build improvised shelters and how to find edible life when the tide is out. "When the tide is out, the table is set," the instructors tell them, as the students search the tide pools for marine life.

After another day in the classroom, it's back into the field under full pack. For half the class, it's OTB drills on Long Island, a deserted island near Kodiak. The students have to waterproof their packs and swim them in. Just as they did in BUD/S and SQT, the scout swimmers come in and recon the beach while the others wait offshore. When the area is secure, the rest of the platoon-size class swims in. This is a tactical exercise, with weapons. The platoon patrols inland, still wearing their MASs with packs and fins loosely slung. The men find a secure location and set up a perimeter. Half of them shuck their MASs and ruck up for land travel, then they take positions on the perimeter while the other half changes out. There is no talking, just a gentle rustle of equipment. After a short patrol to another beach location, they call the boats back in, climb back into their MASs, and return to the sea. Each time they do this they become a little quicker at it, a little more proficient, a little quieter. In the afternoon, the class is told to abandon their rucks and make for the woods. The men grab only a light kit called a jump bag and, of course, their weapons. This bag is attached to their rucks, something they would grab in an emergency if they had to flee or in the event of a helo crash in enemy territory. In a real-world situation, they are taught to fight for their ruck, as it contains what they need to live and continue the mission. This is training—a simulated emergency. They grab their jump bag and begin their E&E, or escape-and-evasion procedures. Two instructors also grab their E&E kits and follow their students into the woods.

The woods on Long Island are damp to a fault, and the trees and ground are matted with a thick blanket of moss. Once the men are well into the interior of the island, they fan out and begin to build shelters from fallen branches, pine boughs, and sections of moss-covered turf. They build small, smokeless fires and begin the process of gathering and drying out firewood. The teaching continues. They put out snares for game, but when the snares fail, one of the instructors shoots a rabbit. The animal is skinned and roasted over a makeshift spit; each man gets to sample cooked hare. As the sun goes down and the temperature drops, the student survival pairs huddle in their shelters, keep their warming fires banked, and shiver the night away. In a makeshift shelter nearby, two SEAL instructors shiver along with their students. At dawn they patrol back to the shoreline, recover their gear, and begin more OTB drills. All the while they play the tactical game, moving quietly, observing 360-degree security.

The other half of 5-02 is on the ropes. The students are taught not so much to be proficient climbers as to be good followers. It's the lead climber's job to establish a route and scale the cliff. Lead climbers in a platoon are specialists, like snipers and communicators, and are trained and certified accordingly. The lead climber's job is important and dangerous. SEALs have to deal with "bad rock"—the scaly loose material found in coastal areas; it's a job that demands a great deal of confidence and professionalism. Again, this is not recreational climbing. SEALs will want to do their climbing when it's dark and when the weather is ugly—when the enemy least expects them to scale a dangerous cliff. Once atop the cliff, the lead climber or climbers deploy ropes and other equipment to bring the platoon and its gear up the cliff. If it's a nonvertical cliff, the student SEALs climb with their rucksacks, shackled into the climbing line deployed by the lead climber. If it's a vertical wall, the students have to use a system of ascenders, prussik knots, and leg loops to climb the line. This involves scaling the line without using the rock to assist in the climb. Then the packs are brought up the face on a rigged trolley system. The last man to climb breaks down the pack line and ascends the line. The platoon recovers its gear and moves on to the objective. The rock work at Kodiak is done under the supervision of Chief Don Bishop.

"We want all of these guys to learn the basic skills of getting themselves and their gear up a difficult face," Bishop tells me. He is from

Colorado and came into the teams with climbing experience. Bishop, with four operational tours at SEAL Team Eight, has been a lead climber and climbing instructor for twelve years. Like Mike Loo and Scott Williams, he is the teams' best in his discipline. "They have to work as a team—some guys are on the ropes, some are providing security, others are at the bottom busy with rigging, and some of the guys are on top hauling up the gear. When we get everybody up, we'll take everybody back down. Then rerig and do it again."

Going back down, the students rappel with their packs clipped to their climbing harnesses. They have all rappelled before but not with this much weight. They learn to use a French prussik, a self-belay system that allows them to free both hands to use their weapon during the descent. All lines are recovered, ascending or descending. At the top of the face and at the bottom, they remain tactical. SEALs not on the lines are on the perimeter to establish sectors of covering fire. There is 120-foot rock wall near the Det Kodiak facility that rises straight up from the surf. The members of Class 5-02 climb this wall, haul their packs up, and recover their climbing gear. They then redeploy the ropes and descend. Up and down, several times—out of the surf and up the rock wall, then back down the wall to the surf. They make the last climb after dark and fade into the woods to set up camp.

"We're only five minutes from the barracks," I observe to Master Chief Williams. "Why don't they just go back there and sleep?"

"You learn nothing in the barracks," he tells me. "Every time you set up at night, and I mean a tactical setup—shelters dispersed, guards out—you learn something. This is the way they will do it in the platoons. When the guys are home, they need to be with their families at night; but when they are at a remote training site, they need to be in the operational environment, or as close to an operational environment as we can make it." Then he adds with a grin, "The wind is coming up and the temperature is dropping; it's a good night for them to be out here."

After two days on Long Island, half of 5-02 comes back in for a night to dry and refurbish their gear. Then they ruck it up and head for the cliffs, while their classmates secure their climbing harnesses and file into the boats for the trip out to Long Island. For many of the men in Class 5-02, it is the first time they have ridden in or worked from an eleven-meter RHIB. The eleven-meter RHIB is a jet-pump-driven, rigid-hull inflatable boat, and the tactical workhorse of the NSW special boat units. Following the Long Island and cliff evolutions, the entire class gets two days at the facility for more classroom work and gear prep. The students also have a written test on all material covered to date, which is the basic skill set for this course. The final exercise is not called an FTX but rather a combined skills exercise. They will be out for four days and three nights, and they will put into practice everything they have learned so far. They will come from the sea, cross the beach, and tactically move up into the mountains. After three nights in the Alaskan coastal winter, they will recross the beach and return to the sea.

"The class was again divided into four squads," Ensign Taylor told me after the skills exercise. "We had a twenty-minute ride up Middle Bay to where the boats dropped us off. There we dropped off the scout swimmers, then brought the rest of the squad in. Once ashore we set a perimeter and changed out of our MAS gear, then headed up into the hills. The first day we humped about seven miles to the fifteen-hundred-foot level. It was in the high twenties, and we camped the first night in the snow. We found a low depression off a ridgeline with some scrub for cover. Once we had made camp, Chief Bishop had us hike out and see how visible we were from different vantage points. The next day we packed up and continued on toward our objective, which was Center Mountain."

"Any tactical gear?" I ask.

"Just weapons and first line gear. The second day out, we stopped on a steep slope to learn and practice self-arrest with ice axes. About that time the wind came up and the temperature went down—way down. We got caught on an exposed north face and had about a two-hour hump to get to a ravine that offered some protection. The temperature had gone down to about eight degrees and the wind was gusting close to sixty knots. We have great gear, but by the time we got away from that wind we were freezing our butts off. Some of the guys were getting frost nips—white patches of skin where there was exposure to the wind.

"There was still too much wind to set up shelters, so we built two-man snow caves, fired up our stoves, and hunkered in for the night. We were pretty comfortable, but we still had to put out guards. Even with thirty-minute shifts, it got pretty cold when you were outside the snow cave. The next day, the wind was still up, so the chief said it was time to head back. We never made it all the way to Center Mountain, but we sure learned a lot. That afternoon, Chief Bishop went through the ice up to his chest on a stream crossing, so we had to put him through a rewarming drill. The stream was a good bivouac area, so we set up there for the third night. With our help, it took about eight hours to dry out his gear. It was great training. We got dry and warm and were ready to carry on with the mission. As it was, we walked out the next day in a full-on blizzard. By the time we got back to the Det compound on the cape, there was two feet of snow on the ground."

"This was a good class and they got good training," Master Chief Williams tells me after all the squads returned to Cape Spruce. "I'm happy with their performance. When the weather turns on you like that, your mission quickly turns to one of survival. Had they made it to Center Mountain, we would have been able to rope up and traverse some ice faces, but not in that wind. You know," he adds with a grin, "two of those guys had never even seen snow before they came here. Now they've been out in rough country in a blizzard. They've learned a lot in the past few days, and they'll take a lot of good information to their platoons."

This is the last training evolution for the SEALs of Class 5-02. While the snow piles up in Kodiak, the men repack their gear and load it onto pallets for the flight back to the Strand. The storm that kept them from reaching Center Mountain delays their return to Coronado for two days. On their return to the Naval Special Warfare Center, the former SQT students are detached and scatter to their new duty stations. They no longer belong to the Center; they're now platoon SEALs.

CHAPTER 4

The Men

The new SEALs returning from Kodiak Island go straight to their new teams. After more than twelve months at the training command, it's an exciting time for them. For those going to the East Coast teams, it's a long way from Alaska to Virginia by way of San Diego—longer still for those assigned to Swimmer Delivery Team One in Hawaii. For the new SDV SEALs, there is SDV School in Panama City, Florida. Depending on class convening dates, they may go directly to SDV School or to their new team until the next class starts. Most of these new SEALs have never been to their new operational command. When they do reach the team, they will begin the serious preparation that will lead to operational deployment. After twelve plus months of basic and advanced training, the new SEALs face eighteen months of predeployment training. The preparation that Navy SEALs today go through for operational deployment is a much different business than it was only a few years ago.

Every SEAL a corpsman. Under the watchful eye of a medical instructor, an SQT student gives first aid to a fellow student in a simulated tactical situation. *Photo by Dick Couch*

THE NSW 21 CONCEPT

Basic and advanced training of Navy SEALs continues to evolve and improve to meet the changing conditions and requirements of Naval Special Warfare. Yet these evolutionary changes are quite modest when compared to the changes that have recently taken place in the predeployment training and operational deployment of SEAL platoons and SEAL teams.

Teamwork is important in BUD/S and SQT, but the basic trainees and SQT students do not train for any length of time as a dedicated team. The "team" they have known so far is usually five to fifteen men organized into a squad or a boat crew for training purposes. These teams are changed or reconfigured to meet different training venues and scenarios. In the numbered SEAL teams, the basic combat team or element is the SEAL platoon. The platoon has many variations of tactical employment, but it is the SEAL platoon that lives and trains as a unit. More than that, it's an operational family unit. When our new SEAL arrives from Kodiak at his team, he is assigned to a platoon. But before a "new guy," as the recent Trident holders are called, and his platoon begin serious training as a combat team, there are a number of individual schools and courses he, and the other members of the platoon, must have. These schools lead to required qualifications and designations that collectively allow the platoon to perform as a operational combat team. Many of these qualifications are mission- and theater-specific for certain special operations requirements. And there are also some procedural and individual qualifications that platoon members must go through before they begin their formal platoon combat training. New SEALs, fresh from SQT and Kodiak, face a different and far more structured platoon training and operational deployment regime than did Class 228 when it graduated in 2000 from SEAL Tactical Training, the forerunner of SQT. Let me explain.

Prior to January 2002, there were six numbered SEAL Teams:

Teams Two, Four, and Eight on the East Coast and Teams One, Three, and Five on the West Coast. SEAL Team Six was disestablished several years ago. The Naval Special Warfare Command, or WARCOM, carries the responsibility for keeping twelve combat-ready, operational SEAL platoons forward-deployed and at the disposal of the theater commanders. There are other NSW assets available and in place for theater commanders, but the central standing requirement is twelve operational SEAL platoons. This load was shared equally by both coasts with each team equipping, training, and deploying two freshly trained platoons every six months. This kept six platoons from each coast overseas and on the job. This is why there were combat-ready SEAL platoons in the Central Command and Persian Gulf region on 11 September 2001. These forward-deployed platoons were in Afghanistan within weeks of the al-Qaeda strikes in New York and Washington, D.C. The platoon SEALs conducted strategic reconnaissance missions and sent back critical intelligence to assist the forces that would soon arrive to vanquish the Taliban.

Because the "old" teams were manned at eight platoons each, this evolved into a two-year rotational cycle for the deploying platoons. Within their team training regimen, SEAL platoons would train for eighteen months and deploy for six. Under this arrangement, the team commanding officer had no operational or tactical responsibility. Basically, his obligation ended with the deployment of his platoons and their assignment to the theater commander. Team commanding officers were, in many respects, the senior training officers, and much of the team command structure was a training cadre. The individual platoons deployed with most of their operational gear: weapons, diving rigs, parachutes, and so on. The deployed platoons still called their East or West Coast teams home, but their team's primary responsibility for their deployed children amounted to equipment replacement, personnel issues, and assisting deployed SEALs with family problems at home. Once overseas, the deployed SEAL platoons made their home at established overseas Naval Special

Warfare Units or with units of the fleet assigned to carry SEAL platoons. Operationally, these platoons fell under the control of the theater command. Once in theater, the platoons were assigned NSW support elements in the way of special boat detachments or other assigned personnel to assist with mission planning and execution. This all changed with the advent of the Naval Special Warfare 21 concept.

NSW 21 is built around an enhanced SEAL team, or "SEAL squadron." The squadron is a six-platoon SEAL organization that has a reinforced command-and-control structure and trains with an expanded complement of NSW small craft, SDVs, and supporting NSW and non-NSW elements. After a period of interoperability training with these additional NSW components, the squadron deploys as a unit. Once deployed, the squadron receives ongoing logistical and administrative support from the Naval Special Warfare Group commands on each coast. While the squadron deploys in mass with its entire complement of people, the reverse is true of the equipment and platforms. The SEALs have their personal weapons and personal gear, but much of their operational equipment remains forward-deployed. Going forward, there will also be enhanced NSW Group–driven intelligence and mission-support capabilities at the disposal of the deployed squadrons. Basically, we are now deploying SEAL teams— or, more accurately, SEAL squadrons—not just individual platoons. The deployed squadrons still report to the theater commanders for fleet and special operations tasking, but there is now a trained, integrated NSW support organization to extend the reach of the operational SEAL platoons. And there is a dedicated, forward-deployed SEAL squadron command structure to help the theater CINCs better use their SEALs.

The most visible change of NSW 21 is that there are two new SEAL teams on each coast: Team Seven in Coronado and Team Ten in Little Creek, Virginia. The number of operational platoons remains unchanged. Formerly, there were six teams with eight platoons. Now there are eight teams, each with six platoons. Instead of simply prepping platoons for deployment, the two new teams and the six reconstituted teams now deploy with their platoons. What is not so visible is the consolidation of administrative, logistical, and training functions under the Naval Special Warfare Groups. NSW Group One in Coronado and NSW Group Two in Norfolk now support and train the teams on their respective coasts. During the last six months of the eighteen-month predeployment workup, the six-platoon SEAL team acquires its NSW augmentees and becomes a SEAL squadron. Change is always hard. The transition from six to eight SEAL teams and the team-to-squadron evolution was not without its growing pains. But the benefits to the men and the SEAL mission have been significant.

There are three defined six-month phases that lead to a SEAL squadron deployment. The first of these three phases focuses on individual training. It's also called the professional development, or PRODEV, phase. For the veterans returning from overseas, it's a chance to see their families and take some of the leave that has been accumulating on the books since their last deployment workup and overseas deployment. For the new men fresh from the training command, the new guys, it's a chance to get acquainted with their new team and their first platoon, and to get some specialized schooling. From SQT Class 2-02, twenty of the newly qualified SEALs were assigned to SEAL Teams Seven and Ten. Since they are the newest teams, they are just beginning their eighteen-month predeployment workup. It's a good time for the new men to get to their team; they step right from the training command and into an environment preparing individual SEALs for deployment. At the time of SQT Class 2-02's graduation, SEAL Squadrons One and Two were deployed overseas. Twenty-two of the new SEALs from Class 2-02 had orders to the two deployed squadrons. Upon returning from deployment, every SEAL squadron will revert to SEAL-team status and again begin the training cycle, starting with the PRODEV period. Those with orders to Squadrons One and Two were sent to various special warfare schools and temporary duty while they awaited the return of their squadron/team. Then they began their PRODEV period with their new platoon mates. The new SEALs from SQT Class 5-02 and Kodiak are bound for SEAL Teams Three and Four. For this book, I observed the PRODEV portion of Team Seven's training.

SEAL Team Seven was commissioned in Coronado on Sunday, 17 March 2002 (Saint Patrick's Day); Team Ten on the East Coast on 19 April 2002. The last time a SEAL team was born was when Team Eight came to life back in 1986. The new team on each coast is manned largely with veteran SEALs from the other three teams on that coast—and our new guys from SQT. To create the new team on the West Coast, there was an expansion draft of sorts, much like when professional baseball adds another team to the league. In the case of SEAL Team Seven, platoon SEALs from Teams One, Three, and Five were assigned to Team Seven. The platoon SEALs coming to Seven are from platoons most recently back from deployment, so Team Seven inherited many of the SEALs with combat experience in Afghanistan. These returning platoons were broken up and scattered among the six platoons forming up at Team Seven for PRODEV. Much the same process is going on at SEAL Team Ten in Little Creek, Virginia, where veterans from Teams Two, Four, and Eight are returning from deployment.

On paper, SEAL Team Seven, as with all the numbered SEAL teams, has a complement of 128 SEAL operators: 21 officers and 107 enlisted men. This is the manning level at the time of their commissioning. Manning for all the teams under the new order is subject to operational and administrative considerations. The teams are further assigned 11 technical support people: 1 officer and 10 enlisted. The team structure is further broken down into three task units of two platoons each. Deployed, each task unit will have a task unit commander drawn from the senior team leadership. Most typically, the team commanding officer, executive officer, and operations officer will serve as task unit commanders. This places the senior leadership of the team forward-deployed with their operating platoons. The task units are staffed as needed depending on the theater requirements, but they can include additional support personnel and operational planners. Amid all this change, the basic fighting unit of the Navy SEALs remains the SEAL platoon.

SEAL platoons are comprised of 2, and in some cases 3, officers and 14 enlisted men. A deployed SEAL squadron is able to field between 96 and 102 SEAL "shooters." Much of the work of the senior leadership of a deployed SEAL squadron is to see that these shooters maintain their skills and get to the fight well equipped and well briefed, and that their mission taskings are in keeping with what they have been trained to do. These mission taskings may vary and could require only two SEALs or two full SEAL platoons to get the job done. Often SEAL platoons operate in two squads of 7 to 8 men, but a SEAL platoon can mix and match to meet the special operations requirement. There are also non-SEAL operational assets assigned to the squadron and may be detailed to a platoon or SEAL operational element. And, as we will see, the extended SEAL squadron duties may require little or no shooting, and may involve a personnel mix other than just SEAL.

THE LEADERSHIP

The commanding officer of SEAL Team Seven is Commander Joseph Rosen. As the first commanding officer of this unit, he inherits no existing personnel, command policy, or infrastructure; he's starting from scratch. His first task is to stand up his six platoons. This requires that he early on make the critical choices of platoon leadership, both officer and enlisted. Each platoon will be led by two key leaders—the platoon officer in charge (OIC) and the platoon chief petty officer. The chemistry of these six pairs of SEAL leaders will, to a large degree, determine the success and combat effectiveness of SEAL Team Seven when it gets to the fight as SEAL Squadron Seven. The six platoon OICs at Team Seven come with a wide variety of backgrounds and platoon experience. Three of them have recently completed tours as assistant officers in charge (AOICs) or assistant platoon commanders in other SEAL platoons. And three of them are former AOICs from SDV platoons.

Platoon OICs are known quantities in the teams; their reputations are well established. They are Navy SEAL lieutenants who have typically been on two platoon deployments, occasionally with only one and a few of them with three. This is the pinnacle of a young SEAL officer's operational career; platoon OIC is what he has been working for since he reported for BUD/S training. These officers have proven themselves operationally and administratively, and have been recommended by their current command or their former command to lead a platoon. All SEAL officers who have aspirations for a career as a Navy SEAL must successfully complete a tour as the OIC of a SEAL platoon. Without this, they will progress no further. The average time in service for an incoming OIC is between five and seven years. If he went straight to BUD/S as a new ensign, he has that amount of time in the teams. By most military criteria, he is very senior to be commanding an element of this size, but this is not uncommon in special operations units. Each of these officers is different; each comes through this pipeline with a different set of experiences and deployment history. Lieutenant Dan Canapa is perhaps more different than most.

Lieutenant Canapa is the OIC for Foxtrot Platoon, SEAL Team Seven. Like many platoon OICs, there is little to distinguish him from the men he leads. He is twenty-seven years old, five-foot nine, 165 pounds, and single. He has blond hair and blue eyes, wears designer sunglasses, drives a Jeep Wrangler, and likes to surf. Canapa graduated from the Naval Academy in 1996—and took his commission as a second lieutenant in the Marine Corps. His father was a career Army officer who met Dan's mother while in Australia. As a service brat, he has lived in numerous places and has been in the military, or been a military dependent, his whole life. At the Naval Academy he competed in lightweight crew. I asked Dan Canapa why he decided to go into the Corps when he left Annapolis.

"I couldn't get one of the billets in my class directly to BUD/S, so I went into the Corps. I wanted to lead men on the ground, and," he says with a smile, "I didn't want to go aboard ship."

"I didn't think you could transfer from the Marine Corps to the Navy as an officer, let alone into BUD/S."

"At the Naval Academy they told me it would be impossible. I grew up in an Army family so I learned early on that in the service, you can always find a way. Heck, they told me I couldn't get into the Naval Academy. People have been telling me I couldn't do things all my life. I knew I could make it happen and I did."

"How did you like the Corps?"

"It was great—the best thing I could have done prior to coming into the teams. I made three deployments as a Marine officer—one as an infantry platoon commander, one as a weapons platoon commander, and one as the company executive officer. I think it would help all team guys to have some infantry experience. That's how the British Special Air Service does it. A man has to have five or six years in the infantry before he can go into the SAS. It's much the same with our Special Forces."

"So you had an infantry platoon as a second lieutenant?" I ask. "How many men in a Marine infantry platoon?"

"I had about fifty in my platoon."

"Now you have a platoon of sixteen SEALs. If you'd stayed in the Corps, you'd be a company commander by now, probably finished with your tour. How big is a Marine infantry company?"

"Upwards of a hundred seventy men."

"That's bigger than SEAL Team Seven."

He smiles. "I know, but then special operations is a whole different approach to war. We need Marines because we need naval infantry, but they're not special operators. They do things we can't, but there are a whole lot of things we can do that they never will, not even in their Recon platoons. It just takes too long to learn the business of special operations."

Dan Canapa came to BUD/S Class 226 from the Marine Corps;

captain, USMC, to lieutenant, USN. From BUD/S, he went to SEAL Tactical Training on the East Coast and on to SEAL Delivery Team Two in Norfolk. On the way to STT he, like all BUD/S graduates assigned to SDVs, went to SDV School in Panama City, Florida. At the three-month SDV School, the new men must master two underwater systems. The first is the Mk-16 scuba. The Mk-16 is a highly complex, mixed-gas diving rig that allows SDV crews to dive deeper and longer than they could on an open-circuit scuba or the Draeger LAR V oxygen rebreather—the standard tactical rig in all the teams. Once they master the Mk-16, they begin learning to drive the Mk8 SEAL Delivery Vehicles—the SDVs. These are fiberglass wet submersibles, which means the seawater in the boat is at the same temperature and pressure as the seawater outside the boat. These SDVs can carry up to six SEALs and can launch from surface craft as well as a submerged submarine. SDV operations, and SEAL operations launched from SDVs, are among the most sophisticated and complex of all maritime special operations. The SDV SEALs refer to the other teams as SEAL nondelivery teams. Dan Canapa comes to Team Seven with a very good reputation in SDV operations. He may be inexperienced in special operations land warfare when compared to other SEAL OICs, but then he has three years' experience as a Marine infantry officer.

Because of his circuitous route to BUD/S, Lieutenant Canapa will make his first deployment as a SEAL platoon OIC a little more than seven years from the day he graduated from Annapolis.

"So why Team Seven?" I ask. "You were ready to begin the workup as an OIC for an SDV platoon deployment."

He gives me a grin. "It was tempting; I liked SDV Team Two. Maybe if I'd got to the teams as an ensign, then I could have done an OIC tour with SDVs and then come to the regular teams for another OIC deployment. But in order to screen for lieutenant commander, I have to deploy as an OIC with a regular team. That's fine. This is a great team, and we have a great platoon."

The Foxtrot AOIC is Lieutenant Sean Quinlan. He is not a big man, perhaps five-nine and 150 pounds. He grew up in Boston and graduated from the Naval Academy in 1998. Quinlan spent seven years in the Sea Scouts in junior high and high school. The Sea Scouts, more often than not, is a route for young men and women who are interested in sea service, but they normally enlist in the Navy. Sean Quinlan took his Sea Scout experience to Annapolis. There he participated in the offshore sailing squadron and captained one of the Academy's forty-four-foot racing sloops. But the SEAL selection committee, the same one that also passed on Dan Canapa in 1996, elected not to take him in their draft of sixteen new ensigns from the Annapolis Class of '98. This is not unusual, as many of the Naval Academy ensigns are culled from the varsity athletic teams. So Quinlan went to sea. He qualified as a surface warfare officer on a guided missile frigate and entered BUD/S with Class 236.

Those of you who have read *The Warrior Elite,* the prequel to this book, know that I went to great lengths to identify the traits that a young man must have or must develop to be a SEAL warrior. If a simple selection process were all that it took, then much of the gauntlet that is BUD/S would be unnecessary. There were ensigns in BUD/S Class 228 who came directly from the Annapolis Class of '99 who performed magnificently. There were also ensigns from that same class who didn't make it; one of them was the first man to quit during Hell Week. He was a varsity athlete at the Naval Academy and a strong BUD/S trainee. So why did the selection committee, composed exclusively of veteran Navy SEALs, pass on Sean Quinlan? And on Dan Canapa?

At twenty-six, Quinlan looks like he is about sixteen, so I can imagine what he looked like at twenty-two. It again points to the fact that the heart of a warrior does not necessarily come with what Hollywood would have you believe is the look of a warrior. Perhaps the screeners at Annapolis did Sean Quinlan a favor in not accepting him for direct entry to BUD/S, sending him instead to the fleet. It will, in all probability, cost him a SEAL deployment, but he brings some maturity and two years of fleet experience to the business of being a

SEAL platoon officer. Having been the primary damage control officer on his frigate, he has run a shipboard division and knows the
administrative side of the Navy, for which all platoon officers are
responsible. He has been a leader; he has had to direct the activity of
a group of enlisted professionals, and he has been responsible for
their performance and well-being. That leadership experience served
Sean Quinlan well during his BUD/S and SQT training.

Yet leadership aboard ship is different from leadership in a small
combat unit and in a warrior culture like the SEALs. Like Sean
Quinlan, I came to the teams from a surface warship. There was no
other way for me, because no Annapolis graduates were allowed to
come directly to BUD/S at that time. The few of us who got to the
teams all went to sea first. Aboard ship, the officer and enlisted duties
are more segregated than in the teams; officers are more mid-level
managers and the enlisted men are more like technicians. The advice
of Mike Loo—"It takes a shooter to lead a shooter"—did not apply
aboard ship. Perhaps that is why the relationship between officers
and men aboard ship is so different than it is in the SEAL teams.

Navy SEALs are intelligent, proud, determined, resourceful,
aggressive, persistent—and the list goes on. But they also are very
adaptive to their environment and culture. It has been my observation that while they can be very independent, one of the reasons they
are in the teams is that they are group-centric animals. They want to
belong. And they will conform to the norms and the culture of the
team and the platoon—especially the platoon. If there is an alpha
wolf in the platoon pack, it is the platoon chief. The ultimate authority lies with the platoon OIC and, in his absence, the AOIC, but both
rely heavily on the experience and guidance of their chief. Generally
speaking, there is only one chief petty officer per platoon—or perhaps it is fair to say that there is room for only one chief petty officer in each platoon. If one of the first class petty officers makes chief,
unless it happens well into the platoon workup and deployment, he
will leave the platoon, much like a young bull will leave the herd
when he grows to maturity and the old bull refuses to give ground.

The platoon chief is usually the oldest man in the platoon and the most experienced. Every SEAL officer's goal is to become a platoon OIC; every enlisted SEAL's goal is to become a platoon chief.

Chief Glenn Schroeder was a senior first class petty officer in Bravo Platoon at SEAL Team Three when he learned that he had been advanced to chief petty officer. The platoon was well into its predeployment training, and Schroeder, the platoon leading petty officer, had worked very hard to get Three Bravo combat ready. It was his fourth platoon. He and the Bravo platoon chief worked very well together; they were also close friends. But with the standing up of SEAL Team Seven, there was a need for senior petty officer talent at the new team, and Schroeder suddenly found himself in a platoon with two chief petty officers. His reputation had preceded him to Team Seven, and he was quickly slotted as platoon chief for one of the new platoons.

Glenn Schroeder is thirty-three years old, perhaps average for a SEAL chief petty officer, but he looks much younger. He graduated with BUD/S Class 177. He grew up in Houston, joined the Navy in 1989, and went into SEAL training right from boot camp. He is married and has two boys.

"I got married right after my first platoon," he told me, "and it's been great, even with the long separations. She understands the business I'm in, so it's never been a problem. And she's done a terrific job with our boys given the amount of time I'm not home."

Schroeder is rated as a parachute rigger, but he is not in Foxtrot Platoon to pack parachutes. His job is to lead, mentor, manage, and train his platoon. Seven Foxtrot began with two men: Lieutenant Canapa and him. As men became available from other teams and commands, Schroeder began to sort through the available talent and build his platoon. He works with the platoon officers; but on most issues concerning personnel, the officers will defer to their platoon chief. Platoon manning is always something of a food fight, and Schroeder had to jockey with the other platoon chiefs at Team Seven to find the best men he could.

"I was able to find a few veterans who were in my previous platoons, guys I knew were solid operators and who had the mix of qualifications we were looking for. And we have four new guys—three from SQT Class 1-02 and one from Class 2-02. That's more new men than I'd like, but I made my calls to BUD/S and SQT to get some good ones. I think we got a great kid from 2-02. He got good marks in SQT."

"Which one?" I ask.

"A kid named Kwan Park, a Korean-American."

I remembered him well. He was still a seaman in SQT, but he was very serious and focused during the advanced training. At the time I thought he would be a solid choice for a new guy in a platoon. "What will he be doing in the platoon?"

"We're going to make him the backup platoon communicator. He's in comm school right now." Chief Schroeder grins. "I told him I expected him to be first in his class—or else."

"What do you look for in a new guy?" I asked.

"We want guys who are self-starters and conscientious, and who will work to fit into the platoon organization. In the platoon, we have six veterans in each of the six department-head jobs: diving, air operations, ordnance, intelligence, communications, and first lieutenant. Each of these men plays a key role in the platoon. Usually no one wants to be the first lieutenant, but I have a man who's very good with boats and motors. He handled first lieutenant in his last platoon and knows the equipment. And I have a great lead comm guy; he's been in comms for two deployments. Everyone coming off deployment now says that communications and real-time imagery is very important. I also need a good man in intel. The intelligence petty officer also has to be sharp. He will play a vital role in mission planning and on those special reconnaissance missions where our primary job is to gather intelligence. I'm lucky; I have two outstanding petty officers in comms and intel. Each of the new men will serve as an assistant to one of my department heads. We try to get them to a department where they have an interest, but sometimes that's not always possible. Then there is the matter of squad assignment. If a department head is in one squad, we want his assistant in the other squad. And we want only two new guys per squad, so we mix and match to make that happen. The chips fall into place, and it usually works well. The guys make it work."

"Any veterans from Afghanistan?"

"Most of my experienced platoon SEALs have deployed to the Gulf, but only one—one of our corpsmen—was downrange. He was in the middle of it, and has a lot of combat medical experience. He also has two Navy commendations for being on the scene at traffic accidents and saving lives. The guy's an incredible medic as well as a great shooter."

Within the Navy shipboard divisions and aviation squadrons, there is the recognized enlisted leadership position of the senior chief petty officer within that division. There is also a key leadership position of the senior non-chief petty officer. This is the leading petty officer, or LPO. Aboard ship, the chief petty officers, like the officers, have their own quarters and dining facilities, and are afforded a separate and more habitable environment. In the berthing compartments where the men live, life is more cramped; there is much less privacy. So the influence and leadership of the senior man in the compartments, the leading petty officer, is a very important one. When I was a division officer aboard a destroyer, my division chief lived in the chief's quarters and I bunked with another officer in a small stateroom. Down in the berthing spaces, my division LPO provided direct supervision and leadership of the enlisted sailors. In my SEAL platoon, my chief and I bunked with the rest of the platoon on deployment; it's that way in the platoons. But there was still a leading petty officer. I asked Chief Schroeder to tell me about the role of a platoon leading petty officer and about Foxtrot Platoon's LPO.

"Our LPO is Rick Gladden. I didn't know him personally, but we made him LPO based on his reputation. He was the leading petty officer at SQT, so we knew we were getting a talented guy. We'd heard nothing but good things about him. We were lucky to get him, and it's worked out very well. If the platoon is working in split squads, I will be in one squad and Rick will be in the other. That way we can support the squad officers. The LPO is chosen for seniority and experience. One usually follows the other, but not always. Sometimes it's difficult for a man to step out of the sled-dog role and take on direct responsibility for the men in the platoon. But it's an important job and a prerequisite to making chief petty officer in the teams. I think the LPO has the toughest job in the platoon. It's like this," Chief Schroeder says with a chuckle. "The LPO is the mother of the platoon and the chief is the father. One of Mom's jobs is to keep Dad happy. Mom also has to make sure that the kids are at the right place at the right time and dressed properly, which means they're in the right uniform and have all the right equipment. If there are problems with the guys, discipline or otherwise, the LPO has to make it right. If the men aren't on time or lack the proper gear, it's the LPO's responsibility. No LPO wants his chief to have to step in and deal with the platoon SEALs on these issues. I know Rick doesn't want me to do this, and I don't think I'll ever have to in Foxtrot Platoon. Rick's doing a terrific job."

I remember Petty Officer First Class Rick Gladden. I first met him in 1999 when he was an STT instructor, before STT became SQT. He was with Mike Loo for three years, and it shows. Gladden is a wall; he's six-two, a solid 225, and hard as nails. He's thirty-one years old and has a degree in sociology and criminal justice from the University of North Carolina. Gladden is a veteran of three platoon deployments at SEAL Team One.

"My job is to monitor the platoon department heads. I give them the latitude to handle the work as they see fit. Bottom line, the job has to get done. I try to lead by example and be a resource for my men."

"Much of the discipline in the platoon rests with you. How do you handle it?"

"I give direction and I set boundaries for what is acceptable and what is not acceptable. The guys know where I stand and where they stand."

"What about the new guys?" I ask.

"As far as I'm concerned, a new guy can't get into trouble. Each new guy works under one of the platoon veterans, usually a department head. If a new guy misbehaves or does something stupid, I go straight for the responsible party—the platoon veteran. That's the way it works in this platoon."

"You like being a platoon LPO?"

"Like it? God help me, I love it!"

The executive committee of a SEAL platoon is called the "top four": OIC, AOIC, chief, and LPO. These four leaders, occasionally with the addition of another key petty officer or an assigned third officer, make the platoon decisions. Collectively or in various combinations, they dictate the life of the platoon. The major issues that concern training, personnel, and administration of the platoon will reflect the collective wisdom of these four men. But when it comes to making the hard or significant decisions, they are invariably made by the OIC with the close consultation of his platoon chief.

Cooperation, chemistry, and professional respect between the platoon chief and platoon OIC is critical. Together, these two men will make it happen. If they don't, Commander Joe Rosen will hold them accountable. Perhaps nowhere else in the American military do an officer and a senior enlisted man in the same unit have the same shared military training and operational experience: As Joe Rosen stands up SEAL Team Seven and works through the myriad of details and issues that confront a special operations commander preparing men for war, nothing will command more of his attention than ensuring that the relationship between his platoon chiefs and platoon OICs is a solid one.

"I have a lot of demands on my time right now with getting this team stood up, getting the new men aboard, and making sure they get to the right schools," Rosen told me, "but I will be making time in my schedule to walk around and watch my platoons work. And I will be spending as much time as I can with the platoon leadership."

At Team Seven there are no platoon third officers, or third-Os.

The standard SEAL platoon configuration is two and fourteen—two officers and fourteen enlisted men. In some teams, new officers, primarily ensigns with no fleet experience, are assigned to platoons as third-Os. This has been standard team practice for a number of years. In this role, they assist with the officer duties as assigned and gain experience. Much of the platoon work is done in squads with the OIC and AOIC serving as squad leaders. Tactically, the third officer then becomes another gun on one of the squads. After a deployment, third-Os move up to the AOIC slot and the AOIC becomes the platoon OIC. Almost always, the platoon OIC and platoon chief move on. But this is not how it is done at Team Seven. Captain Bob Harward, Commander, Naval Special Warfare Group One, has given his SEAL team COs the latitude to use their ensigns fresh from SQT as they see fit. Team Seven platoons will work up with two and fourteen. The new Team Seven ensigns will be tasked with becoming subject-matter experts in areas that will support the operating platoons and serve the deployed SEAL squadron. I ask one of the new officers from SQT Class 2-02 about this.

"I guess it's kind of bittersweet, being a Smee." Smee is team jargon for subject-matter expert. "We all want to get to a platoon and get some operational experience. But the skipper has given us some very interesting taskings. Mine is close air support, or CAS. I'm going to every military school available to become a CAS expert. One of the other Smees is specializing in communications and sniper operations. Another is the mobility Smee; he works with the desert patrol vehicles and Humvees, and yet another is the combatant craft Smee. We even have a guy in school learning to fly drones. Still, we all can't wait to get to a platoon."

During the Vietnam era, SEAL platoons deployed with two officers and twelve enlisted men. Occasionally, one of the officers would be a warrant, and it was not unknown for the platoon AOIC to be a senior chief petty officer. The squad was the basic operational element in Vietnam. It was a squad-size unit business, with variations to fit the mission and requirement. In the 1980s, platoons began to deploy in

sixteen-man configurations. Because there was often a surplus of officers coming into the teams, they began the practice of deploying platoons with a third officer. As with many changes, there was resistance
to this idea. Some of the chiefs and LPOs felt that they were being
asked to baby-sit new officers. But the idea of getting a new officer
immediate platoon experience had many advantages. Chief among
them was that the platoon OIC would be going out on his third
deployment, and that it allowed the new ensign to experience his first
SEAL operations as an operator—often as a pure shooter. OICs and
AOICs typically let the third-Os share the administrative load, leaving most of the tactical leadership decisions to the two senior platoon
officers. Third-Os are often consulted, but they seldom participate in
platoon and squad leadership decisions. After a while, the senior petty
officers got used to the practice, and liked having the third-Os doing
an apprenticeship, of sorts, in the ranks.

"I like to see them in the file dragging a sixty and about four hundred rounds of 7.72," one platoon chief told me. "Then when it
comes his time to lead, he'll know what it's like for his AW man back
there humping the pig and a big load of ammo."

The platoon chiefs and LPOs felt it gave them a chance to help
groom their future platoon officers. Now that there is the prospect of
a change that would remove the third-Os from the platoon, most of
the chiefs and LPOs I talked with don't like it. As with most organizations dominated by type A individuals, they have a strong opinion
of the way things should, or should not, be done. They can be resistant to change. But they are team guys, and they will take any situation and make it work.

THE SKILLS

During the six months of PRODEV, SEAL Team Seven will do everything it can to get its individual SEAL operators ready for tràining as
a platoon. Following PRODEV, the individual platoons will enter six

months of Unit Level Training, or ULT. Among the SEALs, they simply call it platoon training. To prepare for this most important component of the deployment workup, the platoons must bring a diverse collective skill set to the ULT phase of predeployment training. The PRODEV period is when this preparation takes place. This range and balance of individual skills will keep the platoon SEALs busy for the entire PRODEV period. Commander Rosen will also insist that his SEALs who have leave on the books take it during this period. There will be breaks in the deployment workup during ULT and the team-to-squadron transition, but only a day or two here and there. He also knows that his veterans who have just come back off deployment need time to reconnect with their families, and perhaps even time away from the teams.

I found that there are two skill sets that govern individual SEAL training in preparation for platoon training. One is the instruction from Naval Special Warfare Command that presents a set list of qualifications that relate to the administration and the safe operation of a platoon in a training environment. Each platoon must have a certain number of men in the platoon with these qualifications and certifications, including jumpmasters, diving supervisors, range safety officers, riggers, aircraft loadmasters, rappel masters, and fast-rope masters. The list goes on and on. The schools and courses that confer these certifications range in length from several days to a week. These qualifications allow SEALs to train with the prescribed safety and supervisory requirements established by WARCOM. There are administrative platoon requirements that mandate that some members in the platoon be trained in the proper handling of classified material and military instructions. There are very specific skills required by a set number of men in the platoon, such as qualified snipers, SEALs qualified in the use of Stinger ground-to-air missiles, men trained in SEAL communications, and men who have had formal training in chemical-biological environments. Then there are a few individual qualifications that certain members of the platoon must bring with them; there is simply not enough time during

PRODEV to accomplish this training due to the course length. A platoon will typically have two corpsmen who have successfully completed the Army Eighteen Delta and the Navy Special Operations Technician certification, training that can take up to a year or more. The WARCOM instruction states that at least eight platoon SEALs will be HALO parachute (military free-fall) qualified and all must have completed Survival, Evasion, Resistance, and Escape (SERE) School. By the book, there is much individual training required of the platoon SEALs.

The second skill set is one that is recommended by the ULT trainers at the NSW Groups. There is a great deal of overlap in what the WARCOM instruction mandates and what NSW Group training cadres want their platoons to have prior to entering ULT training. The ULT core requirements reflect that which is needed to train a SEAL platoon to go to war today. This is based on a continuing flow of information from deployed squadrons—what they find they need but may not have. In light of 9/11, the ongoing commitments in Afghanistan, Iraq, and the Philippines, and the prospect of future conflict in the Middle East and possibly central Asia, there is a great deal of focus on unit training to address contingencies in these AOs. And there is a great deal of focus on land warfare. So the Naval Special Warfare Group One and Group Two Training Detachments, or TRADETs, tell the platoons what they need to have accomplished when they show up for Unit Level Training. Huge whiteboards are found in the Team Seven spaces with the names of SEALs along the left-hand margin. Across the top margin are listings of schools and qualifications. Much of what the PRODEV period is about is to get the proper number of Xs in the right boxes.

Platoons entering ULT must be ready to conduct combat-swimmer operations in accordance with current SQT course-training standards. This means each platoon SEAL must have all his personal diving gear and combat-swimmer equipment properly configured and ready for training. He must be current on the LAR V Draeger. He must also check his in-water trim and have his pace count, with and without a limpet mine, recently calibrated. In the classroom, the platoon SEALs have to conduct a refresher on diving medicine and underwater emergency procedures. For the new guys out of SQT, these are all current skills, and they have up-to-date information. For some of the platoon veterans, the last time they prepared to conduct combat-swimmer operations was during their last predeployment training. All this is to prepare them for three weeks of unit-level combat-swimmer training.

Platoon SEALs have to begin platoon training with their shooting skills in order, both pistol and rifle. They are required to shoot only a marksmanship score, but in practice, all SEALs are expected to shoot expert on the standard Navy pistol and rifle course. On the range, each SEAL is expected to have his M4 rifle zeroed in at three hundred yards. There are also requirements for the individual SEAL operators to sight in their primary and secondary close-quarter combat weapons, and to perform combat-proficiency drills. Basically, SEAL platoons in PRODEV have to put themselves through a mini SQT weapons training course to bring their skills up to par for Unit Level Training. During ULT, approximately half of the platoon or squad training involves shooting drills or scenario-based training with live ammunition. Platoon SEALs are expected to be able to shoot individually and as a team, and shoot well. They will report to ULT with all their personal weapons, iron sights, and scopes sighted in and calibrated. These are the weapons with which they will go to war.

There are a number of qualifications for which the skill set is perishable, and for which requalification is either prudent or required. In the way of land navigation, the platoons in PRODEV will have conducted navigation drills with map and compass and with GPS. They are to have maintained current static-line and free-fall qualifications. All are to have had level-one training in Close Quarter Defense, the same course given during SQT. All SQT graduates have this when they get to their teams. Those few veteran SEALs who may have missed this training during their last predeployment workup will try to find an opportunity during PRODEV to get to a CQD class. All platoon SEALs must attend a full week's formal training on operations in a chemical or biological environment. This includes recognizing and assessing an enemy's capability from the perspective of strategic reconnaissance missions to conducting special operations in this environment. There is a medical refresher in PRODEV that is a full and comprehensive review of tactical combat casualty care. All platoon SEALs must have and maintain an American Heart Association CPR qualification. And there are a host of fieldcraft items that include preparation and refinement of their first, second, and third line gear. They must have all this gear, collectively called load-bearing equipment (LBE), fully waterproofed and neutral in the water so they can conduct over-the-beach operations with any or all of it, and tow it behind them on a long swim. There is day and night imagery training, and everyone in the platoon must be able to capture, download, and electronically transmit digital imagery.

These are the basics—the individual skills that each platoon SEAL must have and be current in to begin Unit Level Training. The skills, for the most part, are not new, but they have to be practiced individually and, when possible, as a team. There are many more skills that fall into the "better-to-have" or "we'll-need-this" category. Commander Joe Rosen and his platoon commanders will do what they can to cram this training into their six months of PRODEV. The deployed SEAL squadrons and platoons are sending back a constant stream of information and lessons learned that will alter some of the things the platoons do, both in PRODEV and ULT. There are a number of core skills worth mentioning that the platoons must have as a result of training that may get pushed into the six-month PRODEV period, or may only be accomplished when a SEAL is pulled out of the deployment rotation for this highly specialized or technical training. A few of the men from SQT Class 2-02 will have the chance get some of this course work in before they get to their first team assignment. One of those from Class 2-02 is Petty Officer Mark Garrison.

Mark Garrison is from Chicago and has a degree in history from Southern Illinois. After several years of teaching high school history and social science, he decided he wanted to be a warrior and a healer. At twenty-eight, he was one of the oldest men in BUD/S Class 237. After graduating from SQT with 2-02, he was sent to Fort Bragg for the Army Eighteen Delta corpsman training. The Joint Special Operations Medical Training Course conducts training for all Army Special Forces and SEAL corpsmen. The school also trains Air Force special operations personnel and Ranger medics. Graduates of this program are qualified paramedics and experts in combat casualty care. SEAL corpsmen periodically rotate back through this Army facility to update their qualifications. All students train at a $25 million facility where they learn a full range of clinical and diagnostic skills—skills they learn in a laboratory setting, then practice under field conditions. Eighteen Delta students are also sent to civilian hospitals where they train in civilian emergency room and trauma centers. They even get to deliver babies.

"This course is meeting all my expectations and then some," Garrison told me. I first met him during SQT and was glad to see a Navy face at this Army facility. He's not the only one; there are several other SEALs-in-training and a senior SEAL corpsman on the Eighteen Delta staff. "There's a lot to learn. We get a lot of training on infectious diseases—what to look for and how to make diagnoses. SF medics have to learn how to deal with everything from malaria to intestinal parasites. We're here mostly for the trauma and treating battlefield casualties, but we get it all. I can't wait to get back to the teams. I have to admit that Fayetteville, North Carolina, is not San Diego, California, but they treat us well here. And what I'm learning will help my platoon—when I get to my platoon."

The course is conducted in two phases. First there is the twenty-two-week Special Operations Combat Medic Course that emphasizes combat trauma. Then there is the twenty-four-week Advanced Special Operations Medic Course. This latter course qualifies special operations medics for independent duty and the Eighteen Delta certification. The teams often send SEALs for the first course, then rotate them back for the advanced course after an operational deployment. In Garrison's case, he will be at Fort Bragg for a full year or more before returning to the teams.

"Do you ever wish that you hadn't become a corpsman? You'd be training for deployment right now."

"I think about that a lot. If we go to Iraq, a few of the guys in my class will probably see action there. I hope the trauma care I'm learning here is never needed, but this war on terror isn't going to end anytime soon. When I do get to my platoon, I'll be ready to do the job."

"How do you get on with the other students in the class?"

"Oh, they give us SEALs a hard time and call us squids, but it's all good fun. We get close to our Army and Air Force classmates, but it's not the same as BUD/S or even SQT. They're good guys, but they're not team guys."

"How much longer?" I ask.

Garrison looks at his watch and does a quick mental calculation. "Seventy-three days. Then it's on to Virginia and SEAL Team Two. I can't wait."

Several men from SQT Class 2-02 are scheduled for SEAL communications school. Each deploying SEAL platoon must, at a minimum, have two communicators. In my time they were simply called radiomen, because they carried the tactical radio in the field. Their only job was to talk to support elements and to call for air support. At that time we had only a single backpack radio with a range of only a few miles. All that has changed, and the change is ongoing. The six-week comm course is a standing requirement for platoon communicators. Because of the evolution of technology, they must go through this training every deployment cycle. Some new SEALs from 2-02 will attend the course along with veteran SEALs from their team.

Like most SEAL training, the NSW Communications Course is conducted by the Naval Special Warfare Center in Coronado. The course was developed and is conducted by Ken Reeves. Ken is a civilian communications specialist, and it's his job to train SEALs, both regular and SDV-team SEALs, Special Warfare Combatant Craft (SWCC) crewmen, explosive ordnance disposal (EOD) specialists assigned to the SEAL squadrons, and the communication technicians of the NSW mobile communications teams. Reeves is your basic techie—middle-aged and a little overweight with an affable, easy smile. He's turned out in a short-sleeved white shirt with a plastic pocket protector and a striped tie. He knows radios like BUD/S trainees know about cold water, and he has a very important job. Basically, it's his responsibility to train SEALs, and all those who may have to support SEALs, in standard military and special operations communications. Communications are critical to special operations.

"The radios change constantly," Ken says, handing me a PRC-148 intersquad radio, "so we have to continually change and update our training. There are a number of radios in our inventory and many radios used by other military units, so we have to know about all of them. A great deal of our work is done with satellite communications, and SATCOM technology is cell phone technology. When it works, it works great, and since most of our radios have embedded cryptology and frequency-hopping capability, it's very secure. Nice thing is, the radios keep getting better, smaller, and easier to operate. But the guys still have to know how to communicate if the SATCOM goes down, or they have to operate in an area where there is no satellite coverage. Depending on location or operational security considerations, they may have to do it the old-fashioned way with high-frequency radios.

"We spend a lot of time with HF communication, as well as with UHF and VHF, but mostly with HF. If SATCOM isn't an option, they have to know how to bounce and bend radio waves off the ionosphere. So it's important that they know how to rig tactical antennas and to improvise to get the right antenna length for their designated frequency. It takes a little time and practice. We have an FTX where we set up a base station at La Posta, and we send them out in teams in vans all over the Southwest. They travel a five- to six-hundred-mile loop and make SATCOM and HF comm checks."

"You mean," I ask with a straight face, "that you have SEALs out in Arizona at roadside rest stops stringing wire and phoning home?"

"That's it," Reeves laughs, "just like the Verizon commercials on TV. 'Can you hear me now?' It's a lot of fun for the guys and very competitive. The SEALs don't like to lose at anything, but some of the comm techs from the mobile comm teams, or MCTs, are very sharp. It keeps everyone on their toes. This is one of the few courses where the SEALs train directly with their support elements. It's good for the SEALs and their support guys to learn to communicate here before they have to do it for real on deployment. For the SEALs and the boat crews, the success of the mission and their lives may depend on communications. We take it seriously in this course, but we do have a lot of fun."

"What about computers?" I ask. "You teach that here as well, right?"

"That's right. The SEALs will go on an operation with a mix of radios, depending on the mission, but they almost never leave the forward operating base without a computer. We use an NT-based platform that we call a toughbook. It's a ruggedized PC designed to interface with our radios and cameras. All NSW comm types have to know how to handle a computer and how to transmit voice, data, and imagery. When they get back to their platoons, they will show the other platoon SEALs how to do it. The computer helps us do this and do it faster. We cram a great deal into this six-week course. In addition to the field work, there is a written final. If the students don't perform to standard, we don't certify them for deployment as communicators."

"You have Petty Officer Park in one of your comm classes," I say to Ken. "How's he doing?"

Reeves hesitates a moment. "Oh, yeah, Park. Sharp kid and a hard worker. He's doing very well."

"Any chance he might graduate number one in the class?" I clearly remember the explicit instructions given him by his platoon chief.

Ken considers this. "Possibly, but as I said, some of the comm techs from the MCT are awfully sharp."

SEALs receive language training at the basic tactical level and, on occasion, on a full-immersion basis. The latter involves living with a family of native speakers for an extended period of time. Normally, language training is not as intense as that received by the Army Special Forces, whose primary mission is to live with and train irregular foreign allied forces. The teams are now seeing a number of Hispanics with native or near-native Spanish, and a few French speakers. A selected few with some background or aptitude are sent to the Defense Language Institute in Monterey, California, for a year of language training. With the current focus on the Middle East, most deploying platoons will have two or three men who have had a course in modern standard Arabic. It's a three-month course that is taught by a civilian, bilingual contractor who has native Arabic skills. Arabic is a difficult language, and there are many dialects throughout the Arab world. Several of the Foxtrot Platoon SEALs at Team Seven were scheduled for this short course in Arabic.

"Basically, we learn some tactically useful vocabulary," one of the Team Five SEALs told me. He was a member of BUD/S Class 228 and preparing for his second deployment. "It's enough that we can conduct a field interrogation and make ourselves understood at a very basic level. What I personally got out of the course was an appreciation for their culture and how these people think—what they value. I think now I know enough to not be impolite and the proper way to show respect. That can be very important when you come into some village carrying a gun. I'd like to think it can help me contribute to the mission."

"Think the war will wait for you?" At the time, Team Five was just finishing its platoon training and was six months from its scheduled deployment date—mid-April 2003. The platoons at Team Five know they could be deployed early if they were needed.

"We talk about that, and there're lots of rumors. We'll go when we're told and do what we have to do. In the meantime, we'll train as hard as we can. My wife and I just had a new baby; it's our first. I'm just thankful for the time I do get at home. But if we have to go early, we'll be ready—I'll be ready."

SEAL snipers are a very important component of a SEAL platoon, and their capabilities consist of more than just long-range shooting. Sniper training is one of the most sought-after courses in the teams and usually reserved for veteran SEALs coming off their first or second deployment. By the book, a platoon is required to have two snipers, but most platoons I observed had four. In recent times, SEALs have sent their sniper candidates to the Marine Corps for training or even to the Army Marksmanship Unit at Fort Benning, Georgia. Now, with few exceptions, SEAL snipers are trained in-house at the Naval Special Warfare Center. The Center has taken ownership of this training due to the SEAL-specific sniper requirements and the nonshooting skills the platoons need of their snipers. The course is a combination of the Photo Intelligence Course, or PIC, and a precision shooting-and-stalking course.

"It takes us twelve weeks to get a guy through this training, and it's a very demanding course. There are a lot of eighteen-hour days; it's hard on the students, and it's hard on us. This is a premier course at the Center, and a lot of guys want to come here. But not all of them make it; not all of them are cut out to be snipers. A few of them, good SEALs—solid platoon guys—don't complete this course. It's just not for everyone."

Senior Chief Bob Greenwood runs the sniper course. He was a First Phase instructor at BUD/S and is a very experienced SEAL operator. He is a veteran of Teams Two and Eight and saw action during the Gulf War. As he winds down his career in Naval Special

Warfare, he was asked to take the operational taskings within the various SEAL mission profiles and develop a course to support those requirements. While it takes a shooter to lead a shooter, it also takes a shooter to train a shooter. The senior chief is a good shooter—and even more important, he's a great trainer. Before a sniper candidate touches a gun in sniper training, he must complete the two-week PIC course.

The Photo Intelligence Course is run by John Connors. He's a first class photographer's mate and an expert in tactical photography. His father was a professional photographer, and John studied photography at the Rochester Institute of Technology before he joined the Navy. The snipers come to him to learn photography first. Precision shooting and photography might seem like an unlikely combination, but SEAL snipers—or more accurately, scout-snipers—typically have the best fieldcraft skills in the platoon. If the mission is special reconnaissance, or SR, then it is the snipers who will creep forward to the objective. And if it's an SR mission, they will make the shot with a camera, not a rifle.

"I have them for two weeks, and we take a lot of pictures," Connors told me, "and it's all digital photography. The great thing about digital work is that you can see the results immediately, but they still have to learn to shoot in low-light-level conditions. Later on with the guns it will be elevation and windage. Here they work with shutter speed and f-stops. We have them out working most nights. As with conventional cameras, they learn to 'fool' the camera in order to capture an image under limited-light conditions. Then they have to learn how to take the images and prepare them for transmission back to higher headquarters. That's the communicator's job, but we want our guys to know how to do it as well."

"That means computers, right?"

"That's right. Most of these guys have some computer skills, but some just know how to send and retrieve e-mail. When they leave here they can set up and manage image files in a database, download images from the camera, and prepare images for tactical SATCOM transmission. We get through that as quickly as possible and get them on the cameras, shooting pictures. And, of course, we do a lot of telephoto work." Connors grins. "We send them out on urban tactical missions. The team COs are getting a little tired of getting bagged on 'Candid Camera.' Just yesterday one of the guys came in with a great shot of his CO fumbling with his car keys on his way to work, well before the sun was up. This is not portrait photography; we want these guys capturing images in the most challenging environments—long range, in the rain, in the fog, at night, whatever. And the technology is always changing. We're now starting to do a lot of work with tactical video systems. Real-time, long-range, secure tactical video is not that far off."

After the PIC course, the students begin ten weeks of scout-sniper. This breaks down to about four weeks of scouting, or stalking, and six weeks of shooting. Toward the end of the training, the student snipers will be many hours on a stalk to take a single shot. Sniping is a subtle blend of art, technology, and patience. The success of the sniper is that proper blend of the right man and the right gun—or the right camera. The scout-sniper staff at the Center are senior petty officers who have extensive operational and shooting experience. Collectively, they have been to just about all the military, civilian, and federal law enforcement precision-shooting schools, and many foreign military sniper schools. I ask Senior Chief Greenwood what he looks for in a sniper candidate.

"First of all, they have to come to us shooting well with iron sights, preferably well above the standard expert level. And they have to come to learn. I'd rather have a guy with good personal discipline than natural shooting ability. Most of our shooters are veteran SEALs, although we see a new guy now and then. Sometimes it's easier to teach a new guy because he hasn't been shooting that long and hasn't acquired too many bad habits. And given the nonshooting requirements of the platoon snipers, we like it if they have a communications background, but it's not a requirement."

During the scouting portion of the course, the students learn the basics of stalking and all the cover and concealment artistry that go along with that patient skill set. They also learn observation techniques, range estimation, and sketching techniques. At times a sketch, made over time with carefully noted observations, is more valuable than a digital image. SEALs are often called upon to move quietly for extended periods of time to get close to a target. Their mission may be to make observations for a future direct-action operation or in support of a precision air strike. In Afghanistan, they waited and watched an area for days before the Marines landed at what would become Camp Rhino. In another instance, they moved in silently to observe an al-Qaeda compound that was targeted for an air strike. The compound housed the personal residence of Osama bin Laden's physician. On close inspection by a scout-sniper team, it was learned that the compound was largely inhabited by women and children. The air strike was canceled. In Iraq, they performed SR missions associated with the oil platforms at Umm Qasr before conducting the direct-action mission to seize the platforms. There can be any number of missions for a SEAL scout-sniper. Just one of them may be long-range shooting.

SEAL snipers were busy in both Afghanistan and Iraq. Since most of the Afghan operations were, and still are, in rugged, open country, there's ample opportunity for long-range shooting. More than a few Taliban and al-Qaeda fighters have died instantly and unexpectedly from a SEAL sniper bullet. In Iraq, most sniper work was counter-sniper operations. SEALs on patrol in urban terrain feel much better when they move under the protective eye of a sniper. Sniper teams watch their teammates, or simply find a good perch and wait for some luckless enemy soldier or Fedayeen Saddam to take a shot at a member of the coalition forces.

Within the military sniper communities, there is much debate as to who are the best shooters. SEALs tell me that the Marines have historically been the best, and that they still teach good fieldcraft, but that their snipers have poor equipment and don't get enough bullets through the guns they do have.

"I went to the Marine sniper school a few years ago," a SEAL from Team Five told me, "and I was shooting as good as their instructors—with my gun. Then one of their instructors took my gun and *really* did some incredible shooting. I think we shoot a lot better than they do now; we have better training, and we have better guns."

The Army Marksmanship Unit boasts the best military shooters, but they are professional shooters and do nothing but shoot. Few of them make operational deployments, but many Olympic shooters come from the AMU. One thing that is not in doubt is that student shooters in the SEAL course put more bullets downrange than in other sniper training schools, and they do this with a variety of rifles. The SEAL sniper armory is a veritable smorgasbord of sniper weapons.

SEALs entering sniper training are quite familiar with the M4 and the M14. During SEAL scout-sniper they will fire the MK4, a refined version of the standard M4 with special optics and a night-vision scope. The sniper M14s are specially configured from high-grade components for precision shooting using state-of-the-art scopes and match-grade ammunition. We seldom used snipers in Vietnam, but when we did my SEALs used this same M14 with a 10X Redfield scope. If there is a "standard" sniper rifle in the teams, it is the Stoner SR-25, a semiautomatic rifle that shoots a 172-grain, .308 round. This allows a SEAL sniper to reach out to eight hundred yards or more and engage a target with multiple rounds. Perhaps the most popular rifle among SEAL snipers is the .300 Winchester Magnum. The WinMag 300 fires a 190-grain round and is accurate out to twelve hundred yards—about three quarters of a mile. The SEALs like the gun for the same reason hunters do; the trajectory of the round is flat and the bullet is fast and heavy, which translates to accurate long-range shooting. The heavyweight in the SEAL sniper-gun locker is the .50-caliber sniper rifle. This weapon is deadly out to two thousand yards and is typically used for hard targets like vehicles, a parked aircraft, or a radar installation. Basically, the .50 is shoulder-fired artillery—a heavy-caliber weapon, and used primarily when the mission calls for surgically disabling a hard target. I'm not a particularly good shot, but when I fired the .50, I was able to hit a fifty-five-gallon oil drum at fourteen hundred yards and hit it consistently.

The joke is that you can always recognize a SEAL sniper in training because he walks around with one shoulder lower than the other from the kick of the weapons. A student shooter will get as many as 100 rounds a day through the WinMag 300 and up to 150 with the M14 or the SR-25. Forty rounds with the .50 caliber is a big day. But shooting is just a part of it. The real skill is getting the gun to the advanced firing position (AFP). The SEALs train on the ranges at Camp Pendleton for much of their shooting, but the long stalks take place at Camp Billy Machen. You can usually tell the student snipers at Billy Machen—they look like tramps in a train yard. These are men who spend their waking hours in the dirt. A shot may require that a student sniper take six hours to cross a mile or two of open desert. They don't crawl, they slither, carefully working their way to get to a good AFP. All for a single shot. That's the snipers credo: one shot, one kill. Most people have seen snipers in their shaggy, woodland-pattern Gillie suits. In the desert, they look like dun-colored lumps to blend with the sand and hardpan.

"It's incredibly hard work and takes all your concentration to make a good stalk," one of the student snipers told me. "You may study a dry wash for ten minutes before you decide how you're going to cross it, or how to get over a rise without creating a silhouette. You have a timeline, but you have to balance the timeline with moving carefully—not too fast, not too slow. Then, when you get to the AFP, it's a different game. Your mental focus goes into making the shot. That means you have to slow your breathing, slow your pulse, and very carefully get your gun ready for the shot. No matter how much water I drink, I lose about five pounds on a long stalk, and I feel like I just came off a ten-mile ruck hump."

"Just for the one shot?"

"That's right. One shot, one kill."

As I watched Foxtrot Platoon at Team Seven and other platoons during PRODEV, I was struck by a common thread: BUD/S, SQT, and the culture of the teams have left their mark on these men. They have no notion of an eight-hour day. If their training calls for twelve- or fourteen-hour days, they do it. This is not unusual, especially if the trainers are SEALs, nor is it unexpected or resented. The adage that a SEAL must "train as you fight" is not an empty phrase—training for the fight is not a nine-to-five business. The guys work very hard, and this is the time during the operational workup when they will have the most time off—and with their families.

More than ever, SEALs know that they are training for the fight, so they do all in their power to prepare themselves to contribute to the warfighting ability of their platoon. And that is what they will do for the next six months—train to fight as a platoon.

CHAPTER 5

The Platoon

THE TRAINING DETACHMENT

Okay, if everyone will find a seat, we can get started. This will be your in-briefing for platoon training. For those of you who don't know me, my name is Brian Schmidt. For the next six months you are all assigned to the Group One Training Detachment for your platoon workup. It's called Unit Level Training or ULT here, but it's still platoon training. TRADET will exercise TACON [tactical control] over you; you belong to us and we are responsible for your training. It's a big job, and it's an important job. We take it very seriously. It's a job that won't get done unless we work together. We have to work hard, and you have to work hard. So I want to get a few issues on the table—talk about our expectations of you and your expectations of us. Some of you are new to the teams; some of you were in the teams when I was in high school. I have my job; you have your job. This is serious business, and I don't want there to be any misunderstanding of our role and your role."

Lieutenant Commander Brian Schmidt is the OIC of the Naval

Big punch. SEALs train with a variety of shoulder-fired rockets. Here, an SQT student prepares to launch an AT4 rocket. *Photo by Dick Couch*

Special Warfare Group One Training Detachment, or TRADET. He is also an officer with an immense responsibility; he is the man tasked with preparing SEAL platoons for war. Prior to NSW 21, each SEAL team maintained a training cell tasked with training their team's platoons for deployment. The Naval Special Warfare Groups on each coast then evaluated the platoons and certified them operationally ready for deployment. Now the NSW Groups do it all. Schmidt gathered the talent from the team training cells and the group evaluation cadres, and built the Group One Training Detachment. There are eighty-six men in the training detachment. Chief Warrant Officer Mike Loo at SQT might argue the point, but SEAL instructors at the Group One TRADET, and their counterparts at Group Two on the East Coast, represent possibly the richest concentration of SEAL talent in the Naval Special Warfare community. The petty officers range from master chiefs to second class petty officers. The men they have to train are no longer trainees or students in BUD/S or SQT. At a minimum, they are all qualified SEALs. Most are highly experienced and talented SEAL operators, many with combat experience. Schmidt and his training cadre have to train them all, and train them to a standard. The platoon SEALs understand this; indeed, their life in the operating platoons is one of constant training. That they have done this before in preparation for their last deployment is not at issue. This does not mean that the training cadre does not have to exercise some refined ego management skills, nor can they forget that the SEALs they are training may possess expertise in some areas that exceed their own. Nonetheless, the trainers must train, and the platoons must use this time to build and hone their combat skills. The bottom line is that everyone understands this. Lives depend on this understanding.

The platoons come to Brian Schmidt and ULT with their individual qualification updated and validated. In this ULT rotation, the platoons are from SEAL Team Five. Some of the platoons have been able to accomplish some team training during their PRODEV period— perhaps they fit in a week of close-quarter defense training or work on some squad patrolling drills—but most of their work has been devoted to individual skills. Now it's time to build the team.

"As we begin this training period, I want to share with you my philosophy on SEAL platoon training. We are here to train SEAL warriors, period. You are here to train to go into combat. That means you have to work together and take care of each other. This training is hard. This training should be hard, and I don't mean BUD/S or Hell Week hard; it should be harder than BUD/S or Hell Week. We have a lot more responsibility than BUD/S instructors, and you have more on the line than any BUD/S student. You are going to war. In BUD/S or SQT, you had only to do what you were told and take care of yourself. For the most part it was individual training and responsibility. To some extent, this was true even in PRODEV. Now you have the responsibility for your platoon mates as well as yourself. No one wants to go to war with someone who is not ready to fight, so you have to help us see that everyone in the platoon is up to standard and good to go. We have to help each other and train each other.

"I'm going to cover a few things that don't go here. I shouldn't have to say these things, but so there are no misunderstandings, I'm going to say them anyway. I have no time for whiners or guys who don't look out for their teammates. The same goes for those who don't take responsibility for their own actions or who blame others. Take care of your gear; take care of your teammates. I expect you to be professional and accountable at all times. If you have problems at home, get them taken care of. I don't mean to be insensitive, but that is not our job. Time will be in short supply once we get going, and we will not cut you away because there is a problem at home. There are exceptions to this, but you need to get things squared away at home so you can focus on training for war." Schmidt pauses to look at his notes. "We are going to want to know what you think about this training, but not right now or in the middle of a training evolution. Put it in your critique. Unless it's a safety issue, drive on and get the training done. If something is wrong or there's something that we can do better, we'll get it fixed for the next platoons we train.

"Things I expect as the OIC of this training. I expect you to know your people, I expect you to know your equipment, and I expect you to know the routine—to know what is expected in a training evolution and be ready to work to make it happen. I expect you to plan, rehearse, and inspect. Leaders inspect their men before they go on an operation, even a training mission. Leaders get inspected by their teammates. When on a training exercise, I expect you to stay in the game, to stay tactical, and to see it through. If something breaks or there is a problem, stay tactical and fix it; don't go admin. And finally, I expect you to conduct a good debriefing—talk about what went right and what went wrong. Our goal is to see that you get good training. We need your help and cooperation. I know my cadre will work very hard to see that we reach that goal. This is my commitment to all of you. I expect you to be on time for each training evolution, at the right place, and with the right gear. Big-boy rules apply, but no shortcuts; everything you ever learned about safety applies here. There will be a safety briefing before every high-risk training evolution. We want to prepare you for the fight, but we have to train safely so we can get you to the fight. Any questions?"

There are none.

"Thanks for your attention. And now we have a little treat for you. My staff is going to pass out a written exam. Basically, it's much the same as the final exam for SQT. Knowledge on a test may be no substitute for operational experience, but I want to get a baseline on everyone's professional knowledge. It will let you know where you are, and let us know what we may need to concentrate on during your platoon training."

While the members of SEAL Team Five are busy with their examinations, I ask Brian Schmidt what he is going to do with the test scores.

"Post them. Hey, it still pays to be a winner in this game, but it's more than that. It will let some of the old guys know that there is some information they need to work on in order to get current. And it will also let them know that some of the new guys are bringing a lot of good knowledge and information with them from the training command."

"Will you give them the same test at the end of their platoon training?"

"I hadn't really thought about it. Maybe we will."

For ULT, I followed two platoons through the platoon-training phase of their deployment workup. The six SEAL Team Five platoons will be organized into three task units for deployment. The platoons that I observed were Five Echo and Five Foxtrot, and they will comprise Task Unit Charlie. Echo and Foxtrot are sister platoons. These platoons, along with a few SEALs assigned to the task-unit command element, will train together during the platoon workup. Echo, Foxtrot, and Task Unit Charlie make up Team Five's CENTCOM task unit. They will deploy to the Central Command, which means they will have primary responsibility for operating in the Middle East. Given the emerging focus on Iraq and the continuing SOF requirements in Afghanistan, other platoons will also train with an eye to operating in the Middle East, but at Team Five, Echo and Foxtrot are primary. The other four Team Five platoons and Task Units Alpha and Bravo will train and deploy to PACOM, or the Pacific Command. SEAL platoons are very versatile, and once deployed, their AO and mission tasking could be just about anywhere. By the time they deploy, operational requirements may dictate that there be four or more Team Five platoons committed to CENTCOM. All six platoons will receive comparable training, but there will be some theater-specific training, and Task Unit Charlie will do a few things differently from Task Units Alpha and Bravo.

FIVE ECHO AND FIVE FOXTROT

Echo and Foxtrot, as sister platoons, will train together. Because of their Middle East tasking, they will pay particular attention to desert and mountain warfare training. Nonetheless, they will deploy with the same complement of maritime special operations skills as the Team Five platoons with responsibilities in the Pacific Theater. And the four platoons slated for primary duty in the Pacific, Alpha through Delta, could well find themselves with operational tasking in the Middle East. Any platoon at Team Five could find themselves engaged in the Middle East—or in the Philippines, Malaysia, or the Horn of Africa. They know it, and so does the TRADET cadre.

Echo Platoon will train for deployment with two officers and fourteen enlisted men. They lost only three SEALs to the expansion draft to form SEAL Team Seven. And they have three new guys, SEALs who will be making their first deployment. One of the platoon SEALs is from BUD/S Class 228. Another was a BUD/S instructor when Class 228 was in training. Of the two sister platoons, Echo has the most experience, including three first class petty officers. Most of the veterans have made deployments to the Central Command—Gulf deployments, as the platoon SEALs call them. New to the platoon but not new to SEAL platoon duty is Petty Officer Matt Reilly, the shooting instructor from SQT. Reilly finished his tour at the Center and is back for operational duty. Foxtrot Platoon begins platoon training with three officers and fourteen enlisted men, although the third officer may be assigned other duties as Team Five prepares for deployment. Not counting their third-O, Foxtrot has four new SEALs—a high number for a SEAL platoon. One of them is from SQT Class 2-02; he joined the platoon only two months before the start of platoon training. Most of the veterans have experience in the Persian Gulf, and two of them were on the ground in Afghanistan.

Five Echo and Five Foxtrot are typical SEAL platoons. The average age in Echo Platoon is twenty-eight and a half years. Foxtrot is a little younger because of the new men—twenty-seven years. On average, both platoons have about two years of college per man. Even with the youth in Foxtrot, the average deployment experience in both platoons is two deployments per man. Average time in the Navy, or time in service for Echo Platoon, is eight years; for Foxtrot Platoon, seven years. There are four men in each platoon who had prior fleet or non-Navy military experience before they came to the teams. The two platoon rosters, at first glance, would seem to have a typo, because the platoon commanders have the same name. It's not a typo; the OICs of these sister platoons are brothers.

Lieutenant John Rasmussen is the OIC of Five Echo. Echo Rasmussen graduated from BUD/S Class 218. He has been a third-O and an AOIC and completed both of these deployments at Team Five. He will be going back on this deployment with platoon command experience. On his last deployment, his OIC became ill, and he completed the tour as the platoon OIC. Phil Rasmussen, eleven months older than John, graduated with BUD/S Class 216. He has *four* deployments behind him; one as an AOIC and two as a SEAL task-unit liaison officer—once aboard a carrier and once in Europe. Liaison tours for officers do not require the lengthy workup period of a platoon deployment. Still, Phil Rasmussen has been overseas a great deal. He returned to the West Coast from his tour in Europe not long after 9/11. A week later, he found himself in Kandahar on the Special Operations Task Force, South. Now that he's back in the platoons, he's Foxtrot Rasmussen. These two brothers seemed almost destined to be in the teams. They grew up in San Diego, and their dad was a Vietnam-era frogman. Both were water polo standouts in high school and both played rugby in college, John at UCLA and Phil at Long Beach State. They were both good ruggers, but Phil was a little better; he was a first-team All-American for three years. Both attended Officer Candidate School and went directly to BUD/S from OCS. I was proud to have a hand in this; I interviewed them both as candidates for BUD/S. I can assure you that these men are not the same fresh-faced college grads I met back in 1996.

"Just when did they decide they wanted to be SEALs?" I asked their dad. I did not know him on active duty, but we served together in the Naval Reserve.

"You want the real reason or the politically correct reason?"

"How about both?"

"While they were growing up, they saw how much fun I was having on the weekends in the reserves. They've wanted to do this ever since they were little boys. They didn't play cowboys and Indians; they played frogmen. The PC answer, which is also true, is that they are both very patriotic. They feel very strongly about serving their country."

"You have to be proud of them," I offered.

"I am; very much so. I'm also a little worried. They're still my boys, and they both will be going in harm's way."

"It was just the same for us back in the late sixties," I remind him, "when we volunteered for BUD/S, remember?"

"Yes, I do remember," he replies, "but it is not the same, not for me. These are my boys. You don't have any kids, do you?"

"No," I replied. He knows that I don't, but he felt the need to remind me. And rightly so. I can share his feelings as an old warrior, but not as the father of a warrior, let alone two warriors.

The AOICs are both Naval Academy graduates. Lieutenant Sam Crenshaw of Echo Platoon has a third-O tour behind him, which qualifies him as a one-tour wonder. He graduated from Annapolis, Class of '97, and from BUD/S Class 221. He is from Fresno, California. Lieutenant Todd Bollinger came to BUD/S after a tour aboard a guided missile frigate and is a surface-warfare qualified officer: Naval Academy, Class of '98; BUD/S Class 235. He will make his first deployment as AOIC of Foxtrot Platoon. Only Foxtrot Platoon will have an assigned third-O. He will train with the platoon when he can, but he will be detached part of the time to attend UAV (unmanned aerial vehicles) school. Unmanned drones are becoming an increasingly important surveillance platform, a mission for which SEALs are often tasked. What Predator drones and the new Global Star drones can and cannot do will affect future SEAL mission tasking.

The Echo Platoon senior leadership is with Chief Petty Officer Cal Rutledge and Leading Petty Officer John Lopez. Rutledge, another Californian, will be going out on his fifth SEAL deployment. He is a quiet, firm man with an easy smile. At thirty-seven, he is the oldest man in either platoon. Chief Rutledge recently returned to Team Five from a tour at SQT. He has had two deployments with Team Five and two with Team One. Lopez is Puerto Rican and has had three deployments, all with Team Five. Both have attended college, but neither is a college graduate. They have a great deal of experience in this platoon, and one or the other has been on deployment with everyone in the platoon but the new men. I ask Chief Rutledge how he manages his platoon.

"The heart of a good platoon are those second class petty officers going out on their second or third deployment, and we have several. We also have two very capable first class petty officers besides John. They know the business, and we know what they're capable of doing. They've had all the schools, and they have a great deal of experience. I'm lucky; I have proven performers assigned in all the platoon departments. We have four good snipers and one of the teams' best combat shooters in Matt Reilly. My job is to see that they perform at the top of their game. In many cases, it's giving them the job and staying out of their way. Nothing pleases me more than when some other platoon's comm guy has to come to my comm guy because he needs to know how to do something. I want all my E-5s and E-6s to become LPOs and go on to become platoon chiefs."

"How do you handle discipline in the platoon?"

"Unless it's something serious, it stays in the platoon. These guys are here because they want to be in the fight. For the most part, if there's a problem, John handles it."

"We really don't have many problems in that area," Lopez adds. "Occasionally, a few of the guys will show up late for quarters or a training evolution. I just muster the whole platoon forty-five minutes early the next evolution. I only have to do that once or twice, and it becomes a nonissue. If one of the new guys gets into trouble or is having problems, I hold his department head responsible. A new guy can't have any problem as far as I'm concerned. If one of them is having difficulty, I go straight to the department veteran he's working for. It's his job to train him and hold him to standard."

In Foxtrot Platoon it's Chief Will Hanford and his LPO, Petty Officer Ron Kendall. Kendall has had three platoon deployments, all with

Team Five. He is quiet and deliberate, and has a wealth of knowledge on SEAL operations and the Persian Gulf. When Foxtrot was forming, Chief Hanford sought Kendall out for his LPO because of his experience and knowledge. The members of his platoon call him Data, after the *Star Trek* character. Kendall has five new men, counting Lieutenant Bollinger and the third-O. Like John Lopez in Echo Platoon, he has counseled his department petty officers on what he expects from them in mentoring the new guys. In SEAL platoons, enlisted veterans are expected to mentor all new men and look after them. In the mentoring department, Chief Hanford will be grooming Kendall to replace him as platoon chief when he rotates out of the platoon after this deployment.

Hanford is a chief corpsman who joined the Navy from Oklahoma to become a SEAL. He came to the teams in a roundabout way. Selected Navy corpsmen serve as Marine Corps medics, so after his initial medical training, Hanford found himself as a corpsman assigned to a Marine Recon platoon. The Marines did not want to let him go, but he finally managed to get orders to BUD/S. He's a fully qualified Eighteen Delta medic and Navy SOT corpsman. He has had three platoon deployments with Team Five and made the equivalent of three deployments as a Navy corpsman with Marine Force Recon, working his way up to assistant Recon team leader. Ron Kendall is measured and quiet, but Will Hanford is right out there, animated and willing to talk about his platoon.

"The guys are doing a solid job so far; I think we're going to have a great deployment. I'm excited. I like a relaxed platoon, and I try to keep things easy and upbeat—moving forward. One of my jobs is to make sure that we draw lines about what is acceptable and not acceptable behavior, both on and off duty. We have to perform well and build a combat team. The new guys? Sure, I have concerns with the new guys. Before they got here, I talked with their instructors at BUD/S and SQT—about where they are strong and not so strong. I think we have them paired up with the right veterans and working in areas where they can excel. And Ron is doing a great job with them."

The other platoon SEALs are a mix of experience from a variety of backgrounds. One of them in Echo they call the Rainman—after the Dustin Hoffman movie character. He's a big SEAL and spends a lot of time in the weight room. He can also do multiplication and long division in his head. Another in Foxtrot is called MacGyver, after the character from the TV series. He is a crafty second class petty officer who can fix anything. Once they were driving across the desert to a training range in a six-by-six truck. The truck's clutch broke and the platoon faced a long walk home. MacGyver took a weapons cleaning rod from his pack, crawled under the vehicle, and repaired the broken clutch.

"The men have been assigned to the platoon for a while, but we're really not a platoon yet," Chief Rutledge tells me. "The guys have been off to schools, getting individual qualifications, and taking leave before we get into the main part of the workup. And a few of the guys haven't been in the platoon all that long. We need to get away together, and that will happen out at Camp Billy Machen. We'll be out there for four weeks and probably only take two days off the whole time. That's when we'll become a platoon—long days and nights on the ranges. And there will be an evening here and there where we can get together over a few beers. It's all part of the making of a platoon."

"Over half the guys in the two platoons are married," Chief Hanford says. "We haven't had many platoon social events because the guys need to be home. From here on out, we'll be away from home a lot. Most of that time we'll be together, either as a platoon or as a two-platoon task unit. For the next eighteen months, these men will be away more than they will be home—they'll spend more time with their platoon mates than with their wives and girlfriends."

The two platoon chiefs and their leading petty officers know their men well; it's their job. They also supervise the off-duty conduct of their platoons. The platoon OICs will have to answer up the line for any misconduct on the part of their men, but the platoon chiefs, as well as the leading petty officers, are keepers of the standard, and their job does not stop when the workday is over. They know that if one of the platoon SEALs has a DUI or gets into a bar fight or misuses government property, their OIC will have to answer for it. When that happens, the platoon chief and the platoon leading petty officer know they have not done their job. SEAL leaders, officer and enlisted, are responsible for their men—period. So, again, they have to know their men well. They have to know when it's okay for the platoon to have a drink, and when it's okay to have more than one drink. They will come to know who are the ones that may have a tendency to get into a fight and who are the peacemakers. If there is a new guy who is not yet twenty-one, duty driver will be one of his platoon collateral duties. Navy SEALs are typically not men who can be preached to or threatened, nor do they respond well to punishment—save having their Trident pulled and being separated from the teams. But they can be led, and they have a phobia about letting a brother warrior down—leaving a teammate. So, for the most part, the platoon chiefs and leading petty officers have only to set the standard and hold their men accountable for their actions. It's their job.

This is a book on SEAL advanced training and about how SEALs train for deployment to an operational theater. These men are warriors, but few of them are warrior-monks. Can they have a few beers and get a little boisterous? They can. I have been with these men on duty and off duty, and I've seen it. While the current generation of Navy SEALs has an equally robust appetite for good times and good fellowship as the one in my day, they indulge in it far more responsibly. There is a good reason for this. From day one in BUD/S, through SQT and into the teams, responsibility and accountability is drilled into these men. More important, the senior enlisted leadership in the operational components know that if there is irresponsible conduct, on or off duty, then it is a failure of their leadership.

LAND WARFARE

"Sir, you up? How about you, sir?" Both Echo Rasmussen and Foxtrot Rasmussen give a thumbs-up, meaning all their men are present. "Okay, we're good to go. This is your first day of land warfare, and your first block of platoon training. My name is Petty Officer Lynn Kunkle. Call me Lynn or Uncle, as they called me in my last platoon. I will be the leading petty officer for this block of your training. With me here today is Chief Tom Atkin and Petty Officer Sean Billingsly. About myself: I graduated in BUD/S Class 184, and I have four platoon deployments at Team One and Team Three. I volunteered for the training detachment because I believe in it. We are here to help make you the best combat-capable special operators in the world. We're going to ask you to stay focused on training and help us get you ready to go to war. We want you to maintain a warfighting mentality. Stay tactical and play the game for real, or as real as we can make it in a training scenario. The guys who will be training you put a lot of pride and dedication into their work. We expect the same from you. And at the end of most field evolutions there will be a debrief. In the debriefs, we want you to tell us what happened or what you saw. Then we will tell you what we saw. We are going to be critical; we may even nitpick you after an evolution. Be thick-skinned; use this criticism to improve your skills. Better here than when you're doing it for real on deployment.

"Now, there are a lot of ways to do things. There's our way; the tactics we took from the training cells of Teams One, Three, and Five. There's the way you may have been doing it on your last deployment. We'll work with you on that. What we will insist on is that you never take the easy, wrong way just because doing it right is harder or takes more time. The basics always work. For you new guys who are preparing for your first deployment, I want you to pay particular attention to us and to the veterans in your platoon. You're full-fledged SEALs now, and you probably think that you've been training your whole life. Not so. BUD/S, SQT, and your PRODEV training just bought you a seat at this table. From here on you are going to have to work extra hard. In the next few months we're going to teach you how to fight.

"For the most part, this is scenario-based training. We'll minimize the intelligence and lengthy mission-planning work. We'll just want you to come up with a sound plan and make it happen in the field. Have a wheel book and pencil at all times. Write things down. Train safe. This is platoon training, so we expect you to practice combat safety. Again, the basics always work. Twelve hours from jigger to trigger, and that is one rule for which we will tolerate no violations. Come to a training evolution ready to focus on training. And we expect you to demonstrate discipline and good leadership at all times.

"So, are there any questions before we get started? No? Good, let's get to it.

"We're going to be in the classroom for the next few days with a few field exercises toward the end of the week, so stay with us. It's going to be death by PowerPoint for a few days, but we'll get out and get dirty soon enough. Let's take five, and Chief Atkin will be up here to give you your equipment class."

Lynn Kunkle grew up in Oregon and has been in the Navy for fourteen years. He is thirty-three years old and hopes to make chief petty officer this year. His goal is to sit exactly where his ULT students now sit—as a platoon chief. Kunkle spent three years in the fleet and decided to come to BUD/S when he started working out with a few of his shipmates who wanted to become SEALs. His friends never made it, but Kunkle did. He is a Christian, something he will bring up in private conversation, and very serious about training SEALs. His professional knowledge is matched by his sense of humor. Comedian Bill Murray could take lessons on being Bill Murray from Lynn Kunkle. He has the same mannerisms and delivery, and there is a striking resemblance. He is a very funny man and a very effective instructor.

Chief Atkin, who will supervise this block of platoon training, spends two hours on first, second, and third line gear. It could be a class from SQT or even BUD/S, but the information goes much deeper. The veterans have their gear set up, but there is always a way to do it better. Atkin talks about what may and may not work so well with the standard-issue equipment. They talk about the merits and shortfalls of Rhodesian vests, of the commercial providers like

Blackhawk and London Bridge. He talks about how much better the Australian ponchos or "hootches" are than our standard-issue ponchos. No matter whose gear it is, they must spray-paint it lightly to take off the shine. These two platoons are CENTCOM platoons, so they will train for desert and mountain warfare like that found in Afghanistan or Iraq. Their first, second, and third line gear will reflect a combination of desert and upland patterns. For the most part, they will wear desert cammies in their land-warfare training.

Chief Atkin goes into a litany of small things they need to or should do. "If you're going to be in the desert, or anywhere for that matter, have a cleaning kit for your weapon and clean it daily. Carry spares. You guys with M4s, carry an extra bolt and extra set of iron sights. Go out and buy a pair of high-quality, lightweight pruning shears. Nothing works better for cutting vegetation for a hide site. Stuff a beekeeper's hat in your ruck. They're good for bugs and good to break up the outline of your head when you're sitting on an observation position. We're not going to tell you what to wear or how to wear it. We will inspect you to see that you have your basic load and that it's set up so you can easily get to the important stuff, like bullets and bandages. But there must be a standard in your platoon about the placement of your medical kit." The list of do-betters and consider-this-item goes on. The veterans take a few notes. The new guys take a lot more. Some write in small, vest-pocket-size wheel books. Most have green ledger-size books and keep a log.

Later that day, the two platoons muster outside with their first, second, and third line gear. They look uniform, up to a point, but each man has a slightly different harness, vest, or H-gear for his second line gear. Sometimes it's to accommodate ammunition for the weapon they carry, sometimes because they are right- or left-handed, and sometimes because they found, made, or bought something that works.

"Where did you get that vest?" I ask one of the SEALs. It looked like one that SEALs of my era used in Vietnam—kind of a canvas bra with magazine pouches.

"I found it when we were cleaning out an old storage locker." He had sewn new plastic fasteners and Velcro strips on the front of the pouches. When I asked about this he explained, "I use the plastic catches when we're on patrol; they're very secure. Then I can unsnap the catches before the fight or after the fight begins, and use the Velcro. Speeds up my changing out mags."

"Is it comfortable if you have to lay on your stomach for a long time?" Lynn Kunkle asks.

"No problem. I sewed a pocket on the backside for my map case, cravat, and gloves. I also stash a few PowerBars there. Works great."

There are special sessions for the MK43 and MK46 gunners on how to set up special vests and webbing to carry their load. "You can always tell a squad of SEALs on patrol," Kunkle reminds me. "Seven or eight guys dressed differently all doing the same thing."

In the next few days, the training detachment races through classes on fieldcraft skills. They review basic camouflage, both personal and in LUPs and OPs—layup positions and observation posts—and how to go to ground in a hide site and remain unseen. They cover the basics of stealthy movement on SR missions. The instructors quickly get through the basics, and move on to more advanced techniques of cover and concealment. They talk about target surveillance, sketching, range estimation, and communication while on these special reconnaissance patrols. Along with their combat sketching practice, they play KIM games—keep-in-mind exercises—in which they have to describe a scene or detail a list of objects they have only had time to observe for a few moments.

"All this high-tech stuff we have now like digital cameras and Predator drones are great," Petty Officer Sean Billingsly tells them, "but if there is to be a follow-on direct-action mission, the operators who have to conduct that mission will want to know target-specific information—what's the structure made of, does the door open left or right, are there signs of physical security. What would you want to know if you had to come back there on a DA mission? And get only as close as you need to be to get the job done. If you can see what you need to see at three hundred yards, don't come in to one hundred. And sometimes there's nothing to see. The guys who went in on an SR at Camp Rhino in Afghanistan sat there for days and watched sand. Their job was to make sure that when the Marines arrived there was nothing but empty desert waiting for them. It was boring, but it was necessary."

Echo and Foxtrot, and the other Team Five platoons, also receive classwork in tracking and stalking. Even for some of the veterans, it is their first formal training in this discipline. Again, it's Lynn Kunkle.

"I spent three months in New Zealand at the advanced SAS tracking school. I learned a lot from those guys. Now, we're not here to make trackers out of you, but if you know how a tracker works, you can delay him. Notice I said 'delay.' A good tracker can follow you no matter what you do. I'm going to show you what you can do to slow him down or deceive him for awhile. Pay attention, because we will be tracking you out at Camp Billy Machen. One, to see how easy you are to track, and two, to see if you've learned how to effectively deal with a tracker. Tracking is a visual skill; it's not some mumbo-jumbo thing or some mystical art. Trackers bleed; they can be killed. When people move through an area, they leave signs, or spore, as Africans call it. The antitracker skills we're going to show you are dangerous. They will slow you down or could make you more vulnerable as you move. You don't want to use them unless you think there is a chance that someone is following you. You need to make that call depending on the AO and the mission. In some situations, like when you are going to a LUP, you may want to put an overwatch on your trail. If a tracker comes along behind you, and he doesn't have a battalion of bad guys with him, you can ruin his day."

At the end of the week, the platoons travel to Border Field, south of Coronado, for an overnight tactical exercise. First, the four squads do some daylight patrolling and construct some hide sites. Then they have a tactical dinner and wait for darkness. The instructors set up in a bivouac area. The squads try to probe the perimeter of the camp, pushing the envelope, trying to see what they can get away with.

Getting caught or seen is okay—tonight. This is the first and last time during the platoon workup that they will not be called to task if they are seen while on an SR mission.

This first-week classroom and local fieldwork is important. For the most part, it is a review; the SEALs have all done this before. Yet like many things during an operational workup, it has to be done again, and it has to be done with new guys in the platoon and new SEAL veterans in the key leadership positions. It's also a time for the cadre to take subtle ownership of the platoons they have to train.

"These guys showed up to get ready for war," Chief Atkin tells me. "We're going to give them a good platoon workup."

Five Echo and Five Foxtrot will spend the next thirty days at Camp Billy Machen. It is the middle of the summer, and the desert is a very brutal place. The days are always over 100 degrees, often as high as 115. The platoons work mostly at night, but in reality, they work day and night. There is a great deal of similarity between the training of SQT Class 2-02 and platoon training. They work through several days of demolitions, improvised explosives, and booby traps—classroom work, field setups, and walk-throughs. They do a great deal of shooting. There are instinctive-fire drills and drills with grenades. They shoot as individuals and in squads, using all the weapons in the SEAL inventory, including mounted .50-caliber machine guns and 60mm mortars. And there are the IADs, day and night. They set ambushes and conduct assaults and CSAR exercises. Much of their land-warfare training in the desert begins with individual, skills-based training that rapidly progresses to scenario-based training in which they must plan, shoot, and fight as a team. Together, the platoons consume hundreds of pounds of demolitions and an impressive amount of small-arms and supporting arms ammunition:

126,000 5.56mm rounds for the M4 rifle.
75,000 5.56mm linked rounds for the MK46 machine gun

4,000 7.62mm rounds for the M14 rifle

175,000 7.62mm linked rounds for the MK43 machine gun

4,000 .50-caliber rounds

2,000 7.62mm short rounds for the AK-47

2,000 9mm rounds for the 9mm pistol

2,000 12-gauge, oo-buck shotgun rounds

1,000 40mm grenade rounds

750 60mm mortar rounds

26 LAAW rockets

150 Carl Gustaf rockets, all types

40 AT4 rockets

200 hand grenades

This ordnance is not simply sprayed around the desert. It is used in individual skill-building and live-fire, scenario-based training. The schedule looks a great deal like the SQT regime at Camp Billy Machen, and there are some commonalities. The platoon SEALs shoot for accuracy on the sniper ranges. There are rattle-battle drills, because there is no substitute for running, shooting on the run, and changing magazines on the run. Scores are kept and scores are posted. Winners and losers. Who is good and who is better is deeply embedded in team culture. But most of the training goes deeper than SQT.

Along with the familiar demolition drills and explosive charge calculations, there are lessons in improvised explosives. One platoon will make booby traps wired to small amounts of explosives placed at a safe distance. Then the other platoon will patrol at night and try to avoid the trip wires and pressure plates that initiate the training charge. When they fail, and they often do, everyone gets a good scare. It is stressful and tiring work; the point men sweat bullets as they pick their way along the booby-trapped route.

The point-man courses and instinctive-fire drills are more complex and comprehensive than in SQT. On one course, the individual SEALs walk a prescribed route and fire at pop-up silhouettes. There are items of tactical importance along the way that they must observe—a ration can, expended shell casings, perhaps a cigarette butt or a candy wrapper. The objective is a small abandoned building. The platoon SEAL is allowed only a few minutes to search the building to find any items of intelligence and make observations—a kind of KIM game in the field. There are booby traps along the route and in the building. Patrolling on the way out, they find more booby traps, items on the ground, and silhouettes to shoot. The learning does not stop after the field training. Debriefings are especially important, as they will do this exercise many times. Perhaps not the same course—but the skills of moving well, reacting properly, and becoming more observant get better with repetition. And the scores are posted; winners and losers.

The AW men have daylong drills with the MK43s and MK46s. They work on various load-bearing configurations and drill on shooting techniques and reloading drills—boxes, not magazines. They run, shoot, roll in the dirt, and learn how to effectively use their machine guns to complement the SEAL riflemen. They do this for three days. These are fully automatic weapons. There are things the AWs cannot do in the fight, and things only they can do. There are things to learn, relearn, and rehearse—which spares to carry, how to maintain the gun in the field, how to clear a jam, how the MK43 and the MK46 complement each other, how much extra water to carry because the AW men often pack the heaviest load. Since the MK46 is a relatively new weapon to the SEAL arsenal, this machine gun is new to many of the AW men. Some missions may require that they carry one machine gun of each caliber. Others may demand two 43s or two 46s—or more or none at all. In a small unit on a special operations mission, there may be no need for a machine gun; but when you need one, you generally *really* need one. A SEAL AW man may hump that pig and four hundred rounds of ammo for that one-in-a-hundred chance that you really need it.

The platoon SEALs learn to use the M4 rifle and the M203 grenade launcher as a system. With an M4, a SEAL can put a round through a man at three hundred yards. He can do this at greater distances if he's good, or if he has a well-sighted 4X scope on his M4.

With the M203 slung under his M4, he can also take out a man with a grenade at up to three hundred yards or more. More important, this can be done even when the enemy is hiding. The 203 is an indirect-fire weapon, and a grenade can be lobbed over a shallow rise or a berm to find its mark. Most of the veterans use Kentucky windage with their 203s, but there are snap-up sights for the M4/M203s. The new SEALs do very well at this. The sound of the M4 40mm drills is very distinctive: *Bang! Bang! Tonk! Boom!* The platoon SEALs practice dynamic drills in which they learn to shoot where the enemy is going be rather than where he was a few moments ago. They also learn to use the M203 as an area-fire weapon to keep the enemy's head down while they maneuver for a kill shot with the M4. This training is a long way from SQT, where they blasted target hulks on a grenade range.

Night and day IADs are also a step up from SQT, not so much in content but in the intensity and the leadership. In SQT, these live, fire-and-maneuver drills were well-choreographed evolutions, with a great deal of instructor oversight. In platoon IADs, the platoon leadership drives the action. As with all of the higher-risk evolutions, they will dirt dive the IAD—walk before they run, day before night. Then they will do it again and again, formally with the IAD as the objective of the evolution, and repeatedly on an impromptu basis during other scenario-based, desert-training evolutions that involve assaults, CSAR exercises, and DA missions. The TRADET instructors carefully watch the platoon's execution and discipline, and the professional skill of the individual SEALs, but they also watch the platoon leadership. Can the officers and senior petty officers react quickly, effectively, and safely to a threat? Can they manage a running gunfight at night when they're tired and haven't slept in a while? Can they improvise? Can they do this night after night? This level of training at this tempo requires the best efforts from the best in this business. And training is never over—not for a Navy SEAL, and certainly not for a SEAL platoon preparing for war.

There is training and equipment that the new SEALs and even

some of the veterans have not seen. Night-vision equipment, satellite communication radios, and GPS technology gets smaller, more effective, and easier to use every year. Much of it is commercially available equipment adapted for military use. And there are dramatic changes in mobility, specifically with respect to the vehicles that SEALs train to use in desert and mountain environments. These are the desert patrol vehicles (DVPs) and the specially configured HMMWVs (high-mobility multipurpose wheeled vehicles). Both are the product of off-road racing technology adapted for special operations. The SEALs have long used and perfected the use of the dune buggy–like DVPs. The newer versions have more power and more range, in some cases are bigger, and can be adapted to different SEAL requirements and missions. And there are maintenance and driving requirements that change with the vehicles and the tactics. The use of HMMWVs, or Hummers or Humvees, by SEALs is relatively new, so Naval Special Warfare has retained Ray Hall International. They are competitive, off-road specialists who focus on racing HMMWVs. The SEALs are not racers, but they recognize that the people who do race HMMWVs have some very valuable knowledge for the military off-roaders. They teach the SEALs how to drive, and what the HMMWV can and cannot do. They learn base-camp and on-the-mission maintenance procedures, and what is likely to break and what is unlikely to break. Special operations and off-road racing both strain the vehicles. With the help of Ray Hall and his racing techs, the SEALs are able to develop a parts-failure history for their HMMWVs so they can load out with the appropriate type and quantity of spare parts. It's just another way that it pays to be a winner.

Mission planning and the complex command-and-control, communications, and operational-support infrastructure integral to a special operations mission are not overlooked, but they are highly compressed to allow for more field training. However, the canned scenarios reflect ongoing, real-world scenarios and contingencies that SEALs are engaged in now and may be called on for in the future. There are a host of classified mission-support capabilities and operational on-call support systems that go well beyond the scope of this book. The bag of tools at the disposal of a SEAL element in the field, like their professional skill set, is impressive and growing.

An important part of the training at Camp Billy Machen is, for want of a better term, the bonding of the platoon. Some of the platoon SEALs have been on deployment together, some for more than one deployment. There are new SEALs and veteran SEALs new to the platoon. And no matter how many SEALs are holdovers from the previous deployment, things change and times change. The veterans in the platoon are two years older—two years more mature than the last time they trained as a platoon for deployment. For two of the veteran SEALs in Echo and Foxtrot, this is their first operational deployment as married men. For many, this is their first operational deployment since 9/11. This time there is every expectation that they will see action. Most of the men I talk to will be very disappointed if there is a fight and they don't have a hand in it. Perhaps what drives the forces of change in a platoon most are the new men and the change of leadership. New guys are new guys, and because of the fine work of the basic and advanced training cadres, the new men are technically good to go. They listen, work hard, and quickly assimilate into the platoon culture. But the platoon leadership, officer and enlisted, sets the tone for the platoon.

"It's good that we have this four-week block of land-warfare training at the beginning of our platoon workup," Chief Cal Rutledge tells me. "During PRODEV, most of our training was individual training, and when we did train as a platoon, it was never for more than a day or two. Sometimes it takes getting away from the team area and the going-home-at-night, coming-to-work-in-the-morning routine to get the platoon really together. God knows we don't see enough of our families, but we need to be off the Strand as a group to make this happen. As the platoon chief, I need to watch these guys work as a team and see how we perform in the various squad and platoon roles. And I need to see them work when they're tired—really tired. I need to see my officers lead, and they probably need to see me work with the men. It's certainly a critical time for the leading petty officer to take charge of his platoon. It's a big transition for him, and a big responsibility. It is a validation of his ability to do the job, and if he can have the guys ready to train—mentally and physically—on time, every time, day in and day out. Now it's twenty-four/seven. We don't get a lot of sleep and we even get a little cranky, but we have to get the job done. The LPO is the ramrod of the outfit, and the guys in Echo know that."

Chief Hanford of Foxtrot Platoon agrees. "We will be out of the area training a great deal before we deploy, but this first outing is especially important. Myself and the LPO learn a lot about the guys and our officers. Especially after we get into the meat of the training. The days are brutal and the nights are long. We get beat down, but we have to function and perform—as a team. There are a few times that we don't go out at night after a day on the ranges, times where we can knock back a few beers and relax together. Some of the guys don't drink, but whether it's beer or Gatorade, it's all the same. And there are a few occasions when we can get into town for a sandwich and a little away-from-camp downtime. It's important. Platoons have personalities, just like people. They change from group to group, deployment to deployment. It's my responsibility to see that my platoon develops a good personality—that we are comfortable with ourselves. If the LPO or I see something off duty that is out of line or we think may affect our combat capabilities, we get right on it."

"How do you handle internal problems?" I ask.

The two platoon chiefs approach this differently.

"I'm a proactive kind of guy," Will Hanford says. "Some might think I'm an in-your-face kind of guy. But I want to head off problems. And that's up the chain as well as down. Periodically, I hold a bitch session with the platoon. That's the time to get any pissing and moaning out of the way. If the guys have problems with the platoon leadership or the way the training is going, we deal with it. They get anything on their mind off their chest. I usually learn something and we keep any tension out of the platoon. It works pretty well."

Chief Rutledge is a little more circumspect. "I work closely with my LPO on any problem issues. John has a good feel for when a guy has a bitch and when he's unhappy about something. He's a good communicator and most problems never get to me, although we will often talk about them, sometimes before John has to deal with them and sometimes afterward. If I get involved, it's usually about a personal issue, something we need to work on together or even take up to Mister Rasmussen. One thing we're all committed to is to getting a resolution in place that solves the problem so we can get back to training. We have a big job ahead of us; this will likely as not be a combat deployment. We don't have as much time to prepare for it as we'd like, but then, that's the way it always is."

The final week of training at Camp Billy Machen is full-on, scenario-based training. Each morning at ten o'clock the platoons are given a problem: special reconnaissance, direct action, CSAR, POW recovery, or a combination of these. The mission-planning phase is shortened to provide maximum time in the field. The training cadre expect a good concept briefing of the operation and a basic plan. The platoons talk about what support and additional intelligence they would ask for and could reasonably expect to get in a real-world situation. Then the platoon OICs issue a quick warning order, and the men set about getting their gear ready. Most of the afternoons are taken with rehearsals and time-on-target drills (TOTs). It is very hot work, especially with a combat load, but rehearsals are important. So they do walk-throughs and run-throughs in the hot afternoon sun and drink gallons of water.

"This was an incredible block of training for us," says Lieutenant John Rasmussen of Echo Platoon. "This is my third platoon workup, and we've never had this caliber of training. It was real, it was fast paced, and every night we got something thrown at us that forced us to improvise or amend our tactics en route. Much of the time we had helicopter gunships available to get some CAS training. We had seven missions in eight days; every night we were running and gunning. The planning is important, even critical, but to rehearse all day and patrol all night really tightened us up tactically. The guys are moving very well now, and the platoon morale couldn't be better."

Foxtrot Rasmussen—Phil—said much the same thing. "This was great training, especially the IADs. I'll bet we did a different IAD every night. We knew it was coming, we just didn't know when or where the threat would be coming from. The training cadre really challenged us. They used a lot of explosive charges and simulators against us in the field. They were out there all night, posing as opposition forces; they made it real. And you could tell they put a lot of time in on the targets. The guys in the platoon won't put out a hundred percent unless they're challenged. It's the best land-warfare training I've had in the teams."

John echoes his brother's sentiments. "I can't say enough about the cadre. They worked as hard—often harder—than we did. I saw them with that thousand-yard stare more that once. They took our training seriously. When we get to the fight, we'll be ready, and we have them to thank for it."

After four weeks at Camp Billy Machen, the platoons enjoy four days off, then head back to the desert—a different desert. They fly to Fort Hood, Texas. Fort Hood, just north of Austin, is where the Army exercises and trains its armored forces. Many of the armored columns that roamed across Iraq in March and April of 2003 trained at Fort Hood. There, Five Echo and Five Foxtrot will hone their land-warfare skills at a different location and spy on the Army. They will conduct IAD, TOT, and CSAR drills and be in the field on multiday exercises, but the focus of their training will be on special reconnaissance. At Fort Hood, they spend most of their time in the field, rucked up in full first, second, and third line gear with full face paint for full-on combat patrol.

Midway through their training at Fort Hood, they are sent out on a two-day surveillance exercise. Without notice, the platoons are recalled after eighteen hours and retasked. This time they are in the field for over four days, hiding by day and conducting sneak-and-peek operations at night. Sometimes the Army has force security personnel out looking for them and sometimes not. It allows the platoons a rare opportunity to scout main-force elements and report their composition and disposition back to higher headquarters, just as SOF forces scouted the Iraqi Republican Guard divisions during the Gulf War. Typically, the platoons go to ground in an LUP for the day and move only at night, although this exercise called for some daytime travel so they could practice daylight movement.

"This was an important block of training for me," one of the radiomen told me. "I had to make my comm windows and get our surveillance reports out. The snipers were out taking pictures, so I had a lot of imagery to handle. We also had to make detailed reports on what was needed if we were to bring in main-force elements— what were the best routes in and out, where were the best helicopter landing zones, that kind of thing. It was great training."

"We got close enough to read the numbers on their HMMWVs and to hear some of their call signs when they were on the radio," one of the platoon SEALs reported. "And we had a few close calls with some of their patrols, but we were never compromised. Well, except for the one time."

"Oh?" I said.

He laughs. "We were in the LUP one night and we heard this cracking and breaking of brush. Then this mule deer charged right in the middle of us. He knocked me down and trampled two of the other guys. Scared the hell out of us. At first I thought it was Uncle Kunkle or one of the other instructors screwing with us because they'd found our hide site. But it was a deer. Frankie has this hoofprint bruise right in the middle of his back. He got trampled."

"Any other critters out there?"

"Just snakes. A lot of rattlesnakes, and we did see one coral snake." He sees the look of disbelief on my face. "Truly. He had the yellow bands. Came right through the LUP. Sleep is important when you're out on an SR mission. Tough to get back to sleep after a coral snake comes through the LUP."

The platoon returns to the Strand after sixteen days of training at Fort Hood. The men get a few days off, then plunge into their three-week Combat Qualification Course. This is the end of their formal land-warfare training, but they will revisit these skills as they continue with the platoon workup.

COMBAT SHOOTING

The ULT Combat Qualification Course, or CQC, will involve a great deal of shooting and will bring the shooting indoors. Most recently, SEALs have ranged across Afghanistan and Iraq over desert and mountainous terrain—long-range movement in a hostile environment. But SEALs also have to be able to fight at close quarters. This means house-to-house or room-to-room combat on land, and compartment-by-compartment combat at sea aboard ship. The dramatic events in Afghanistan and Iraq have focused the nation's attention on special operations that range across large expanses of territory. But occasionally, these moving battles are punctuated by small-scale, vicious close-quarter engagements. When you are in a confined space and the other guys have guns, all the air cover and precision-guided munitions in the world will not help. Senior Chief Petty Officer Trent Larson is in charge of the CQC training for Five Echo and Five Foxtrot.

"The platoon SEALs know how to shoot, and with the exception of the new guys, they know how to fight in close quarters. Over the next three weeks we will work with them to refine their shooting techniques and help them build the team skills to safely enter and occupy a building while being opposed."

Foxtrot and Echo Platoons begin their CQC training at Camp Pendleton. On a hill above the rifle ranges are a small-arms combat range and a kill house. The combat range, much like the one at La Posta, allows shooters to move and shoot, engaging targets with primary and secondary weapons. The platoons do this hour after hour, running and shooting, changing magazines and changing weapons.

They work singly and in pairs. The platoon chiefs run the training, setting up different targets with different objectives. For the most part, they focus on shooting mechanics and smooth transitions. But there are timed drills and scores are kept—winners and losers. I was delighted to see the recent SQT graduates shooting competitively alongside the veterans. The newest SEAL, the young petty officer from Class 2-02, shot better than most.

The combat shooters wear body armor and Kevlar helmets. On their second line gear they carried an assortment of breaching tools, including axes, pry bars, bolt cutters, and sledgehammers—the tools of a basic burglar. Five Echo and Five Foxtrot now carry modified M4s, not MP5s. The business of close-quarter shooting by SEALs will be done with a .556 primary weapon, not the 9mm MP5. I ask several of them about this.

"It's not as bad as I thought it was going to be," one of the veterans from Foxtrot told me, holding up his M4 with the ten-inch barrel. "It tends to ride up a little more than the MP5, but you get used to it. It's a gun we know very well, and I personally think the .556 round will prove its worth in a fight. It may not have the pure stopping power of the nine millimeter, but it makes for a much lighter gun in a confined space."

"And when you get back out in the open?"

"Take the long barrel out of your ruck and you're back in business."

The SEAL kill house at Camp Pendleton is the first of many the platoons will work in. A kill house is a very special and expensive building, built from the ground up to accommodate live-fire training. It has movable partitions and ballistic walls with thick rubber sheeting to minimize backsplash from fragmented rounds. The kill house at Pendleton is a three-story affair, with conventional doors and shipboard hatches served by internal and external stairs and ladders. SEALs must train to fight aboard ship as well as inside buildings. There are any number of training scenarios that can be arranged to challenge the SEAL combat shooters. There are configurations that allow the SEALs to rappel into close-quarter shooting situations. The targets are cardboard silhouettes of men and women, in various dress, sometimes armed, sometimes not. In one scenario, a woman may have a gun in her hand. In the next, it's the same woman wearing the same dress—but this time she is holding a purse. One is a clear shooting situation, the other is not.

Time in the kill house begins with walk-throughs to get the shooting pairs working together. There are a number of verbal commands and hand signals that must be rehearsed.

"Moving . . . Move" is heard over and over again. In an opposed situation, the good guys have to let their shooting partners know what is going on. When they move, they have to call out, and acknowledge, what they're doing. If there is a potential danger, they have to call that out as well. Some situations call for the shooters to move back-to-back, or for one to cross the other's line of fire. Entering a room, each has a sector of responsibility; he has to clear his area and let his partner know it's clear. It has to happen by the numbers, but it has to happen fast; eliminate any immediate threat, sweep your area, check out any obstructions or unknowns, and check any doors or closets. They practice in two-man teams and four-man teams. Each time the TRADET instructors coach and critique; each time the dry-fire drills go a little faster, a little smoother. Then it's time to lock and load.

The house goes hot and the room entries are made with live fire. If the silhouette shows a gun, it gets punched with a bullet. If it doesn't have a weapon, it is made compliant: "Get down! On the floor!" The unarmed silhouette is summarily knocked to the floor, and the shooters move on to check and clear the space.

"Clear left!"

"Clear right!"

If there is a second room to be cleared, the SEAL combat pair sets up on the door and prepares for the second entry. The platoon SEALs trade off so that each man gets to run a given drill with a different platoon mate for a shooting partner. This builds trust among the platoon and in their room-clearing procedures. The clearing drills are made with primary and secondary weapons. The crack from those short-barreled M4s in a confined space is deafening. It is exciting work, but it is also hot, tiring, and repetitive work. For some of the veteran SEALs, it's a chance to refine their close-quarter shooting skills. For the new guys, it's their first time in the kill house with live rounds. And for all of the SEALs it is the first time they have shot at close quarters with the shortened M4. After a week at Pendleton, they are ready to move on to the Shaw School.

The Naval Special Warfare Groups try to schedule their platoons in training for a week at a civilian shooting school. There are several, but the SEALs rate the Mid-South Institute of Self-Defense Shooting in Memphis as the best. It's simply called the Shaw School for its owner-founder, John Shaw. Shaw teaches combat shooting to a number of SOF and law-enforcement organizations, and has one of the best kill houses. The Shaw instructors help refine the individual shooting techniques and pass along the most current room-clearing and urban-assault procedures. Five Echo and Five Foxtrot, along with their TRADET mentors, spend a week at Shaw. Here they do much the same thing they did at Camp Pendleton, but in a different kill house. The Shaw shooting instructors are on hand to help, but the training at Shaw is conducted by TRADET. Following a week at Shaw, Five Echo and Five Foxtrot are back at the Pendleton kill house for more team building and live-fire drills. On this third and final week of the CQC, they are inserting near or on the kill house by helo and running through assault drills with live fire. All the while, the platoon SEALs are getting comfortable with the short-barreled M4s and the transition between M4 and Sig Sauer. More important, they are getting comfortable with shooting in close quarters with their platoon mates. It all takes practice.

MOUT AND BEYOND

MOUT is yet another acronym. This one stands for military operations in urban terrain. MOUT training is a logical extension of CQC. CQC focuses on the fight indoors; MOUT training includes the fight inside and outside. SEALs have to be prepared to enter a town and manage a hostile urban environment, as well as clear rooms in a given building. Often this requires more people—and sometimes vehicles.

"There are a lot of moving parts in this training," John Rasmussen explained. "We train with both platoons and learn to support each other. If the target is inside a building, some of the guys have to be managing the external space while others go inside to complete the mission. Like everything else, we walk through it, then run through full tilt. We use the combat town at Fort Ord for much of this training. It's an incredible experience. They ask for volunteers from the Army post there to serve as civilians. On our final problem we had close to two hundred role players in civilian clothes, most serving as innocent civilians and a few with weapons in opposition. The cadre used smudge pots and noisemakers to add to the confusion. It was surprisingly similar to the real thing."

"You said weapons," I say. "Blank ammunition or Sims?"

"We use blanks when there are civilian role players. When it's just us and the opposition, we use Simunitions. It was great training."

"I understand you had Ranger supervision on this one."

John laughs. "We sure did. Ranger Mallory was incredible. I can't say enough about that guy. He organized the training and made it real. He has a huge amount of experience in MOUT operations, and we were lucky to have him working with us."

Master Sergeant Will Mallory is an exchange instructor on loan to TRADET from the U. S. Army's Seventy-fifth Ranger Regiment. Ranger Mallory, as he is known, runs this block of SEAL platoon training. Rangers are light infantry and specialize in airfield and urban assault. His experience and professionalism have gone a long way in preparing SEAL platoons to conduct urban warfare.

Following MOUT training, the platoons begin GOPLAT and VBSS training. In nonmilitary speak, the former is training for assaults on gas and oil platforms; the latter stands for visit, board, search, and seizure of vessels at sea. For the veterans it's high-speed, challenging training they may not have done since their last workup. Most of them have been involved in GOPLAT and VBSS for real while on deployment. Between the Gulf wars, SEALs boarded numerous ships in the Persian Gulf looking for Iraqi contraband; in the last few years, they've been hunting for members of al-Qaeda. For the new men, it's another thing they've never done before. Both of these missions are classic maritime special operations, and like over-the-beach operations, they are something the SEALs do better than anyone else. Prior to and during combat operations in Iraq, SEALs boarded and searched literally hundreds of Iraqi vessels in the approaches to Umm Qasr. Those found with munitions were promptly sent to the bottom.

The economic value of the Iraqi offshore oil terminals captured intact by Navy SEALs is incalculable. Securing and safeguarding those important facilities was critical to the recovery of the Iraqi oil-export industry. In this operation, the SEALs worked in partnership with the "boat guys," the special warfare combat craft crews. Approaching and seizing a structure at sea loaded with explosives takes a special kind of courage.

Exactly how SEALs approach and take down oil rigs and ships at sea is something I've been asked not to put in print. There are those who make it their business to keep SEALs from attacking these targets, and do their best to stop them. It's obvious that the SEALs come from the sea or the air, and it's safe to say they will come at night if they have the choice. It's dangerous business—one that requires nerve, skill, and a great deal of practice—but the platoons do it and do it well. It's also safe to say that if you are a ship captain or an oil platform supervisor, and your operations support terrorism or are in opposition to the interests of the United States, you are a candidate for some uninvited SEAL guests.

Five Echo and Five Foxtrot, like all deploying platoons, have to do the basics, things they learned in BUD/S and practiced in SQT—skills that need to be rehearsed and performed at an elevated professional level. So, like the basic trainees and the advanced students, they must do a series of hydrographic reconnaissances, over-the-beach operations, underwater demolitions, and combat-swimmer operations. They are all competent with land and maritime GPS navigation, but these platoons will be out at night—preferably a dark, foggy night—running nav problems in CRRCs using map and compass. It's cold, repetitious, and often boring work, but it has to be done. These basic skills must be practiced and made current. The TRADET cadre are there to see that it is done right and that the skill level of the platoons is challenged and, where possible, expanded. If the work is done poorly, they are not above directing a platoon or squad element to do it again. The platoon SEALs know this and do their best to get it right the first time. By this time in the platoon training workup, both cadre and platoon SEALs are tired. Getting an evolution right the first time means everyone gets a little more sleep and possibly a little more family time.

Throughout all the training, the platoon snipers are sometimes broken away for different training or to support a platoon or a squad mission profile in a sniper-support role. This is called sniper integration. Their duties are straightforward if the mission calls for long-range shooting or surveillance. But SEALs are often asked to carry out a special operation and move to their objective under the protection or cover of a sniper. This requires coordination, communication, and practice. A SEAL squad may be able to approach an objective with a greater degree of safety if there is a sniper team watching over it. The snipers could be there in case the SEAL squad has to make an emergency extraction. An enemy guard force may not be so interested in pursing a SEAL element exfiltrating from a target if there is a sniper element in the area.

For the most part, the OICs try not to have individual SEALs training away from the platoon. There are exceptions, and training in close air support, or CAS, is one of them. With the importance and precision of the new smart bombs (or JDAMs—joint direct attack munitions), SEALs cannot afford to miss an opportunity for this training. Air-ground coordination is rapidly becoming a force multiplier in special operations. The SEALs need to train and communicate with the pilots, and the Navy and Air Force pilots need to communicate with the guys on the ground. Occasionally, a high-value training opportunity will present itself and the platoon training schedule is adjusted accordingly. The missed training venue will have to be pushed forward to a future date in an already crowded schedule. The platoons and the TRADET cadre work together to make it happen.

At the end of the six-month ULT period, the Team Five platoons and their cadre are exhausted. For the trainers and operators, it is a bittersweet experience. In the time allowed they did what they could, but for all of them there is the nagging feeling that they could have done better—that they could have squeezed in one more training evolution or that the ones marginally done could have been performed better. This is part of the SEAL culture; they know they can always do better. The Team Five platoons will move on for SIT, or squadron integration training. The TRADET cadre will take a few days off, review the critiques from the Team Five platoons, and reevaluate its training syllabus. And the training for the platoons from SEAL Team Seven will be just a little bit better.

"Are you satisfied with the training of these platoons?"

Brian Schmidt gives me a tired smile and hesitates a moment. "I suppose. No, definitely. They're good to go, but I always want them to do better. You see, if they have shortcomings, then we have shortcomings. We're limited here; we train them to perform certain tasks under certain conditions to a certain standard. Standards aside, each of these platoons has its own personality. Some are better in the water than others; some are strong at VBSS or MOUT. They're the guys in the arena. We just hope we've given them enough to do the job when the bullets start flying. Training for war is not a perfect science. We do the best we can."

"What happens when a platoon is having trouble and not performing?"

"They don't get a free pass. If we can't work it out with the platoon leadership, then we have to take it to the team CO, but it's usually not news to him. He and his command master chief are out here enough; they know when they have a problem in a platoon. It's usually leadership, and that usually has to change."

"What about an individual SEAL in the platoon who is having problems?" I ask.

"That's easier. We work with the platoon leadership to correct them. There's very little we see that the platoon chiefs and LPOs are not aware of. If it's a veteran, it's either a problem at home or an attitude problem. The platoon leadership has to take action or I will, and that involves my boss and the team CO. If it's a new guy, we go to his BUD/S and SQT records to see if there is a history of a problem in a specific area or a general inattention to detail. Usually we can work with the guy to correct it, but it's got to be done quickly and with full resolution. A SEAL platoon has to count on every gun in the file. Every gun has to be a go-to guy.

"I'll tell you one thing. We did a better job training the Team Five platoons than we did with the Team Three platoons. And we'll do even better with Team Seven, and following them, Team One."

Later that day, I caught Five Echo and Five Foxtrot in their platoon spaces, getting ready for a few days off prior to beginning SIT. I sought out the Rasmussen brothers and thanked them for allowing me to tag after them during ULT. These two fine officers worked very hard to get their platoons ready for war. I later learned that both of them made it to Baghdad before combat operations were declared over. They managed to get their guns into the fight.

After thanking the Rasmussen brothers, I found the new guy from SQT Class 2-02. He was wiping down his M4 and wrapping it in a soft padded cloth for storage in one of the platoon weapons boxes.

"Glad to have ULT behind you?" I ask. He had missed part of Team Five's PRODEV period, and there was a lot of new information he had to assimilate in ULT. Three years ago, this "kid" was in high school.

"Oh, hello, Mister Couch." Young SEALs are invariably polite and courteous. "Yeah, I guess so. I learned a lot; I just hope I learned enough. We got a great platoon, and I don't want to let anyone down."

"Well, I think the chief and your LPO are pretty happy with you. You shoot as well as any of them."

He grins at that. "Shooting's never been a problem for me, sir. But I got other areas to work on."

"What has been the best thing about joining the platoon and getting into the meat of the workup?"

"I think," he says in a measured tone, "the best thing is that these guys trust me; they rely on me to do my job. That's a lot of responsibility. I didn't really feel that during BUD/S or even SQT. But these are veteran SEALs, and they count on me. I have to do everything I can not to let them down."

I saw this in new SEALs in other platoons. Even some who I thought lacked maturity or seemed to not take training seriously became responsible sled dogs when they got to their platoons. For some men, it has to get real before they get serious. For others, it's the strong example or the strong hand of the platoon chief or platoon LPO. A new guy is like a rookie shortstop on a Major League baseball team. The veteran ballplayers will kid a rookie and even tease him, but they will also help him. They also expect him to play his position on the team. The bottom line is that in the big leagues— baseball team or SEAL team—the rookies have to perform. Only in the teams, it's bullets, not fastballs; firefights *have* to be won. There is no second place in a gunfight. The stakes are that high. For the most part, the new guys I saw will help their platoons. I would expect nothing less. They are, after all, Mike Loo–trained SEALs.

Smile, you're covered. SEALs fully rigged for close-quarter battle—a terrorist's worst nightmare. *Photo by Cliff Hollenbeck*

CHAPTER 6

The Squadron

THE SEAL SQUADRON

In chapter 4, we talked about the NSW 21 concept and how this dramatic reorganization changed and enhanced the operational posture of the Navy SEAL teams. This deployment format dramatically increased the duties and responsibilities of the SEAL team commanding officers. Before we go into the warfighting obligations of these key officers, let's talk about the composition of the SEAL squadron.

Upon the completion of Unit Level Training, the six SEAL platoons return to the tactical control of their team. Given the time spent away from home, platoon training was a domestic deployment of sorts. With their return, the number of personnel assigned to the team is about 130 individuals. Of that number, some 96 plus of those are platoon SEALs—in the vernacular of the teams, pure shooters. Another twelve to fourteen members of the team are SEALs that serve outside the platoon. These SEALs, which include the senior leadership—commanding officer, executive officer, operations officer, and command master chief—will serve as task-unit commanders or in other deployed leadership positions. The other qualified SEALs, including new SEAL ensigns fresh from the finishing school, will serve in the task units or in liaison positions aboard ship, at shore-based command facilities, and as Smees (subject-matter experts). Under certain conditions, these nonplatoon SEALs, including the Smees, may go into the field, either with the platoons or with other NSW elements that support the platoons. There are as many as twenty non-SEAL teammates on the team rosters. These are intelligence specialists, communicators, logisticians, and administrative personnel. While the operational end of the SEAL business is a guy thing, there are females among these non-SEAL teammates. Without these non-SEALs, the teams and the squadrons could not function.

One hundred and eighty days prior to operational deployment, D-180, the SEAL team "pluses up" to become a SEAL squadron. At this time, the new squadron begins six months of Squadron Integration Training, or SIT. When the team commanding officer puts on his hat as the squadron commander, he will ultimately be responsible for up to 220 souls and take them in harm's way. This number is a moving target, as the role of the squadrons expands and is redefined by deployment experience and operational requirements. Soon after D-180, a number of units will change operational control, or "chop," to the squadron. These squadron components greatly expand the team's capability.

The new SEAL squadron will acquire a navy of sorts—its SEAL combatant craft. The platoons own and operate their Zodiac-type rubber boats, the CRRCs and outboards, but the larger craft that SEALs often need to get to the job site are the property of the NSW Special Boat Teams. The largest of the SEAL squadron craft are operated by the squadron Mk V detachment. The Mk V Det consists of one officer, fifteen enlisted men, and two Mk V special operations craft. The Mk V is an eighty-two-foot boat that can carry a platoon of SEALs and is armed with heavy machine guns and grenade launchers. It is powered by two turbocharged MTU diesels rated at over 2,200 horsepower each. It's a scalded dog; the Mk V can run in a light sea state at over fifty knots. Carrying SEALs is just one of its special operations taskings. The Mk V is fast, agile, and, with its pump-jet engines, draws only five feet, so it is an excellent light maritime interdiction and surveillance platform.

The squadron will also take on four detachments of rigid-hull inflatable boats, or RHIBs. Each detachment has up to eight men and two boats. The versatile eleven-meter RHIB are the squadron workhorses. Each RHIB is powered by two turbocharged Caterpillar in-line, six-cylinder diesels with jet-pump drives and can carry a SEAL squad–sized element at close to forty knots. Like the Mk Vs, the RHIBs carry machine guns and grenade launchers, and they can do something that a larger boat can not do: they can parachute. When needed, SEAL squadrons will deploy with an MCADS (maritime craft, air deployable system) RHIB detachment. This detachment allows a deployed SEAL squadron to parachute an eleven-meter RHIB, a crew of three, and a squad of SEALs from a C-130 aircraft. This unique blend of SEALs and special boat combatant craft crewmen allow SEALs to come from the air to the sea well offshore and from the sea, over the horizon, to complete a land attack or a maritime mission.

The combat crewmen who maintain and drive the Mk Vs and RHIBs are special in their own right. The Special Warfare Combatant Craft (SWCC) crewmen are sailors who have been carefully selected and highly trained. SWCC personnel are multitasked in the conduct of their trade; they must be proficient in navigation, communications, engineering, seamanship, and weapons. There are a number of NSW taskings and missions that require the smooth integration of SEALs and SWCC crews. Since the first SEAL teams were commissioned, the SEALs and the boat support crews have been brothers-in-arms. SWCC crews often take the same risks in combat as SEALs and can be tasked independently for maritime special operations. The professional respect that SEALs have for the boat guys is deep and long-standing. A great many SEALs owe their lives to the courage of these special sailors. Indeed, I am one of them. During my last SEAL deployment in Vietnam, there were more Purple Hearts awarded in my special boat detachment than in my SEAL platoon.

The regular team platoon SEALs are not the only SEAL elements attached to the squadron. Two platoons of SDV SEALs will chop to the squadron during SIT. The SEAL Delivery Vehicle Team SEALs come to the squadron in a package that allows the squadron to conduct minisubmarine operations from the Mk V craft as well as from submerged submarines. The SDVs currently deploying with SEAL squadrons are Mk-8 SEAL Delivery Vehicles, wet submersibles that can carry four to six SEALs on a variety of maritime and littoral missions. Much of what SEALs do falls under the heading of direct action and special reconnaissance, and the same can be said of SDV operations. The capability and reach of the SDV SEALs is beyond the scope of this book and, in some cases, beyond the security boundaries established for this work. The SDV platoons chop to the squadron with SEALs specially trained in the navigation, operation, and maritime application of these unique submersibles. They also come with a number of talented technicians to keep these sophisticated craft maintained and operable. In addition to those SEALs and support personnel directly assigned to the squadron, there are support assets in theater, embedded with deployed components of the fleet or with the NSW overseas detachments. The launching and recovery of SDVs from a submerged nuclear mother sub is a complex underwater ballet that requires a host of nonsquadron assets and personnel. In recent years, with the focus of SOF on operations in Afghanistan and Iraq, as well as the pursuit of the fractious al-Qaeda, it is easy to focus on the land-warfare roles of Navy SEALs. Yet the capability that the SDVs and the SEALs trained in SDV operations provide is important and singular. No other SOF elements have this unique role. SEALs are able to come from the sea, the air, or across the land. SDVs allow them to travel a considerable distance underwater and come from under the sea.

SEALs from the regular and SDV teams, along with their SWCC brothers, are NSW assets. Other NSW personnel chopped to the squadron include members of the NSW mobile command teams (MCTs). The squadron will pick up four or five of these special communicators and perhaps additional MCT forward-deployed personnel when the squadron arrives in theater. These communicators do not typically operate with the SEALs or aboard Special Warfare Combatant Craft, but serve to support and maintain the command-

and-control links of the deployed operational elements. The squadron will also pick up additional NSW intelligence personnel to augment the management of tactical intelligence and assist with mission-planning support.

The SEAL squadron also acquires non-NSW assets and personnel for operational deployment. One of these, which can and will accompany SEALs and NSW combatant craft on combat operations, is the squadron explosive ordnance disposal detachment. The EOD Det will normally consist of one officer and six enlisted EOD technicians. These men are trained in the render-safe procedures and disposal of military and improvised explosives. Depending on the requirements of the mission, EOD personnel will accompany SEAL squads and platoons in the field and may be embarked on SWCC assets. Missions that involve MOUT, VBSS, and GOPLAT environments could well require EOD participation. The SEAL and SWCC elements that were so successful in capturing the oil terminals during the recent Iraqi campaign had EOD technicians with them to manage and render safe the explosives planted on those platforms.

"We believe the deployment of EOD personnel with the SEAL squadrons is a good use of our technicians," Captain Mike Tillotson told me just prior to combat operations in Iraq. He is the commander of EOD Group One, based in Coronado. "Much as the SEALs receive specific individual and platoon training prior to the team becoming a squadron, we give special training to our EOD technicians to prepare them for this duty. The detachment normally consists of a lieutenant on his second deployment and a senior chief petty officer. Most, if not all, of our techs have some deployment experience. Because our people will be scattered throughout the SEAL squadron elements, we train them to operate individually and in pairs. Our EOD techs are jump and dive qualified, but we try to get them some additional small-arms training before they join the squadron. They will have specific duties and responsibilities as a member of a SEAL element, but they also may find themselves in a firefight and have to be one of the guns in the fight."

"Do you get volunteers for SEAL squadron duty or do you have to draft them?"

"Oh no," Captain Tillotson assured me, "we have plenty of volunteers. Our EOD techs like working with the SEALs."

Captain Tillotson supervised the shallow-water mine clearance effort in and around the port of Umm Qasr during the Iraqi campaign to speed relief supplies to Basra and southern Iraq. SEALs and EOD personnel often work together in mine-clearing operations of this type, often with the SEALs supporting the EOD techs in this dangerous and important work.

In addition to the EOD Det, other non-NSW personnel assigned to the squadron may include linguists, cryptologists, theater-specific intelligence personnel, and special communications technicians. And it appears there will be others. A Marine Corps detachment will soon deploy support of a SEAL squadron. That squadron will then grow by some eighty-five marines. Future Marine deployments with SEALs will await the results of this first deployment.

While the basic components of the squadron are somewhat fixed, each squadron will be a little different when it deploys than the previous one. A deployed squadron commanding officer will speak almost daily to the squadron commander who will relieve him. Shortcomings and lessons learned are immediately applied to the SIT of the next deploying squadron. This allows the squadron commander to use his six-month predeployment training window to build and configure his squadron assets to meet the most current deployment needs. Just as SEAL training must reflect changing mission requirements, so must the SEAL squadron evolve to meet emerging special operations taskings.

SEAL Squadron Three was deployed for the Iraqi campaign and was relieved by SEAL Squadron Five just after the fall of Baghdad. Every component of these SEAL squadrons was used in combat operations in Iraq. This forward-deployed squadron concept was more than validated in this conflict as these squadrons were able to conduct and coordinate multiple special operations simultaneously.

Operationally, it has proved to be a smarter and more efficient way to employ Naval Special Warfare assets. And this diverse capability is forward-deployed 365 days a year, 24/7.

SQUADRON DEPLOYMENT

Squadron deployments typically last for six months. This allows for some predictability in the lives of the SEALs, boat crews, and other squadron personnel. They will have six months overseas and eighteen months back home—although given the out-of-area training requirements, a SEAL spends a great deal of time away even when he is at "home." When deployed overseas, squadron elements will call designated units of the fleet or the Naval Special Warfare Units their home or home base. The West Coast deployed SEAL squadron can rely on NSWU One in Guam and NSWU Three in Bahrain. The East Coast squadron can make use of NSWU Two in Stuttgart, NSWU Four at the Roosevelt Roads Naval Base in Puerto Rico, and NSWU Ten in Rota, Spain. The NSW units support the deployed platoons and squadron assets for logistic and operational support requirements. They also assist the squadron in joint and combined military exercise participation and, more recently, combat operations. There was a lot of activity at NSWU Three up to, during, and following the Iraqi campaign. The West Coast deployed squadron supports the Pacific Command and the Central Command; the East Coast squadron, the European and Southern Commands. While these theater commanders keep their NSW assets busy with scheduled military exercises, they are ready to respond on short notice. One of the reasons SEAL platoons were available for immediate in-theater duty after 9/11 is that there were platoons aboard fleet units and in Bahrain at the time. Within weeks, they were in Afghanistan.

The focus of the deployed squadrons' attention continues to be the Middle East. The Iraqi campaign may be winding down, but the war on terror goes on. And much of this war on terror will continue to have a focus on the Middle East. So while there are ongoing requirements for SEAL and NSW elements worldwide, the two deployed squadrons continue to disproportionately allocate their resources to the Central Command. General Tommy Franks needed them in Afghanistan and again in Iraq, but those are not the only places in which they are needed. Even as SEALs were fighting in Iraq, there were SEALs in the Philippines, South America, and elsewhere to meet ongoing NSW commitments. I can assure you that those SEAL platoons I spoke with who deployed and were not in the Central Command theater of operations were bitterly disappointed. These are warriors who work very hard to get ready for the fight; they want their number called. Many spend a career preparing for war and never fire a shot in anger or go in harm's way. They are like cops who walk a tough beat but somehow never confront a bank robber or a street thug. Between the Persian Gulf war and 9/11, the life of a Navy SEAL was one of preparing for war, but while on deployment they mostly conducted readiness exercises with allied forces around the world. There were exceptions, but very few real-world operations— very little extended time in harm's way. The post-9/11 realities are such that many, if not most, SEALs will test themselves in combat in the war on terror. At the very least, they will deploy in the face of a tangible and immediate threat. Still, they chafe if a deployment goes by without a real engagement. Part of it is the aggressive nature of a warrior to engage the enemy; part of it is the real desire to contribute to this struggle in a meaningful way. This includes the trainers as well as the men in training. Along with the professionalism and sense of purpose, I noticed a longing, even a sadness, among members of the SQT and TRADET cadres. The guys they were training were on their way to the fight, and they were not. Many are counting the days until they can finish their tour at the training command and return to operational duty. On a recent visit to the TRADET offices I bumped into Petty Officer Lynn Kunkle, a.k.a. Bill Murray.

"I see it's now Chief Petty Officer Kunkle," I said, congratulating him on his recent advancement. He was beaming.

"Thank you," he replied, "and you know what this means?"

"You're leaving the training detachment?"

"That's right, and you know what else?"

"Platoon chief?" I ventured.

"Yesssss! I'll be going to Team Five as a platoon chief. This has been my goal since I got into the teams. This was a good tour, but I'm ready for another deployment. I learned a lot here, and I'll miss the guys in the training cadre, but I'm a platoon guy at heart. And now I'm a platoon chief. Life is good!"

I'm often asked how many SEALs there are for immediate duty overseas. Two continually deployed SEAL squadrons place twelve SEAL and four SDV platoons at the disposal of the theater commanders worldwide. There are other SEAL elements that can be made available, but these are small in number, very specialized, and highly classified. Together, the deployed squadrons can muster somewhere on the order of 250 SEALs available for operational tasking. Under certain conditions, as happened briefly in the Iraqi War, the deployed squadrons were held a little longer and elements of the deploying squadrons left a little early. Much as our aircraft carriers overlapped on their deployment rotation, SEAL squadrons can do the same. With this wartime overlap, there could be as many as 500 SEALs available for duty in theater. For how long? As long as necessary; they're Navy SEALs.

THE SQUADRON COMMANDERS

For the individual SEALs and deploying SEAL platoons, their life has not changed a great deal under NSW 21. Most that I asked say the training and deployment workup is much better and that the command and control that governs their operational activities in theater is greatly improved. Yet for the sled dogs in the platoons, it's still a life of train hard for eighteen months and deploy for six. This two-year life cycle has been institutionalized under the reorganization, but the life of a platoon SEAL goes on. Experience and maturity are measured in the number of deployments, much as some of us mark those attributes by the number of years in a marriage. But the change within the team command structure is monumental. NSW 21 brought a whole new way of life to the senior team leadership, far beyond the two new commanding officer billets created with two new SEAL teams. Instead of simply training SEALs for the fight, they now deploy and lead them in the fight. This was a sea change for the senior leadership in the team and none more dramatic than for the team commanding officers. Before NSW 21, the team COs were essentially the senior training officers, responsible for chopping two fully trained SEAL platoons to the operational commanders every six months. Now they, too, are in the deployment cycle. They must not only train their platoons and other squadron elements, they must also train themselves. They and the senior team leadership are now part of the command and control of the deployed squadron assets.

In writing this book, I worked with the commanding officers of SEAL Teams Three, Five, and Seven. As I spoke with them, I tried to assess their approach and leadership style as they assumed this new and larger role of squadron commander. This was the first time since the reorganization that these three SEAL teams made the team-to-squadron buildup and deployed as a squadron. This is the first time that these three officers, selected from among their peers for command of a SEAL team, have had this much responsibility.

As discussed in chapter 4, the PRODEV period focuses on individual training requirements. The rotation and assignment of SEAL team commanding officers is timed to bring that new CO to the team shortly before his team begins PRODEV. This allows the incoming CO to begin the deployment workup with the SEALs he will take to the fight. Due to platoon assignments and leadership progression within the platoons, the new team CO will inherit six SEAL platoons that have a fixed cadre of veteran SEALs and some of the platoon leadership in place. Platoon makeup will be altered by the departure of the platoon OIC and the platoon chief, and perhaps an experienced petty officer who will leave the platoon and the team for other duty, possibly at BUD/S or SQT. One or two of the first- or second-tour SEALs may leave the Navy. The remaining officer, the AOIC, and senior petty officers are two years older and two years more experienced than when whey began preparation for their last deployment. Most of the time, the AOIC will move into the OIC position, but not always. Occasionally, the LPO will make chief petty officer and move into the key role as his platoon's chief petty officer. As new veterans and new men from the finishing school become available, there is jostling and positioning among the platoons for the best available talent. Reputation is everything in the SEAL teams; new men and veterans alike are known quantities. They all have status and baggage. The outgoing CO and the new CO are contemporaries and often friends; they will talk at length prior to their change of command. Personnel assignments will dominate those discussions. The new CO will inherit a fixed platoon structure, but it will be his inescapable responsibility to validate and confirm the final manning of the platoons. This is now his team.

"Leadership decisions are always the toughest," Commander Shawn Harkness told me when Team Five began PRODEV. "The guy I relieved left this team in good shape, but the key leadership within the platoons has changed. I have to be comfortable with this. During PRODEV, I will be spending a lot of my time with my new platoon OICs and platoon chiefs."

Harkness is the commanding officer of SEAL Team Five. He is a former enlisted man who returned to the teams after a break in service to attend college. Actually, he was beginning his third year of medical school when he decided that the calling of a warrior was stronger than that of a healer.

"It's a matter of talent and chemistry," Harkness told me. "I can make one or two super platoons with the best talent, but I have to field six platoons. And too much talent or the wrong personalities affects chemistry. During PRODEV, my command master chief and I will get out as much as we can to watch the guys. Sometimes it's hard, since many of them are off to schools. But we see enough to know if the platoons are beginning to jell. The officers will bring any problems to me, but first they go through the chain of command. The platoon chiefs go straight to the command master chief. The command master chief and I will make the final decision on platoon assignments and platoon leadership. I have a great CMC. We agree most of the time but not always.

"I guess what it come downs to," Harkness concluded, "is a matter of trust. I have to have absolute trust in the senior leadership of my platoons. Ultimately, it's my responsibility; I have to do everything in my power to see the platoon SEALs have the best possible leadership."

All the team COs I spoke with talked about having to make leadership changes and how difficult that was on all concerned. They spoke about this reluctantly, even sadly.

"I hate to be negative or pessimistic," a team CO told me, "but I have to plan on relieving a platoon officer or one of the senior petty officers in a platoon—perhaps even a platoon OIC or platoon chief. This is critical business, for the platoon and for the officer or petty officer who is taken out of the platoon; it's basically a career-ender. But these platoons are going in harm's way, and I have to have complete confidence in the combat leadership. I have plenty of good shooters; I need men I can trust. And that means I cannot leave a weak leader in a platoon just because I haven't planned on what to do if one of these key leaders is not performing to standard. There's really nothing more serious than platoon leadership."

In two of the three teams preparing platoons for squadron deployment, platoon officers and senior petty officers were relieved of their duties by their commanding officers.

When the six platoons leave the team and chop to TRADET for Unit Level Training, the team CO is left with his executive officer, operations officer, and those SEALs, most of them senior petty officers, who will staff the deployed squadron task units. The skeleton crew that is left at the team area also includes the team admin and support cadre. Most of the Smees are away at school, gaining expertise in their assigned subject-matter area, or out catching some training with the platoons.

"We work a lot of command-and-control issues, and look for opportunities to get some time in at the Group Mission Support Center." Commander Clark Trainor is the CO of SEAL Team Three. "If the opportunity presents itself, I try to get a few of the guys overseas to the deployed squadron or one of the NSW units. Maybe they can learn something that can better prepare us for our deployment."

"Do you ever get out to watch the platoons during ULT?" I asked.

"I do," Trainor said, "but I do this very carefully. Don't get me wrong. I'm very concerned that they get good training, and I certainly want to see my platoon leadership in the field, but I have to respect TRADET; it's their responsibility. I don't want to undercut their authority, nor do I want to disturb the focus of the platoons. It's a matter of trust. TRADET has to conduct training, and the platoon leadership has to see that their men are trained. If one of my platoons is having problems, the platoon leadership and the training cadre will work to solve it. If not, then I'll get a call from Brian Schmidt. That's a call Brian does not want to make and one I don't want to get."

Joe Rosen at Team Seven had this to say. "It's quiet around here with the platoons in ULT. It's like the kids all left home and went to college at the same time. But I can use the time. It allows me to firm up some of the stay-behind requirements for our deployment."

"Stay-behind requirements?"

"When we deploy, I have to have an element here on the Strand to look out for the team while we're away—actually, to look out for the entire squadron. There are operational and family considerations that are very important to us. I'll leave behind a lieutenant who has had a platoon OIC tour and a master chief, and probably one of our admin types. I want them here to handle any personnel or logistics issues that come up and to help us better make use of the MSC [Mission Support Center] while we're deployed." Rosen is an affable man with an easy disposition, but suddenly he is serious. "Now don't misunderstand this, but my job is to keep those platoon SEALs on the job and the rest of the squadron at their stations. They're a combat team, and if someone has to come back on emergency leave, that platoon or squad or support component will have to do the mission a man short. We don't have replacement SEALs or SWCC crewmen, at least not ones that can jump into a platoon or a boat crew that's been together for eighteen months or more. It's a tough decision to release a guy on deployment to come back for a family emergency. If I have a good stay-behind element, then maybe they can step in and help out or defer the problem until we come off deployment. It sounds cold, but I have to keep those guns in the fight. And those guns in the fight have to know that unless it's really serious, the stay-behind element will handle it until we complete the tour. It's no easy thing, balancing the needs of the mission with the needs of the men and their families. No matter how much you try to plan for these things, problems always come up when the guys are away, and each case is different. And, of course, we have to put a casualty assistance plan into place if one of the guys gets hurt or killed. All the team COs and squadron commanders give this a lot of thought. There's a lot more to this business than just getting the team and the squadron ready for combat."

"Ever long for the days when you were a platoon commander and had nothing to do but get the guns trained for the fight?"

"Yeah, those were the days, alright." His smile has returned. "But even now, I insist that my platoon OICs and platoon chiefs take an active role in the welfare of their men. If a personal or family problem of one of their men gets out of hand due to his inattention, they're going to know just how unhappy I am. They all know where I stand on this; I don't think we'll have any problems on that issue."

All the deploying squadrons have at least one ombudsman (or more) in place before they deploy. It is usually the wife of one of the senior members of the team. One squadron had two of them, who shared the duty. The ombudsman's job is to serve as an informal liaison between the families and the squadron commander. She works for him. It's a volunteer duty and an important one. A squadron commander has a lot on his plate. He has lines of communication through Navy channels to the families at home, but the ombudsman has the ability to cut through any red tape and go straight to her squadron commander.

"Our ombudsman is the wife of one of my senior chiefs and a terrific lady," Clark Trainor told me. "She knows the Navy, and she knows the Navy family. I trust her to let me know just how serious a family problem really is. Some of the wives are young and have never been through this before. She will get them through it and let me know if something back home needs my attention. Cutting a man away on deployment is a very crucial decision. His team depends on him; so does his family. The decision lies with me, and there is usually a downside to whatever I decide. Before I make the call, I'll want to talk to my ombudsman."

SQUADRON INTEGRATION TRAINING

At D-180, the platoons return home to their parent SEAL team and the SEAL team becomes a SEAL squadron. The squadron commander now has a great number of moving parts to his organization, an organization he will have to lead into combat in six months. During the six-month squadron integration training period, there are any number of issues on the squadron commander's plate, but there are three that will consume most of his time: training his SEAL platoons; training his command and control, or C2, elements; and the integration of the non-SEAL and non-NSW assets into his squadron.

For the most part, the SEAL platoons are fundamentally combat ready; but in the SEAL culture, there is always room for improvement. One of the first things a squadron commander will do is gather his platoon OICs and platoon chiefs and take a measure of their six-month ULT. Where are they strong? In what areas do the platoons feel they need additional training? The platoon capabilities will be evaluated in light of the emerging needs of the theater commanders; what current events may drive future squadron mission taskings? Platoons will have been training with some idea of which platoons and how many platoons will be assigned to a given theater. As deployment date draws near, platoon theater assignments may be altered to reflect the needs of combatant commanders. This may even drive squadron makeup. Up to and during the Iraqi campaign, an East Coast platoon was chopped to the West Coast squadron to beef up NSW support for CENTCOM. During the course of two successive squadron deployments, the West Coast SEAL squadron deployed with seven platoons and the East Coast squadron with five. Because of the uniform training standards established in SQT and carried through during ULT on both coasts, SEAL platoons are able to mix and match, because they all have trained in much the same way.

"For most of platoon training, we worked only with our sister platoon," Lieutenant Phil Rasmussen of Team Five told me, referring to his brother's platoon at SEAL Team Five. "During SIT, our task unit, Task Unit Charlie, was the squadron's primary CENTCOM task unit. Task Unit Charlie picked up an additional team platoon, Five Delta. Our training operations with them were seamless; everyone was on the same sheet of music. We also conducted some training with the platoon on loan from Team Eight. No problems. The East Coast guys are good to go and then some."

"SIT is when I want to see them in the field," said Clark Trainor. "Platoons, like individual SEALs, have strengths and weaknesses. Some are better at maritime operations than others. Some have become my best VBSS or GOPLAT operators. I have the input from TRADET, but I want to see it for myself. For this there are scheduled military exercises during SIT which will give me that opportunity."

"We were having some problems with the MK43s in our platoons," Joe Rosen said. "Not all of them were resolved during ULT. Early on in SIT is the time to get these equipment deficiencies cleared up. As for platoon training during SIT, I get a continuing flow of information from the deployed squadrons. What our guys are doing right now in Afghanistan, Iraq, and the Philippines will drive our training right up until the day we deploy." He gives me that easy grin. "I have a whole lot of balls I have to keep in the air in getting the squadron ready to go. For the guys in the platoon, it's pretty simple. All they want is to get good equipment, get good training, and get the chance. When you've watched these guys prepare for deployment, you know they have a wide range of skills and can tackle any number of maritime and inland targets. But as we get closer to deployment, my platoons will focus on the basics. They have to move, shoot, communicate, and patch themselves up if they get hit. I want them to get a good review of the basics in the latter stages of SIT. When it's real world and they have to improvise or make last-minute changes to accomplish the mission, well, that's what we do best."

Once deployed, the platoons and other squadron assets will be tasked with missions at the direction of the theater commander. In the case of the Central Command during the Iraqi campaign, General Tommy Franks did not sit in his headquarters in Qatar and dream up missions for his SEAL squadron. Its missions were given to them by the land force and fleet commanders, and in some cases the air commander. These mission taskings come down through the various levels of command and ultimately to the appropriate special operations task group commander. That task group commander will decide who among his inventory of SOF assets is best suited to do the job. Is it an Army Special Forces mission or one for the Rangers? Or is this a SEAL or maritime tasking? If the mission requires SEALs or boats, it will be assigned to one of the Naval Special Warfare task units. These NSW task units are comprised of SEALs, communicators, intelligence specialists, and support personnel from the squadron and from the theater Naval Special Warfare Unit personnel. This NSW task unit commander could be the squadron commander, his deputy, or one of the other senior squadron SEALs.

The task units are responsible for tasking and working with the platoons or other squadron assets to plan, prepare for, and support the mission. During the conduct of the mission, the task unit will usually serve as the primary C2 element for the men on the mission. In some cases, other SOF elements will be assigned to the NSW action element, or NSW assets may serve to support other SOF or conventional forces. No matter how the mission tasking evolves, when there are SEALs or NSW combatant craft committed to an operation, their task unit will be watching over them very closely.

Joe Rosen again: "During SIT, I will find any excuse I can to get my task units out working and communicating—interacting with fleet units, SEALs in the field, and boat units under way. We take advantage of every exercise opportunity, and, when possible, I want them interacting with the Mission Support Center and the group logistical support unit. Sometimes there are FTXs where we can exercise our guys in the field with other ground and air units; sometimes these are computer-driven command-post exercises that test our mission planning and C2 skills. I also try to rotate my platoon officers through the task units during exercise play so they can see what goes on in the task units to support them in the field."

"I was lucky," said Clark Trainor at Squadron Three. "We had the benefit of Exercise Millennium Challenge during our SIT. This was a large, multiservice exercise to test all levels of command, control, and communications during the buildup that supported the Iraqi campaign. I was able to set up two task units, one here on the Strand and another on San Clemente Island. We had the whole squadron engaged. Each platoon got to work up and execute two full-mission profiles, and there were specific taskings for the SDVs, RHIBs, and Mk Vs. The exercise lasted two weeks and the guys got very little sleep. My task unit personnel worked twelve hours on, twelve hours off. But the squadron performed superbly; we had our problems, but the guys worked through them. After Millennium Challenge, I felt a great deal better about taking this squadron to war."

"It's always hard to know how much to push them," Shawn Harkness at Squadron Five told me. "During ULT, I expected my platoons to have that thousand-yard stare, given the amount of time that they were in the field. But how hard do you push the squadron?

This is the first time most of us have had to command a force this diverse, training it for a wartime deployment. And there's the question of time off before you take them overseas. There's a lot to do, but you still want to give them time with their families—that's very important. If there wasn't the ongoing operations in Afghanistan and the Philippines, and the possibility of war with Iraq, I couldn't work them this hard."

The squadron integration training period is largely driven by the squadron commander's vision and what training opportunities come his way in the form of military exercises or training venues that he can orchestrate. Given the growing importance of close air support (CAS), SEAL platoons often travel to Nellis Air Force Base near Las Vegas to work with the Air Force, or to Fallon Naval Air Station in southern Nevada to work with the Navy. When possible, the SEAL platoons were out in the desert directing air strikes for Air Force F-15s and F-16s, and for Navy F-14s and F/A-18s. The pilots need the training, as well as the SEALs. CAS training includes directing training munitions to GPS coordinates and using laser designators to "paint" moving targets for destruction from the air. The Iraqis found out just how good our SOF operators and pilots were at this during the war.

"We devoted a lot of time to CAS training in SIT," said Lieutenant John Rasmussen. "And a lot of time with other elements of the squadron. Commander Harkness went out of his way to make sure that we spent time on the boats and that the operational squadron units got plenty of time working our task units."

"I understand that you have EOD men assigned to your platoon."

"That's right. I have two in my platoon, one for each squad. We've designed some of the training that involves them, like disarming mines or using them to set breaching charges. They're great guys. They don't have the time on the gun like we do, but they can hold up their end in a firefight. Given what we might get into on deployment, it'll be nice to have them in the squad file."

The closer the squadron gets to deployment, the more frequently the deploying SEAL squadron commander will try to speak with the squadron commander he will relieve. And it's not just the squadrons with CENTCOM responsibility. The deploying commanders have to think about their commitments in Central and South America, Korea, the Philippines, Indonesia, and Southeast Asia. On the West Coast, Squadrons Three and Five were deployed during the Iraqi campaign. The SEALs at Squadron Seven were finishing ULT or going into SIT. When their training duties allowed, they had to watch the war on TV like the rest of us. Commander Joe Rosen did his best to help his men understand that the Iraqi campaign was really only a single military campaign in the war on terror. Still, they are anxious to take their rotation in the combat zone. I asked Joe about this.

"In some ways, I feel just like the guys in the platoons; the war's going to be over before we get there, and peace will have broken out. Intellectually, I know that's not the case. There are still going to be a lot of bad guys in our AO, and there are a lot of places for them to hide. The peace may be just as challenging for us in SOF as during the war. We know there will be work waiting for us in Afghanistan and the Philippines. Who knows how many of the Ba'ath Party will have gone to ground in Iraq when it's over. And there will be pockets of al-Qaeda in any number of places, or at sea. For the most part, my platoons are good to go and could be called on if needed in Iraq, but we're a long way from having an integrated, combat-ready squadron. I tell the guys, and myself, to keep working and have patience. There'll be plenty to do when we get there."

A good squadron commander also has to look past the deployment of his squadron, to the time when the squadron will again revert to team status, and he will hand his team off to a new commanding officer. "Even before we deploy, I have to be thinking ahead to what the team will look like when we come off deployment," Rosen told me. "Somewhere between thirty and forty guys will be leaving the team, and that many will be coming to the team. I like to talk with the officers who are due for rotation—counsel them and see what their objectives are, and what I can do to help. There are always a few who want to finish their tour and get out, and maybe one or two of those who I'm going to try my darnedest to get to think about staying in. Sometimes a good deployment will help me to get our best officers to stay for a career. Most will stay in, but they all have attractive opportunities on the outside. It's their choice, but I do what I can to get the best of them to stay. My command career counselor and command master chief will work with the enlisted men, and I will want to talk with some of the senior men. The senior enlisted men are the key to the future of our SEAL culture, and we have to take care of these guys. Time to do this will be in short supply once we get overseas. I want to do everything I can to address these personnel issues before we deploy."

During the busy course of the West Coast squadron workups, the squadron commanders try to orchestrate at least one squadron family social event. These usually take the form of beach picnics or a barbecue—burgers, hot dogs, and chili—at one of the local parks. There is no single day or time that will find all the squadron on the Strand or in San Diego at one time, but they try to catch as many of the squadron members as they can. These are volleyball and touch football affairs, and if there is a quorum of SEALs involved there will probably be a Monster Mash. These are usually run-swim-run affairs, challenging enough for the younger guys to sort out who is fast and who is faster, and long enough for the older SEALs to work up an appetite and a thirst—although there was a lot more bottled water and soda in the ice tubs than beer at the event I attended. I also learned that some of the EOD and SWCC men can run and swim, and that there are some competitive triathletes among the SEAL wives who can run and swim with the best of them.

The spouses and families of Navy SEALs are as special as their husbands and fathers. During my time with the platoons and squadrons, I had the opportunity to meet many of the wives and a few of the children of Navy SEALs. As you would expect, they were uniformly proud and supportive of their men. During the past several years at the training command, I found that few BUD/S trainees and SQT students were married. Something less than 5 percent enter SEAL training with a spouse. So most SEALs marry after they have earned their Trident and, given the rapid pace and steep learning curve they experience during their first deployment workup, most of the new SEALs marry after their first operational deployment. So the majority of these new wives married SEALs, not sailors or civilians who wanted to become SEALs; they married this team animal, and with that came at least some understanding of what they were getting into. They met this guy, and given the pack behavior of off-duty SEALs, they probably met his platoon mates as well. When a SEAL gets married, there is often a liberal sprinkling of teammates among the contingent of groomsmen. Dating and marrying a Navy SEAL, who comes with a charismatic band of warrior brothers, probably has its share of romance and excitement. After the honeymoon—if he can get the time off for one—this woman becomes a Navy wife and the wife of a Navy SEAL. The learning curve for a new SEAL wife is probably as steep as it is for a new guy in the platoons. But for the new SEAL spouses, there is no program like BUD/S or SQT to prepare her for this duty. Most SEALs have no real understanding of just how much time they will spend away from home until they experience it in the platoons. They were told about it, but it takes an operational deployment cycle to really bring this home. The women who marry SEALs have to know their guys are going overseas and that they will be away much of the time when they are home, training for the next deployment. But dating a guy who travels a lot is different from waiting for a man who doesn't come home like other husbands do. I have no statistics to offer on the divorce rate among SEALs compared with that among the population at large or even among other the military communities. I do know there is a recognition among the senior leadership of the NSW community that a good marriage usually makes a good warrior a better one. They also know that a bad marriage is bad for everyone—for the woman who doesn't understand the competing demands on her husband's time, and for the SEAL who cannot focus on his work when things aren't right at home. The life chosen by a

Navy SEAL can be very hard on those who love and depend on him. In that same vein, many of the more mature and capable SEALs I met did not hesitate to tell me that their home life was a great source of strength and peace of mind.

One thing I did see in the women who marry Navy SEALs—especially the younger ones—was that they were a lot like the men they married. By that, I mean that they were fit, capable, well educated, and aggressive. And more than a few are simply drop-dead beautiful. Many are professionals who make more money than their husbands. In talking with some of the junior officers and enlisted SEALs approaching the end of their initial period of obligated service, I learned that their spouses will figure in the decision of whether these men will stay in or get out. As with many military families, the separations are difficult, but it's more than that for some of these talented young women. They have a range of interests and careers. When a SEAL comes off deployment and wants to focus on time with his wife and family, her career may not allow her to drop what she's doing just because he's home. Additionally, Navy SEALs get transferred. Enlisted men are often with the same team for six years or more, but a platoon OIC can count on leaving his team after his OIC deployment, perhaps sooner for a special assignment. The more senior the SEAL, the more often he may be transferred. If his wife is running a business or trying to make partner in her law firm, this could lead to a discussion as to whose career is the most flexible. There is a saying in the naval service: Navy Wife—the toughest job in the Navy. That certainly applies, and then some, for the Navy SEAL wife.

On the eve of their deployments, I ask these squadron commanders about their apprehensions. What, if anything, kept them staring at the ceiling at night?

"If our timing's good, or bad depending on your point of view, we're going to get caught up in a war in Iraq. We're going to be doing a lot of things at sea and on land. Many think what we do and how we do it is all supersecret. But the bad guys often know we could show up at any time, and sometimes they know how we'll be coming. And that means we can have only tactical surprise at best. These are high-risk missions. We train hard and the guys are ready, but they can only be so ready." He turns thoughtful a moment, then continues. "I guess I'm afraid of mines—land mines or even chemical mines—that may be laid just for us. The speed of a mission may not allow us to move as carefully as we'd like, whether it's looking for mines or looking for enemy snipers. And much of what we may be asked to do is out of our control. There are a lot of things we do that conventional forces can't. And if the conventional forces get bogged down in a ground war, there may be a lot more things we'll be asked to do. We're all volunteers and we do this because we want to. Still, I love these guys and I want to bring them all home. But the mission comes first. They know that and I know that."

"This Iraq business," another told me, "it's a bittersweet thing. We hope we get on deployment before it's over, at least the guys do. Just like the deployed squadron hopes it will go down before they leave. We want to do what we're trained to do, but you can't pray for war like you pray for rain. Concerns? I have my share. I've been pushing these guys pretty hard, both the team guys and the rest of the squadron. I have to do everything in my power to see that my squadron is ready for war. But there's a point when I have to step back and give them some time off. Sometimes knowing when they need not to train is the hardest part—when more training does not translate into operational readiness. And they're breakable. This is high-risk training, and when they get tired they get hurt. At this stage of the game, we go with what we have; we don't have a bench to go to. A few weeks ago I had a guy get hurt in training. My command master chief, the platoon chief, the platoon OIC, and I talked about it, and we decided the platoon would go with a man short. We tried, but we couldn't find another SEAL with the experience and maturity to jump in with the platoon. Or better said, we couldn't find a SEAL that the platoon chief and the OIC felt would fit in and help their platoon. Myself, I would have tried to bring another SEAL in; one who had recently come off deployment and was ready to go back. But at this stage of the game, I'm not going to tell my platoon leadership how to do their job, or in that particular case, the composition of their platoon. Truth be told, I can't wait to deploy. Once we're gone, I can trade all these how-can-we-get-ready concerns for a whole other set of worries."

"We'll begin SIT in another two weeks," Joe Rosen told me on the eve of the war in Iraq. "Anything can happen, but unless this is another Vietnam, the main-force fighting will be over long before we get in theater, and this country is not going to do any more Vietnams. Actually, this is a good thing; there's going to be no shortage of work and probably fewer people to do it. Most of the forces will have rotated out, and the rats that went to ground during the war will have to come out sometime." He grins. "Maybe we'll have them all to ourselves." Then he turns serious. "But try to tell the guys that. Platoon SEALs have a way of feeling they're always on the wrong deployment cycle or deployed to the wrong AO—that they just missed the action on their last deployment or that it won't wait for them until they can return in-theater on the next deployment. I try to help them see the big picture, and not just invent something to get them to focus on training."

"I'm not sure I understand," I reply.

He shoots me another grin. "You're like a lot of my guys. You see, we're in a war on terrorism, and whatever we do in Iraq is just part of the bigger picture. In my opinion, when we do go to Baghdad, we will begin a process that will hopefully bring fundamental change to that whole region. But that's going to take some time—in my opinion, a long time. Occupying Iraq is like stepping on a tube of toothpaste with the cap on. Toothpaste is going to squirt out, but you don't know where or how much. But it's going to happen. We want change in the Middle East; there are those who will oppose us every step of the way. And we don't know how or where they may come at us—CENTCOM, the Pacific, Horn of Africa? And how about North Korea? That's the big picture. The little picture, our picture, is that we have to be ready to fight any number of enemies in a large and often very troubled world. In some ways, the squadrons ahead of us had it easy. They trained to a full range of mission profiles, but they were able to focus on Iraq. We don't have that luxury. So I tell the guys that there will be plenty of work, maybe more than the squadron we relieve had. Only we may not know where it will happen, when it will happen, or exactly who the bad guys may turn out to be. We have to be ready to take care of business."

"Anywhere, anytime?"

"Anywhere, anytime."

One of the primary duties of a squadron commander is to set the right ethical tone for his squadron; what he will and won't tolerate in the way of behavior; what are and are not acceptable standards of professional conduct and performance. The squadron commanders set the moral foundation from which their squadron will project its power. I found that they all did this, in their own fashion, with their own personal leadership style. What follows are the words that Commander Shawn Harkness set down in writing for SEAL Team Five, and by extension, SEAL Squadron Five.

> I want to pass on my command philosophy so you know where I stand:
>
> - Honor, courage, and commitment are words I believe in.
> - I will command SEAL Team Five according to the Uniform Code of Military Justice, Navy Regulations, and my own moral compass.
> - Alcohol abuse is not a rite of passage. No matter how much one drinks, he is responsible at all times for his actions.
> - I have a zero-tolerance policy on drugs, sexism, and racism.

- Honest mistakes are acceptable; willful disobedience is not.
- All of our actions must be legal, moral, and ethical.
- Know your job and be prepared to use your skills when needed.
- Understand what it means to turn "IT" on and off.
- Nothing good ever happens after midnight.
- Technicians do their job so we can do ours; respect is a two-way street.
- Keep the Commander informed.
- I am open to your suggestions, but follow the chain of command.
- I am here to assist you in reaching your career goals.
- Weapons, crypto, and other sensitive equipment and publications will be 100% safeguarded and accounted for at all times.
- Work hard, play hard.
- Flexibility is found in the dictionary under Naval Special Warfare.
- Loyalty goes up and down the chain of command.

SEAL Squadron Five deployed in support of combat operations in the Central Command during Operation Iraqi Freedom. The superb contribution of the warriors from Squadron Five is now part of the battle history of Naval Special Warfare.

EPILOGUE

The Fight Continues

Navy SEALs have fought bravely in Afghanistan and Iraq. They have written new chapters in the battle history of the teams. In the early spring of 2003 at Windsor Castle in England there was a quiet, private ceremony to honor a Navy SEAL for his heroism. He was presented with the Military Cross, England's second-highest award for gallantry. On 28 June 2003, an awards ceremony was held in this country to recognize SEALs who had distinguished themselves in combat. Again, it was a ceremony neither the public nor the media was allowed to attend—only family and military guests. Among the awards were a Navy Cross and seventeen Silver Stars. These awards were given in private because of the nature of this fight and to protect the SEALs who must continue it. How do these men feel about the lack of public recognition for their heroism? They fully accept and even welcome their anonymity. They are professional warriors; it's all about the job. Those who count most, their families and brother warriors, know of their bravery and sacrifice.

Many of those recognized were not there to have their decorations

---

First shot of the day. An SQT student shoots from a set perch during a Combat Stress Course. He would never silhouette himself like this in a tactical situation. *Photo by Dick Couch*

for bravery pinned on. They were deployed overseas—back on the job. One of them returned to the fight under unique conditions. During the Afghan campaign, he lost a leg below the knee. Yet he was back in combat with his SEAL brothers for the Iraqi campaign—*on a prosthetic foot*. We fight a vicious enemy; America is fortunate to have a generation of dedicated warriors who are up to the task. Since our nation went to war following the attacks of 9/11, Navy SEALs have been fully engaged in this war. They have conducted hundreds of combat special operations in Afghanistan and Iraq. They are there right now.

I have two mental images of those two very different conflicts. In Afghanistan, it's an Army Special Forces sergeant, caked with dirt and two weeks' worth of beard, standing alongside a Northern Alliance commander. Our sergeant has an M4 rifle in one hand and a radio handset in the other. He's speaking to the Afghan in Pashto, and on the radio he's giving eight-digit grid coordinates in English to the Navy F/A-18 circling overhead. Moments later, a string of explosions march along the line of Taliban resistance. Then the Northern Alliance leader beckons his troops forward and they advance, but none of them get too far from the Special Forces sergeant and his radio. In Iraq, it's much different. The image in this fight is much younger—maybe fifteen years younger. He's a marine on the back of an armored amphibious vehicle, and he's some one hundred miles from any beachhead. When an embedded reporter asks, "You guys are moving awfully fast; what's the hurry?" the baby-faced marine, who is just as grimy as the SF sergeant in Afghanistan, replies, "We have to beat the Army to Baghdad!" Two images in two differently fought wars that nevertheless had the same results: dramatic American victories.

Who are these guys, and why are they so good? What the Soviet Army could not do in Afghanistan in ten years, they did in a few months. The 3rd Infantry Division and the 1st Marine Expeditionary Force overran Iraq in a matter of weeks. It was nearly over before the 101st Airborne and the 4th Infantry Division got into action. Military analysts say we are becoming skilled disciples of John Boyd.

That is, we execute the Boyd Loop—observation, orientation, decision, action (OODA)—far better and far quicker than our enemies. In fighter-pilot parlance, we continue to "turn inside" the enemy and enjoy continuous tactical advantage. Our forces react more swiftly and with far superior technology, so much so that the enemy is kept confused and disordered. The OODA loop also leads to an unprecedented mission compression capability. Simply stated, we're faster. We saw this in Iraq when it was a matter of minutes from the sighting of Saddam Hussein, or one of his doubles, to the arrival of a two-thousand-pound bunker buster. This compressed loop also applies to the relatively low-tech business of special operations. All those years of "train like you fight" paid off. When a piece of perishable intelligence comes in, there is often no time for detailed briefings and rehearsals. A SEAL mission leader almost has to draw the play up in the sand before they board the insertion helo. Then you fight like you train. This happened often in Afghanistan and Iraq. Another reason for our success: Our guys are better than their guys. America is developing a warrior culture with historically unprecedented superiority.

"We do it much faster than anyone else," a platoon SEAL from Team Three told me on his return from Iraq. "We went from the warning order to boots on the ground in a matter of minutes. We did it in a matter of hours during platoon training in ULT, but we did it a lot faster in Iraq."

There is also the issue of courage. For more than two years now, Navy SEALs have been engaged in combat operations. One of them said to me, "Captain, it's just like what it must have been for you in Vietnam; we go out every night." And just like in Vietnam, this dangerous business becomes almost routine—until something goes wrong. Then all the technology, superior equipment, and superior tactics become side issues. Then it's all about the gun in the fight—how well he can react and how much fire there is in his belly. It's all about courage. There have been numerous incidents of courage under fire in Afghanistan and Iraq, but that is a story for another time—and another book.

Large-scale combat operations in Iraq are now in the rearview mirror. As our nation bends to the task of rebuilding and rehabilitating that country, what's next? The conflicts in Iraq and Afghanistan are but campaigns in the war on terrorism and those who aid or harbor terrorists. Looking ahead, there is no shortage of potential adversaries or issues that need attention. There are the fundamentalist Shiite Islamist clerics in Iran, the Wahhabis in Saudi Arabia, and remnants of the Ba'ath Party in Iraq and in Syria, to name a few. And, of course, there is the thorny Palestinian issue. All of these relate to our war on terrorism. We will be engaged in these issues and in Iraq for years to come. For the most part, our engagement will be diplomatic, economic, and political. But the military option is always there. When the cards are dealt around the diplomatic table, Colin Powell's, or his successor's, first two cards will be aces—one for Afghanistan and one for Iraq. What our military did in those two countries will not soon be forgotten by those who oppose our national interests in the region. Economically, we have a lot to offer. Few American secretaries of state have been as motivated as Mr. Powell to offer so large a carrot, nor have they carried a bigger stick. In this war on terror, we can help to rebuild a nation, or we can cross international boundaries with armored columns. Whether our stay in Iraq proves to be a fulcrum from which to leverage this carrot-and-stick approach to further our interests in the region, or a tar baby, remains to be seen.

And what are our interests in this oil-rich, troubled part of the world, specifically as it relates to the war on terrorism? Thomas Friedman, no friend of the Bush administration, tacitly backed the invasion of Iraq, but with a long list of reservations. These reservations centered on our ability to do the heavy lifting in Iraq after the removal of Saddam Hussein. Amid his "if you break it you have to fix it" admonition was the central theme that if we, as a nation, don't enfranchise Arab youth with the wealth of their land, then they will remain ripe for recruitment for duty as terrorists. Young Arab men with nothing to lose will come at us, in wave after wave, generation after generation. I believe this. What Mr. Friedman is suggesting is that if we don't drain the swamp where the rats are breeding, it won't really matter how many of these rats we kill; they will continue to leave the swamp and migrate to our cities in numbers that are legion. I also believe that the first step in this swamp-draining project is to do the right thing in Iraq, no matter how much it costs or how long it takes. And that is easier said than done. Our stay there must be neither too long nor too short. Every mistake and misstep along the way, and there will be many, will be fairly and prominently reported in the *New York Times,* and boldly heralded by al-Jazeera. Yet in the long run, draining the swamps that breed terrorists will be far cheaper than the personal, humanitarian, and financial costs to this nation if we don't. It's the right thing to do, but it will take time.

There are other considerations. What about the recently recruited rats, or the rats that are headed our way? What about the stateless rats that move within the region's many tribal and ethnic areas? They are plague infected and have no home to which they can return. These are Chechen, Uzbek, Egyptian, and Saudi expatriates, among others, who have no place to go; these are very serious rats. I believe we have two wars to fight: the war on terrorism and the war on *terrorists.* This brings us to a particularly nasty part of this complex equation: What do we do about these terrorists? In many cases, they have strong financial backing and lethal technologies at their disposal. And if our diplomatic and economic pressures do manage to end their state sponsorship, will they fight on? I think so. Al-Qaeda needs Saudi money more than it needs the Saudi government to look the other way. So while we do the right thing in Iraq, and by extension for all Arabs who suffer from repressive or inept regimes, we must still deal with al-Qaeda. Perhaps Hezbollah and Hamas will become nasty if we are able to end their patronage in Iran and Saudi Arabia. For all those terrorists who refuse to leave the field, we have a serious and effective antidote: American special operations forces. SOF, along with their brothers in the CIA Special Activities Division, will have to run this vermin to ground. Very simply, they have to be tracked, found, and killed. It's the only short-term solution—until, of course, the swamps are drained.

While the bulk of our conventional forces come home, SOF will remain engaged. They are in Afghanistan, Iraq, the Philippines, the Horn of Africa, and Indonesia, to name a few. In some cases they are working with allies to meet this threat, and in others they operate independently—on patrol in rugged, hostile country. Often, they are forward-deployed at overseas bases or in units of the fleet, waiting for the terrorists to make their next move. We have to keep the pressure on and take the fight to their ground so they will have more difficulty bringing it to our ground. There may be other Afghanistans or Iraqs—wars conducted by SOF or conventional war supported by SOF—but I don't think so. Our battlefield strength and airpower is simply too overwhelming. The people we want will go underground, into the mountains, or into the cities, and we will have to go in after them—with allies if they are willing, or by acting unilaterally if they are not. It is not a nice business. In the past, we have used euphemisms like *low-intensive conflict* or *operations other than war* (OTW). More simply and directly put, we have to find these people and kill them; it's an extermination process. It will be a dangerous and difficult business, and it's going to take a long time.

The professional skill set of the military special operator will continue to be the tools of the trade in this ongoing war on terrorists. New men will have to be trained to shoot, move, communicate, and survive in urban and mountainous terrain. They will have to know how to live in other cultures and speak their languages. They will have to be able to endure hardship, isolation, and extended periods of danger. If one of their own is wounded, they will have to care for them in the worst possible conditions. And the warriors who did this in Afghanistan and Iraq will have to mentor and train the new men just entering this perilous business. The training commands do a wonderful job, but some things can only be learned on patrol in enemy territory or by a combat internship.

The Navy SEAL will continue to train for all this and more. While his duties will still carry him well beyond the shoreline, SEALs will remain our nation's primary maritime SOF component. SEALs will have to board ships at sea, seize oil platforms and port facilities, and conduct a range of over-the-beach operations. They must always be ready to come from or under the sea, at night, and under the worst possible conditions. And as our nation steps back from direct military intervention, if it can, SEALs and their SOF brothers will continue the fight. This means an unending cycle of training and overseas deployment. This continuous, forward-deployed presence means that when a terrorist surfaces, there will never be a Navy SEAL too far away.

In this book, I have focused on the training of SEALs—particularly the advanced training venues and preparation for SEAL squadron deployment. The value of this training has been validated many times in combat since 9/11. The exploits of Navy SEALs in Afghanistan and Iraq are of record—publicly in a few cases, but for the most part within the closed world of the teams. Those SEALs performed magnificently; they trained hard, they had the right equipment, and they got the chance. But I would be remiss if I did not recognize those SEALs who have worked and trained for years and did not get the chance. While a new chapter in the battle history of the teams was, and is, being written in Afghanistan and Iraq, there are SEALs on guard on other parts of the world. Their presence in potentially dangerous but quiet theaters allowed their brothers to focus on combat operations. While SEAL Squadrons Three and Five were heavily engaged in Iraq, SEAL Squadrons Four and Eight were deployed in South America, Europe, and North Africa, ready for emerging contingencies. Those SEALs trained just as hard for war, but they never sent a round downrange. Perhaps to train and not fight, especially while others are, commands the highest degree of professionalism.

Our nation has generally been good about recognizing the contribution of our servicemen and -women, and the sacrifice they make for all of us. This recognition is always highest following periods of war, as was the case with the two recent conflicts. The flags come out on Memorial and Veterans Days, but this war or terrorism and terrorists will be with us for awhile; it might only be won by a commitment to fight indefinitely. Our SOF warriors will be engaged in this fight 24/7. They will be deployed and in harm's way with or without recognition——whether the flags at home are flying or furled. They will continue to fight like they train and train like they fight. So, dear readers, as you go about your daily life with its trials and pleasures, give a thought now and then for the warriors in training—the guns training for the fight. They have volunteered for this: the dirt, the danger, the cold, the long hours, and the long family separations. But their professionalism and sacrifice is no less noble. We are at war, and they stand on guard for all of us.

ABOUT THE AUTHOR

Dick Couch is a 1967 graduate of the U.S. Naval Academy. He graduated from BUD/S Class 45 in 1969, and was the class Honorman. He was also the first in his class at the Navy Underwater Swimmers School and the Army Military Free-Fall (HALO) School. As Whiskey Platoon Commander with SEAL Team One in Vietnam, he led one of the few successful POW rescue operations of that conflict. Following his release from active duty in the Navy, he served as a maritime and paramilitary case officer with the Central Intelligence Agency. In 1997, he retired from the Naval Reserve with the rank of captain. Dick Couch is the author of *The Warrior Elite: The Forging of SEAL Class 228*, and of six novels—*Covert Action, SEAL Team One, Pressure Point, Silent Descent, Rising Wind*, and *The Mercenary Option*. Dick and his wife, Julia, live in central Idaho.

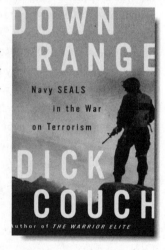